KT-219-339

knit, Swirl!

Sandra McIver

SeaStack Publishing

foreword by Cat Bordhi
photography by Zoë Lonergan

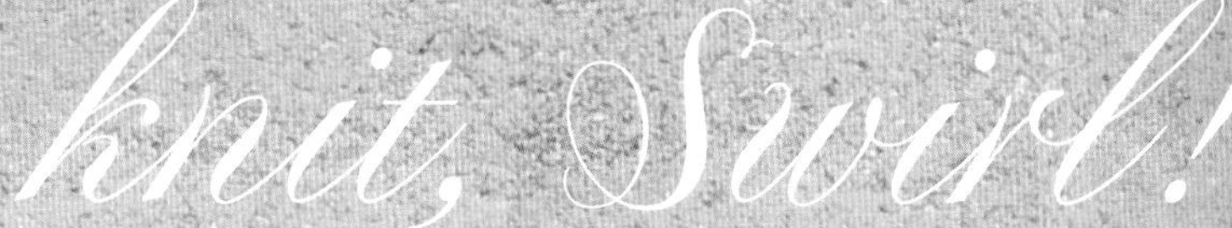

knit, Swirl!

Uniquely Flattering
One Piece, One Seam
Swirl Jackets

Sandra McIver

For *Violet & Willa*

I cherish the thought that one day, when you are much older, you will pick up your knitting needles, open the pages of this book and share another special moment with Ma.

Photography: Zoë Lonergan
Book Design: Zoë Lonergan
Technical Editor: Jeane deCoster

First published in 2011 by

SeaStack Publishing
1360 19th Hole Drive, Suite 201
Windsor, CA 95492

www.knitswirl.com

ISBN-13: 978-0-9819859-1-6

Library of Congress Control Number: 2010940535

Printed and bound in China through Asia Pacific Offset.

10 9 8 7 6 5 4 3 2

Contents

FOREWORD BY *Cat Bordhi*

I will always remember the moment I met Sandra and her sweater on the first evening of my Visionary Retreat, a seminar for knit designers dedicated to self-publishing spirited books of enduring and unique value. She was sitting in the golden glow of a lamp, and as she rose, her sweater, which until then I'd only seen in still photos, moved and swirled like a force of nature, its beauty so commanding that I'm not even sure I managed to say hello.

When Sandra contacted me to ask about attending the Visionary Retreat, I'd already sent out acceptance letters and had no more spots available. Every year I receive far more applications from accomplished designers than I can accept. But when Sandra's compelling images danced in my head day after day, I decided to add one more spot to include this intriguing new designer with the hauntingly beautiful sweaters.

Once we gathered, the excitement that erupted quickly confirmed my instinct. Sandra and her sweater became the darling of our group of high-powered designers. One by one, we discovered that the sweater (which we soon tagged the "Miracle Sweater") made us instantly feel young, graceful, and buoyant. Anyone who donned one began moving sinuously, although some of us had not moved sinuously in years. In her sweater, it was impossible to do anything else—as you will find if you knit one.

The Miracle Sweater seemed so flawless that none of us could have guessed Sandra would spend the next three years relentlessly identifying and mastering every nuance of the structural mechanics (imagine spread sheets of stretch ratios) necessary to perfect its flow and drape and to develop a collection of silhouettes to flatter and fit any woman. In my opinion Sandra has now earned a Ph.D. in Swirl Sweater Engineering. We knitters are the beneficiaries of her epic labor of love and intelligence.

Sandra's sweater is happily free of the shortcomings of other "circle sweaters," such as seams that interrupt the flow and purity of the form, a lack of bodice shaping, limited sizing and few options for variation in color and texture. As you study this book's images, you'll realize that Sandra has achieved an entirely new dynamic that includes several distinct silhouettes, enticing sleeve and collar choices, and curvaceous shaping. The sweater is ingeniously knit in one piece with one seam that runs from cuff to cuff. The three sizes can each be refined for a snug, medium or loose fit, and each sweater can be worn open or double-breasted, pinned asymmetrically or as a cowl neck, with the collar rolled and tumbling, or pulled up into a hood. You can play with yarn combinations (contrasting textures are especially luxurious), colors (hand-painted colors stream harmoniously around the rings), or enhance the fabric with textures. It is astonishing that only simple knitting skills are needed to knit this most sophisticated of all sweaters.

Your Swirl will be as stylish, mesmerizing, and desirable at the end of this century as it is today. I believe this sweater is destined to become one of the most oft-knit, beloved and reliable knitting designs in history. Thank you, Sandra, for your fortitude, your brilliance, and for transcending my greatest hopes for Visionary books of extraordinary and timeless value. This book rings oh so true.

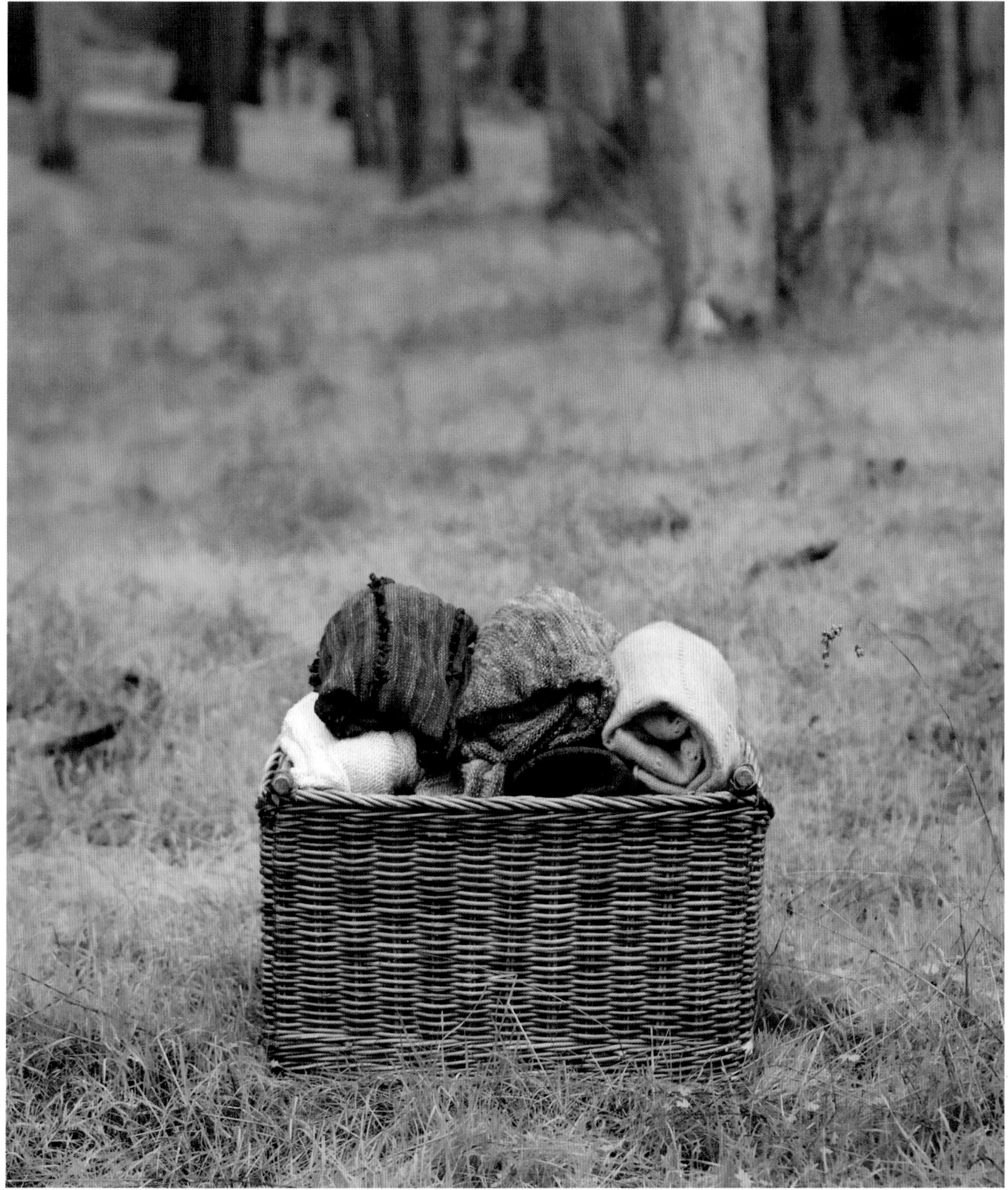

LET ME TAKE YOU FOR A *Swirl!*

Swirl? What's a Swirl? A Swirl is a uniquely flattering, one piece, one seam, circular jacket with sculptured shaping and fluid fit. A Swirl is any one of eighteen patterns in four silhouettes, each with flexible sizing and styling options. A Swirl is elegant drape, lively motion and a mix of color, texture, and pattern across a sweeping form.

The designs are unusual but easily done. Most require little more than basic knitting skills. All offer relaxing, rhythmic knitting at its best. A Swirl begins at the outer circular edge and proceeds toward the center in a series of concentric, welted rings that make up the collar, lapels, front and lower back portions of the garment. Once the circular form is completed, the remaining stitches are worked flat to create the bodice and sleeves. Lastly, one seam is sewn that runs from cuff to cuff, traveling around the front bodice and back neck along the way. The single seam serves as a minimal but essential frame from which the garment flows.

Ironically, this all began with a rectangle that was long and wide and worked in garter stitch. I was captivated by the sculptural qualities displayed as I arched and bowed and twisted the fabric in space. Inspired, I designed a sweater I hoped would capture some of those same traits. While that piece still holds favored status in my wardrobe, it was far from the artful silhouette I set out to create. It was then that a friend came by wearing a circular sweater she had found on a recent trip to Italy. The light went on! I was thinking in static, horizontal and vertical terms when I needed to be thinking dynamically—in the round. The next day I sketched and thought and sketched some more. In my mind's eye I began to see a slowly rotating, three-dimensional image grow from its circular base and take shape around an invisible female torso. With only a concept and the most rudimentary calculations to guide me, I cast on five hundred and sixty stitches and took off on one of the great journeys of my life.

That first Swirl was Strata Sphere. Another twenty-five followed. More often than not, the results surprised me. Some seemed to knit themselves. Others demanded to be ripped out and reinvented again and again. Some—like the one I cut up, felted and turned into a knitting bag—had fatal flaws. I learned from them all and slowly began to understand the complex structural mechanics at work in my designs. What's a Swirl? For a while there, *aswirl* was the state of my mind.

Knitting the first welts of a Swirl is slow going, but each successive welt takes less time than the last. Along the way you find yourself marveling at completing five welts in the time it once took to do one. Shaping the bodice goes quickly, the sleeves less so. Then, suddenly you find yourself speeding down the slopes of the front bodice and, sooner than expected, binding off the last stitch. The pace of my journey has been much the same. Years of knitting, measuring, analyzing, calculating, illustrating and writing are suddenly done. There's only one thing left to do.

Let me take you for a Swirl!

Sandra McIver

CHAPTER ONE *silhouettes and sizing*

All Swirls share the same basic construction—an outer circular form that flows into a bodice and sleeve component. The circular form provides the collar, lapels, front and lower back portions of the Swirl. It is shaped by eight lines created by pairs of decreases that start at the outer edge of the Swirl and continue toward the center, frequently traveling into the bodice for extra shaping. Variations are created by changing the size of the circular form, the arrangement of the decrease lines, the placement of the bodice and the location and shaping of the inner collar edge. The resulting designs fall into four silhouette types based on the shape of their circular form (circle or oval) and the location of the inner collar edge (centered or off-center).

Circles vs. Ovals

In *circle silhouettes*, decrease lines are evenly spaced in order to produce a circle. The bodice is set into the circle so that one of these lines runs up the center back, forming soft points at the back of the collar and the lower back. The welts within the circle run diagonally at all times, creating a fabric that falls on the bias around the torso. As a result, *circle silhouettes* offer gentle draping throughout and are softly flared across the back and hips.

In *oval silhouettes*, the distance between the decrease lines is varied, with the top and bottom sections elongated to produce an oval. The bodice is positioned in the oval so that it is centered between the two decrease lines that define the top section. This creates a straight edge at the back of the collar and at the bottom edge of the garment. The welts of an *oval silhouette* run horizontally across the back and diagonally across the front and side sections. As a result, *oval silhouettes* hang flat across the back with more drape than the *circle silhouettes* at the front and sides. Because *oval silhouettes* allow sections of different lengths, more variation in overall length is possible than in *circle silhouettes*.

Centered vs. Off-Center

Centered silhouettes have an inner collar edge created by binding off a portion of a completed circular form along one row. The result is an inner collar edge that is truly centered and mirrors the shape of the circular form. In *off-center silhouettes*, the inner collar edge begins high in the upper half of the circular form and is created by working decreases at each collar edge as the knitting progresses. The result is an inner collar edge that is off-of-center and shaped a bit like an egg.

In *centered silhouettes*, collars are deeper and more shawl-like, back lengths are shorter, and the torso and upper portion of the sleeve are more generous. By comparison, in *off-center silhouettes*, collars are much narrower, back lengths are longer and, the torso and upper sleeves are more fitted.

Sizing and Yoke Measurement

Swirls, by virtue of their circular construction, are highly adaptable garments. A Swirl of any size will fit and flatter a surprisingly wide range of shapes and sizes. In some cases, the same person could wear all three sizes of a single Swirl design, with size one worn as a semi-fitted short jacket; size two as a classic-fit, mid-length jacket; and size three as an even larger, flowing, drapey jacket. In a Swirl, the key to size is *yoke measurement*—so toss that notion that size is determined by body circumference. *Yoke measurement* defines the range of Swirl sizes available to you.

To determine your *yoke measurement*, stand with your arms slightly raised to the side. Have someone measure the distance from the point under your arm where a side seam and bottom edge of a bra would intersect, then forward and up in front of the shoulder, back around the neck, forward and down in front of the other shoulder, ending at the side seam-bra edge intersection on the opposite side. A diagram illustrating this measurement can be found on page 208.

Silhouette, then Pattern, then Style

After you have defined your size range, consider the characteristics of the four silhouettes as outlined on the following pages and identify the silhouette, or silhouettes, that suit you best. Next, review the pattern choices within those silhouettes, paying attention to the "as shown" size worn by the models. (As a point of reference, all the primary models have yoke measurements of 32-33 inches and wear a size medium. They range in height from 5 feet, 6 inches to 5 feet, 9 inches.) With the "as shown" size, style and fit in mind, identify a size within your size range that will provide the style and fit you wish to achieve. Keep in mind that the longer the listed yoke measurement is in relation to your own measurement, the looser and more deeply draped the finished Swirl will be.

If you feel the available range of yoke measurements do not sufficiently address your needs, there are options for making size one smaller or size three larger. Start by reviewing the notes on *Structure and Gauge* in the *Tips and Techniques* chapter on page 14. Of course, to create a truly predictable circular size, it is always wise to stay close to the stated gauge and yarn type for each pattern. However, in the case of a knit garment based on a circle, nudging your gauge up or down can be a successful method of modifying the size of a Swirl. While not always recommended for changing sizes of more structured garments, nudging your gauge to slightly more stitches per inch will result in a smaller yoke measurement. Correspondingly, slightly fewer stitches per inch will result in a larger yoke measurement. So too will substituting a slightly lighter or heavier weight yarn. Be careful! *Slightly* is the key word here. In a knitted circular form, small changes will have exponential effects. Another option is to substitute a yarn with a different level of resilience. A more resilient yarn will result in a smaller garment and a less resilient yarn will result in a larger garment—even when your stitch gauge matches the stated gauge of the pattern.

The Magic of a Swirl

Remember that knitting is connecting a series of loops together. Knitting a Swirl puts all those loops into a circular shape that is then worn vertically on the body. Gravity rules and those loops are going to magically change shape to create your own personal Swirl.

SIZE - YOKE MEASUREMENT

SIZE ONE	Yoke Measurement of 33in/84cm *or less*
SIZE TWO	Yoke Measurement of 35in/89cm *or less*
SIZE THREE	Yoke Measurement of 37in/94cm *or less*

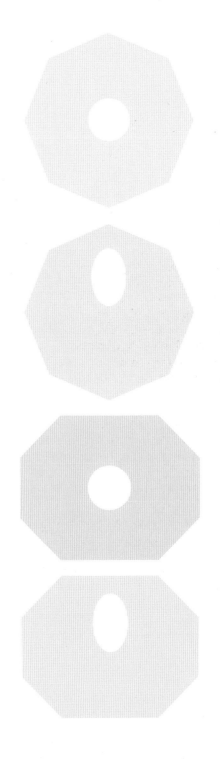

Centered Circle

- Deep shawl-like collar and lapels
- Short back length in relation to collar depth
- Decrease line at center back
- Soft point at back of collar and lower back
- Diagonal welts throughout circular form
- Gentle draping around entire torso
- Softly flared across back and hips
- Generous fit around torso and upper arm
- Some collars may be worn as hoods

Off-Center Circle

- Narrow collar and lapels
- Long back length in relation to collar depth
- Decrease line at center back
- Soft point at back of collar and lower back
- Diagonal welts throughout outer circular form
- Gentle draping around entire torso
- Softly flared at lower back and hips
- More fitted torso; semi-fitted upper sleeve
- Some versions may be worn upside down as waist-length jackets with cape-like collar

Centered Oval

- Deep shawl-like collar and lapels
- Back length to collar depth ratio varies by pattern
- Decrease lines at sides of torso
- Straight edge at back of collar and lower back
- Horizontal welts across back
- Diagonal welts at front and sides
- Gentle to deep draping at front and sides
- Hangs flat across back
- Variety of torso fit; slim tapered sleeve
- Some collars may be worn as hoods

Off-Center Oval

- Narrow collar and lapels
- Long back in relation to collar depth
- Decrease lines at sides of torso
- Straight edge at back of collar and lower back
- Horizontal welts across back
- Diagonal welts at front and sides
- Gentle to deep draping at front and sides
- Hangs flat across back
- More fitted torso; slim tapered sleeve

CHAPTER TWO *tips and techniques*

NO "RIGHT SIDE"
In a Swirl, there is no "right side" or "wrong side" in the usual sense. One side of the knitted fabric is presented in the torso, the other in the collar and lapels. I use the terms out of necessity. I define "right side" as the side facing the knitter when working the outer circular portion of a Swirl, and "wrong side" as the opposite.

YARN AND FABRIC DEVELOPMENT
Each of my designs began with a search for yarns that would provide the balance of resilience and drape required in a Swirl. From there I experimented with a variety of combinations of yarn, stitch pattern, color and texture in an effort to develop a unique and interesting fabric. While I highly recommend each of the remarkable yarns used in the patterns within, I encourage you to substitute and have the fun of developing your own fabric. In the process, keep in mind that both sides of the fabric will be seen and that long colorway repeats will manifest differently in the short rows of a swatch than they will in the long rows of a Swirl. Avoid yarns made exclusively from heavy, non-resilient fibers such as cotton, linen or hemp.

STRUCTURE AND GAUGE
In a Swirl, it is important to consider both stitch structure and gauge. To do this, create a swatch that is worked in pattern, without edging, square (important in a welted swatch) and approximately 8" on each side. If the yarn you are working with is on the less resilient end of the spectrum, you will want to make sure that your stitch structure is fairly tight as it will stretch and loosen with blocking and wearing. If the yarn is highly resilient, you will want your stitch structure to be relaxed but not loose. Before measuring gauge, wash the swatch in lukewarm water with mild soap, roll in a towel and gently squeeze. Block only to the extent that the sides are perpendicular to one another, but the swatch is otherwise relaxed. Allow to dry completely. In a welted swatch, even relatively minor differences in tension in either direction can significantly influence gauge. After trying many different approaches, I recommend the following: Place the swatch on a suitable surface, and pin so the stitches in the center of the swatch achieve the specified stitch and row gauge. If your swatch lies flat with the welts still slightly raised and the stitches show no signs of being stretched or distorted, your needle size is appropriate. If not, adjust needle size accordingly.

MARKERS
Locking stitch markers are indispensable. You will use them to mark decrease points and cuff edges and to pin sides together for seaming. They can be also be used to hold dropped stitches, identify the location of problems to fix later, mark every fifth welt for quick counting, etc. Clip a supply on the start-of-row marker for easy access. You will want to have twenty or more on hand.

MAIN SCHEMATICS
The two large schematics accompanying each pattern evolved from diagrams that I created to assist in the design process. They provide a visual digest of the information found in the written pattern but with more detailed stitch count information. Unlike charts, my schematics are not meant to be read in a particular direction. Instead, they reflect information on a geographical basis from the perspective of a knitter looking at the "right side" of the garment. Before beginning your Swirl, I recommend reading through the pattern, referring to the schematics in the process.

Casting On

The initial stitches of a Swirl are cast on using a method variously called *long-tail*, *double* or *two strand* cast on. There are several versions of this method, each with its own approach to holding and manipulating the yarn to achieve the same result. I prefer a version called thumb method or long-tail using thumb loops (not to be confused with thumb cast on). Sources of instruction in several versions can be found on page 207.

Casting on hundreds of stitches may sound daunting, but it is an easily managed task when done as follows: Make a single slip knot containing two strands of yarn, one from each of two balls of the same yarn. One of these two strands acts as the long tail, the other as the working yarn. Cast on the number of stitches called for in the first section. Confirm correct stitch count. Place a marker, cast on the second section, and confirm stitch count. Repeat the process until all eight sections have been cast on. Place the start-of-row marker and cast on 1 stitch. Remove the extra strand from the slip knot by sliding it off the needle and pulling down. Break the strand used as the long tail, and continue with the working yarn.

No Twist Join

Joining numerous stitches in the round requires that you carefully align the stitches on the needle in order to avoid twisting the cast-on edge around the needle. Here is the way I go about it: Work the first three rows flat, slipping the last stitch of the third row. Adjust stitches so that they are evenly distributed across the cable, with the mid-point marker at the center of the cable. (1) Place right index finger on the mid-point marker, making sure the cast-on edge is below the cable at that point. Use right thumb and middle finger to bend and firmly hold the cable around the right index finger. (2) Place left index finger in the middle of the bent cable so that index fingers touch. Place left middle finger and thumb on the outside of the cable. (3) Squeeze fingers of left hand together, and pull stitches on the cable to the left, spreading the stitches out and orienting them so that their cast-on edge is below the cable. With fingers held in the same configuration, move right hand to meet left hand. Squeeze fingers of right hand together to hold the cast-on edge below the cable, and (4) pull straightened stitches back toward the bend. Repeat the process of the left hand spreading and straightening the next group of stitches, and the right hand maintaining the orientation of the stitches while pulling them back to toward the bend. (5) When you reach the stitches at the ends of the row, hold them in proper alignment while placing the slipped stitch back onto the left needle. Work the first two stitches together to join the round.

1

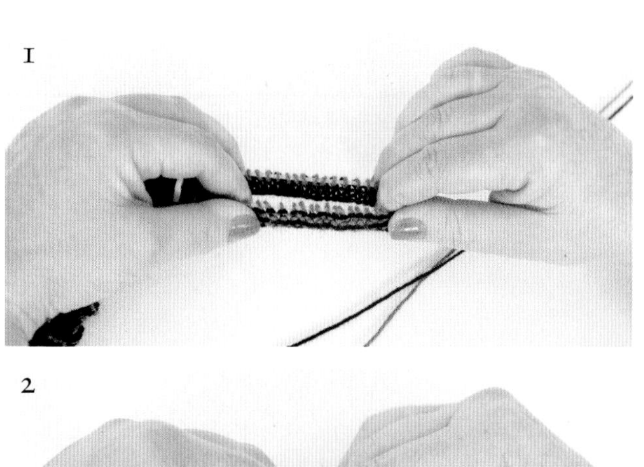

2

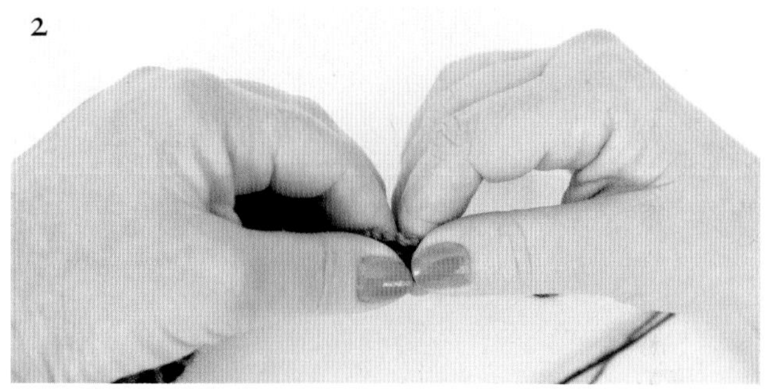

3

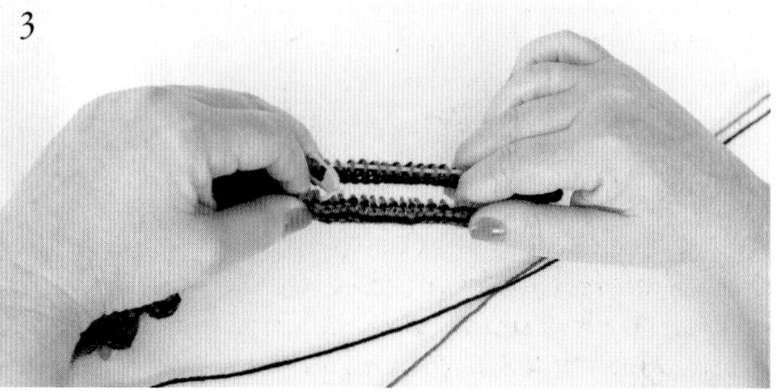

4

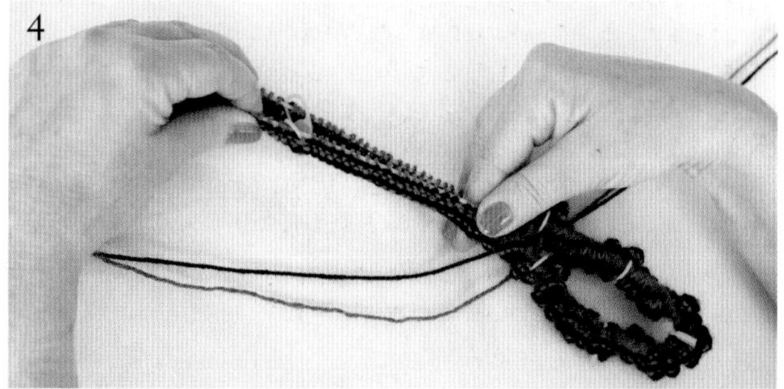

5

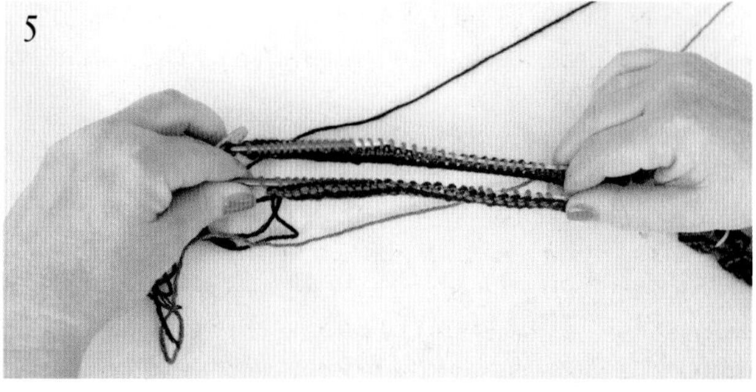

Decreases at Markers

The decreases at markers are basic single decreases (knit two stitches together on stockinette stitch rows; purl two stitches together on reverse stockinette rows) worked two stitches out from the marker on either side. To ensure a uniform look on both sides of the fabric, give a little tug on the yarn to tighten the tension after working the two stitches together. Experienced knitters may be tempted to work "matching" right and left slanting decreases at markers, but doing so results in a less uniform look on the two sides of the fabric.

Joining Yarn

I recommend two methods for joining in new yarn. The simplest is to work one or two stitches with both the working yarn and new yarn together. Leave ends to be woven in with duplicate stitch at finishing. The other is a splicing method that works well with all but the finest gauge yarns. Use a darning needle threaded with the yarn to be joined. Insert the needle in the center of the working yarn end and make short running stitches through its plies for 2-3". After removing the needle, pull the end of the new yarn back until it disappears within the working yarn. If needed, dampen and roll the edges of the join to integrate fibers.

Inner Collar Edge

In centered Swirls, the inner collar edge is created by binding off a portion of the completed outer circular form along one row. In off-center Swirls, the inner collar edge is created by decreases worked at each collar edge, on each row, within the outer circular form as knitting progresses. In both cases it is important that the inner collar edge be elastic enough to be compatible with the inherently expandable bodice-neck edge to which it will be seamed. In off-center Swirls, avoid tightening the stitches at the inner collar edges. In centered Swirls, and in portions of some off-center Swirls, bind off at inner collar edge using *Jeny's Surprisingly Stretchy Bind Off (JSSBO)*.

JSSBO on stockinette row:
Set up: YO in reverse, k1. Lift YO over st just knit and off needle.

Remaining sts: * YO in reverse, k1. Lift both right st and YO over st just knit (can be done in one step or two). Repeat from* for required number of sts.

JSSBO on reverse stockinette row:
Set up: YO, p1. Lift YO over the st just purled and off needle.

Remaining sts: * YO, p1. Lift both right st and YO over st just purled (can be done in one step or two). Repeat from * for required number of sts.

Sleeves and Stretch Factor

As the sleeves begin to take shape, you may notice that they appear short. This is, in part, an illusion created by the lack of a shoulder seam. It is also because the sleeves, by virtue of their lengthwise welted structure, will stretch when washed and worn. Using the test knit version of each pattern, I was able to quantify the stretch factor and adjust patterns accordingly. A finished sleeve stitch gauge is included in each pattern for use when making adjustments for proper fit. If you are substituting yarn, take the resiliency of that fiber into consideration when making sleeve length adjustments. Sleeves that have a simple slip stitch edge or a narrow rolled cuff edge can be folded back to form a deeper cuff if needed and are safe choices when in doubt.

Weaving in Ends

After binding off the last stitches of the bodice, take a moment to study the knitted form. Identify the path the seam will take, and think about how the collar and lapels will fall when worn. You will want to weave the ends in on the side that will be concealed from public view most of the time. Use duplicate stitch (a stitch usually associated with embroidery) to weave in the ends. With duplicate stitch, the ends will be well-camouflaged and well-secured, and the knitted fabric will retain its original elasticity. As its name implies, duplicate stitch repeats the shape and tension of the stitch over which it is worked. Thread a yarn end through a tapestry needle. Working horizontally along one row, follow the contour and path of the existing stitches for 1-2". When working duplicate stitch in a purl row, first interlock the yarn ends then weave each end back in the direction from which it came. In a knit row, simply weave each end away from its point of origin.

Blocking

Blocking is done ***before*** sewing the seam. Prepare an area that is: 1) large enough to accommodate the expanse of a Swirl and allow room for you to maneuver, 2) on a surface that will accept pins (towels spread over carpeting works well) and 3) in a location where the garment can stay long enough to dry completely. Place the T-pins, yard stick, blocking wires (optional but extremely helpful) and small schematic nearby. Submerge Swirl in a sink of lukewarm water and mild soap. Let soak for a few minutes. Drain the sink, then squeeze and press Swirl against the side of the bowl to remove excess water. Being careful to support the entire garment, remove Swirl and set to the side. Fill the sink with lukewarm water, return Swirl and gently swish to rinse. Repeat the rinsing process until the water is clear. Drain, remove excess water and place Swirl on a large towel. Being very careful not to stretch, spread the Swirl out, place another towel on top and roll up. Press on the roll, but do not twist. Repeat if needed to remove excess water. Transfer garment to your blocking area.

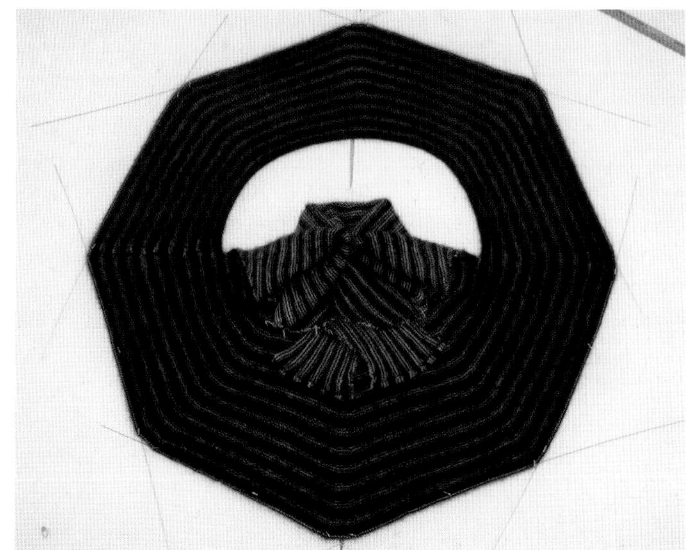

With "right side" up, carefully arrange the outer circle or oval of the Swirl, and fold the sleeves and front bodice so that they rest in a pile in the center. (If you have access to blocking wires, insert a wire from back to front at the base of the first row of the second welt and in line with a decrease point. Thread the wire along the base of the row, across the length of one section and exit downward at the next decrease point. Repeat this process at the remaining 7 sections.) Use T-pins to maintain the perimeter of the Swirl so that: 1) in circle silhouettes, the vertical axis and the horizontal axis are perpendicular to one another and, in oval silhouettes, the top and bottom edges are perpendicular to the right and left edges; 2) opposing sections are aligned with one another; 3) the length of each section is consistent with the small schematic. I have found it useful to use T-pins placed along the sides of the yardstick to create channels in which I can slide the yardstick to check alignment of opposing sections. Do not overstretch the fabric; there should still be raised welts and resiliency in the welted structure.

Once the outer circle is aligned and pinned in place, unfold the sleeves and front bodice. The tendency is for the sleeves to lengthen and the bodice neck and cuff edges to fan out. You may wish to pin some parts of the cuff to encourage proper shaping, but otherwise do not use pins in this portion of the Swirl. The goal in blocking the bodice is to align it properly with the rest of the garment while encouraging the welted structure to stay as compact as possible at the neck edges. The goal in blocking the sleeves is to avoid stretching them lengthwise. The sleeves should be arranged so that the stitches are relaxed and its raised welts touch one another. The sleeves will be somewhat shorter than the finished measurements indicate. When completely dry, remove all pins and wires.

One Seam

Use locking stitch markers to clip the two sides of the seam together, taking care to align cuff edges, the center of the inner collar edge with the center of the back neck and the tapered ends of the front bodice with the ends of the inner collar edge. Working from center back neck out toward the sleeve edges, sew a seam using *mattress stitch* (also known as *ladder stitch* and *invisible seam*). Your Swirl will benefit from resting on a dress form or the narrow back of an upholstered chair for a day or two, allowing gravity to play a role in the final sculpting—or you may decide you would rather achieve the same effect by wearing it every chance you get!

www.knitswirl.com

Need more information? See *Resources*, page 207, or go to www.knitswirl.com for illustrated tutorials of the techniques used in creating a Swirl.

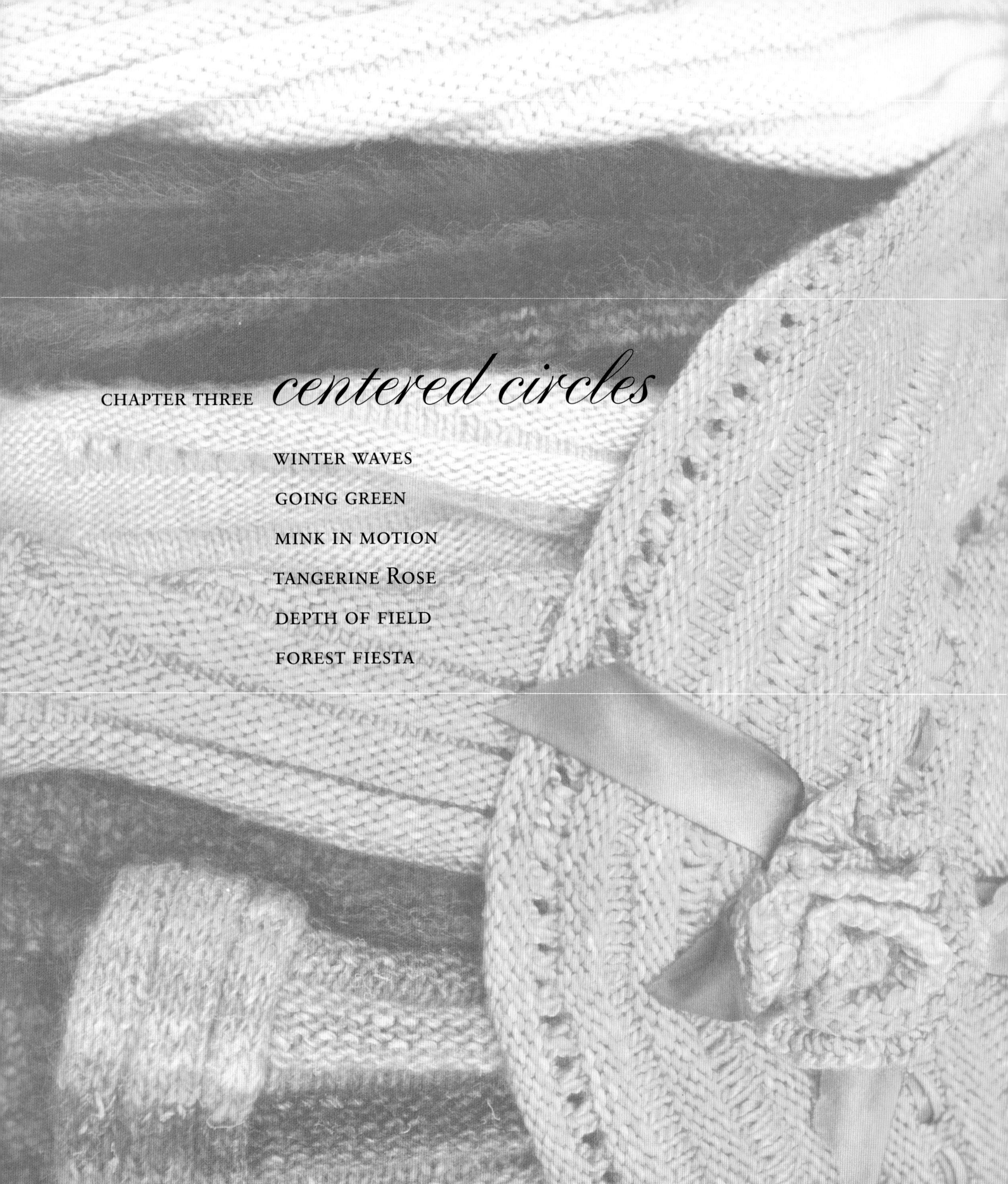

CHAPTER THREE *centered circles*

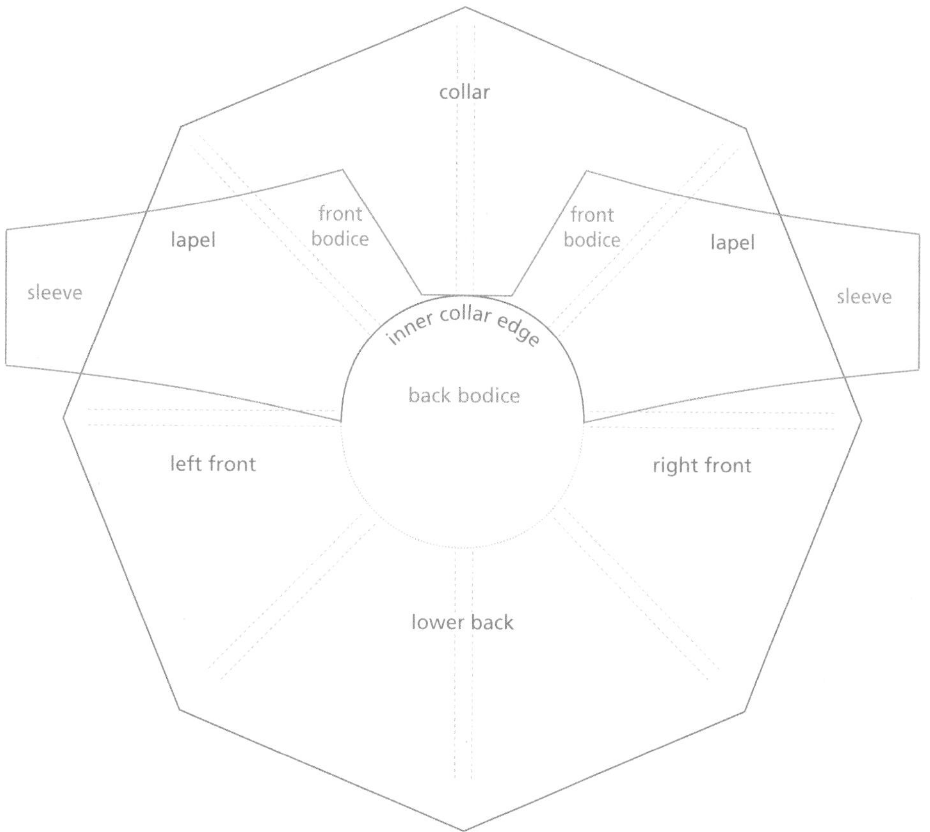

The ***centered circle silhouette*** is ideal for those who enjoy wide swing-style jackets or simply desire more ease around the entire torso. The deep shawl collars and wide lapels typical of this silhouette provide a range of styling options. Sleeve treatments vary within the group from deep dolman sleeves to more fitted tapered sleeves. Two of the patterns, *Depth of Field* and *Forest Fiesta*, were designed with gussets at the sides of the bust in order to provide a better fit for the full-figured woman.

winter waves

Winter Waves offers the Swirl shape in its purest form. Tightly-plied merino wool creates a smooth fabric with excellent stitch definition that allows the concentric welted structure to take center stage while providing the spring needed to support a shawl collar of generous proportions. This coat length version is particularly versatile. The collar can be worn as a hood, rolled under to form a stand collar with narrow lapels, or gathered loosely and pinned cowl-like about the neck. The sleeves are tapered and trimmed with a simple narrow roll.

Sizes
One (Two, Three); shown here in Size Two.

Knitted Measurements
Collar: 15½ (16½, 17)"/39 (42, 43)cm
Center Back: 32¼ (33¾, 35¼)"/82 (86, 89)cm
Center Back Neck to Cuff: 28¼ (29, 30)"/74 (77, 76)cm

Approximate As-Worn Measurements
Collar: 13 (13½, 14)"/33 (34, 36)cm
Center Back: 33 (34½, 36)"/84 (88, 91)cm
Center Back Neck to Cuff: 33½ (34½, 35½)"/85 (88, 90)cm

Materials
Multiple-ply, worsted weight wool yarn, 2024 (2232, 2460) yd/1851 (2041, 2250)m. As shown, 21 (23, 26) balls Karabella Aurora 8 (100% extrafine merino, 1¾ oz/50g, 98 yd/89m) in color #250.

One 40 (40, 47)" size 8 (5.0mm) circular needle or size required to obtain gauge.

Gauge
18 stitches and 26 rows = 4"/10cm

Before beginning, please review Chapter One, ***Silhouettes and Sizing*** and Chapter Two, ***Tips and Techniques.***

Stitch Pattern: Welted Stripes
Continuous, alternating welts of Reverse Stockinette stitch and Stockinette stitch.

Welt 1—Reverse Stockinette Stitch, 5 rows
When working in the round: (RS) Purl all rows.
When working flat: Purl on RS rows, knit on WS rows.
Welt 2—Stockinette Stitch, 5 rows
When working in the round: (RS) Knit all rows.
When working flat: Knit on RS rows, purl on WS rows.
Repeat welts 1 and 2.

Outer Circle
Use a long-tail or double method to cast on 545 (577, 609) stitches, placing a marker in between the following 8 sections of 68 (72, 76) stitches each, with 1 stitch after the last marker. Use a different color marker for the last marker to denote the beginning and end of each row.

Welt 1, Reverse Stockinette Stitch (Note: This outer welt has 7 rows instead of the normal 5 rows. The first 3 rows are worked flat before joining the work into a circle. It is important to the directional integrity of the pattern that the circle be joined at the completion of the third row as instructed.) Row 1: (RS) Purl. Row 2: Knit. Row 3: Purl to last stitch, slip 1. Adjust work to ensure that cast-on edge is not twisted around needle. (See *No Twist Join*, Chapter Two.) Join work into a circle by placing the last, slipped stitch from row 3 back onto the left needle. Two stitches are now on the left needle before the marker. Purl these two stitches together. Continue next rows in the round. Rows 4-7: Purl. 544 (576, 608) stitches.

Welt 2, Stockinette Stitch Rows 1-4: Knit. Row 5: *K2, k2tog, knit to within 4 stitches of next marker, k2tog, k2, slip marker; repeat from * across entire row. 528 (560, 592) stitches.

Welt 3, Reverse Stockinette Stitch Rows 1-4: Purl. Row 5: *P2, p2tog, purl to within 4 stitches of next marker, p2tog, p2, slip marker; repeat from * across entire row. 512 (544, 576) stitches.

Welts 4 - 21 (22, 23) (Note: Continue in Welted Stripes stitch pattern throughout remainder of garment.) Continue decreases at markers in last row of each welt as established. 224 (240, 256) stitches.

Back Bodice and Sleeves
After the collar and lapels are completed and bound off, the bodice is worked flat on the remaining live stitches in the center of the garment. Change to the working-flat version of Welted Stripes stitch pattern after row 1 of next welt.

Welt 22 (23, 24) Row 1: Use Jeny's Surprisingly Stretchy Bind Off method to bind off first 112 (120, 128) stitches, then work remaining 112 (120, 128) stitches. Rows 2-3: Change to working-flat version of Welted Stripes stitch pattern. Work even. Row 4: Increase 1 stitch at beginning and end of row, placing markers one stitch in on each side. Row 5: Increase 1 stitch at beginning and end of row and continue decreases in established manner at the 3 center markers and to the inside only of the 2 outer markers. 8 decreases worked/welt. 108 (116, 124) stitches.

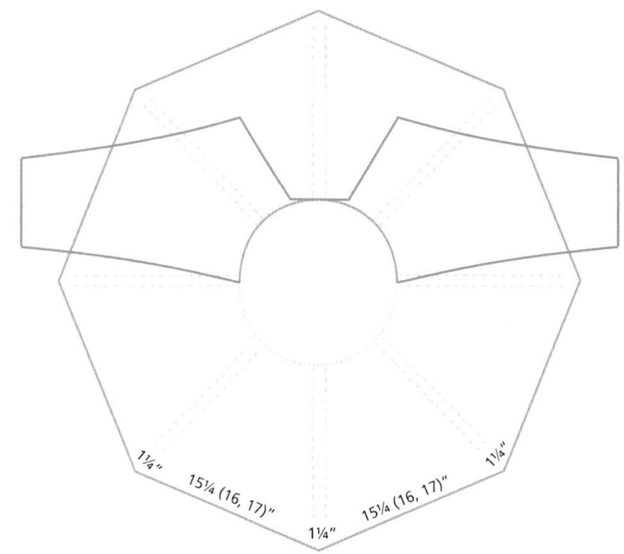

Welts 23 (24, 25) – 24 (25, 26) Continue to increase 1 stitch at beginning and end of each row and to decrease in established manner at markers in last row of each welt. 8 decreases worked/welt. 112 (120, 128) stitches.

Welts 25 (26, 27) – 28 (29, 30) Remove the first and last marker. Continue to increase 1 stitch at beginning and end of each row and to decrease in established manner at 3 remaining markers in last row of each welt. 6 decreases worked/welt. 128 (136, 144) stitches.

Welts 29 (30, 31) – 35 (37, 38) No further marker decreases; remove all stitch markers. Continue to increase 1 stitch at beginning and end of each row. 198 (216, 224) stitches.

Welt 36 (38, 39) Rows 1-4: Cast on 4 stitches at beginning of each row. Row 5: Cast on 6 (4, 4) stitches at beginning of row. (Note: To achieve desired sleeve length, add or subtract 3-4 stitches for each inch, distributed across all rows in this and the next welt.) 220 (236, 244) stitches.

Welt 37 (39, 40) Row 1: Cast on 6 (4, 4) stitches at beginning of row. Rows 2-3: Cast on 7 (4, 4) stitches at beginning of each row. Rows 4-5: Cast on 7 stitches at beginning of each row. 254 (262, 270) stitches.

Cuffs

Welts 38 (40, 41) – 42 (44, 46) Place markers 7 stitches in from each sleeve end to indicate cuff stitches. Work the stitches between the markers even, in the established pattern. At the same time, work the cuff stitches in Reverse Stockinette stitch only. 254 (262, 270) stitches.

Neck, Front Bodice and Sleeves

In the next welt, stitches in the center of the row are bound off to create the back neck and begin shaping the two front bodice panels. Continue to work cuff stitches in Reverse Stockinette stitch and the stitches between the markers in the established Welted Stripes pattern.

Welt 43 (45, 47) Row 1: Work 118 (119, 120) stitches, use basic method to bind off center 18 (24, 30) stitches, work remaining 118 (119, 120) stitches. Row 2: Work in established pattern to second neck edge, add a second ball of yarn and continue row. Rows 3-5: Work even. 118 (119, 120) stitches/sleeve.

Welts 44 (46, 48) – 47 (49, 52) Work in established pattern, decreasing 1 stitch at each neck edge on row 5 of each welt. 114 (115, 115) stitches/sleeve.

Welt 48 (50, 53) Apply in reverse order any sleeve length changes made in welts 36-37 (38-39, 39-40) in this and the next welt. Continue decreasing at neck edges on row 5. Rows 1-2: Bind off 7 stitches at beginning (sleeve end) of each row. Rows 3-4: Bind off 7 (4, 4) stitches at beginning of each row. Row 5: Bind off 6 (4, 4) stitches at beginning of row. 99/93 (99/103, 99/103) stitches/sleeve.

Welt 49 (51, 54) Continue to work decreases at neck edges as established. Row 1: Bind off 6 (4, 4) stitches at beginning of row. Rows 2-5: Bind off 4 stitches at beginning of each row. 84 (90, 90) stitches/sleeve.

Welts 50 (52, 55) – 62 (65, 68) Continue to work decreases at neck edges as established and, at the same time, decrease 1 stitch at each sleeve edge each row. 6 stitches/sleeve.

Welt 63 (66, 69) Continue to work decreases at neck edges as established. Rows 1-2: Decrease 1 stitch at each sleeve edge each row. Rows 3-5: Work even at sleeve edges. Bind off remaining 3 stitches/sleeve.

Finishing

Use cast-on yarn tail to sew first rows on Welt 1 together. Weave in ends. Block*. With tapestry needle and matching yarn, sew neck/front bodice edge to bound-off inner collar edge. Sew underarm seams so that the finished seam is outside on the sleeves and inside on the cuffs. Tack cuffs to reinforce rolled shape.

*Karabella Aurora 8, an "irrestringible" (pre-shrunk) yarn, tends to grow when washed but will regain its original gauge when machine dried. Prior to blocking, hand wash in lukewarm water or machine wash on gentle cycle. Machine dry on gentle cycle, checking frequently, and remove from dryer for blocking while still slightly damp.

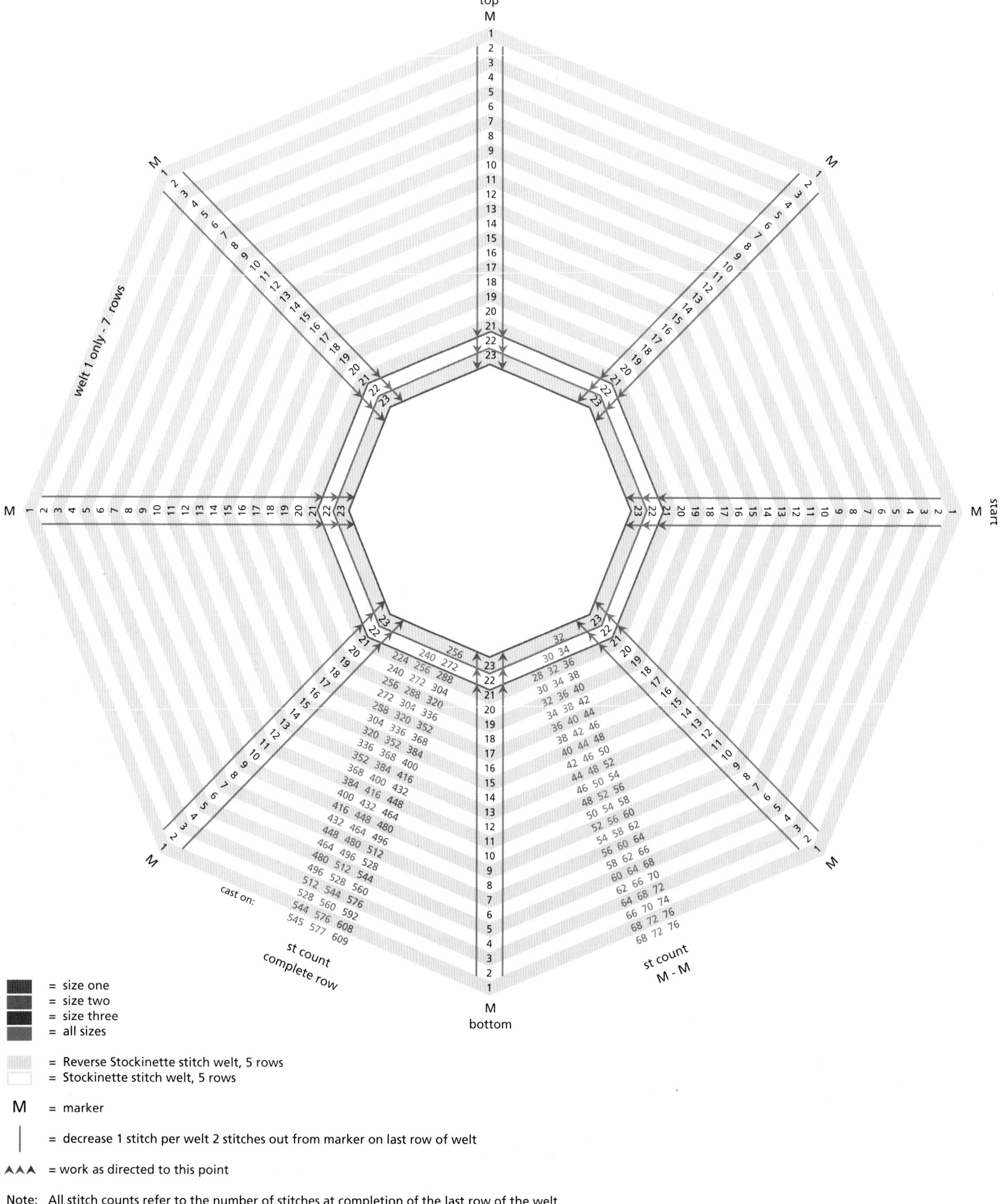
top
M
start
M
bottom
M
welt 1 only - 7 rows
cast on:
st count
complete row
st count
M - M
256
240 272
224 256 288
240 272 304
256 288 320
272 304 336
288 320 352
304 336 368
320 352 384
336 368 400
352 384 416
368 400 432
384 416 448
400 432 464
416 448 480
432 464 496
448 480 512
464 496 528
480 512 544
496 528 560
512 544 576
528 560 592
544 576 608
545 577 609
32
30 34
28 32 36
30 34 38
32 36 40
34 38 42
36 40 44
38 42 46
40 44 48
42 46 50
44 48 52
46 50 54
48 52 56
50 54 58
52 56 60
54 58 62
56 60 64
58 62 66
60 64 68
62 66 70
64 68 72
66 70 74
68 72 76
68 72 76
= size one
= size two
= size three
= all sizes
= Reverse Stockinette stitch welt, 5 rows
= Stockinette stitch welt, 5 rows
M = marker
= decrease 1 stitch per welt 2 stitches out from marker on last row of welt
= work as directed to this point
Note: All stitch counts refer to the number of stitches at completion of the last row of the welt

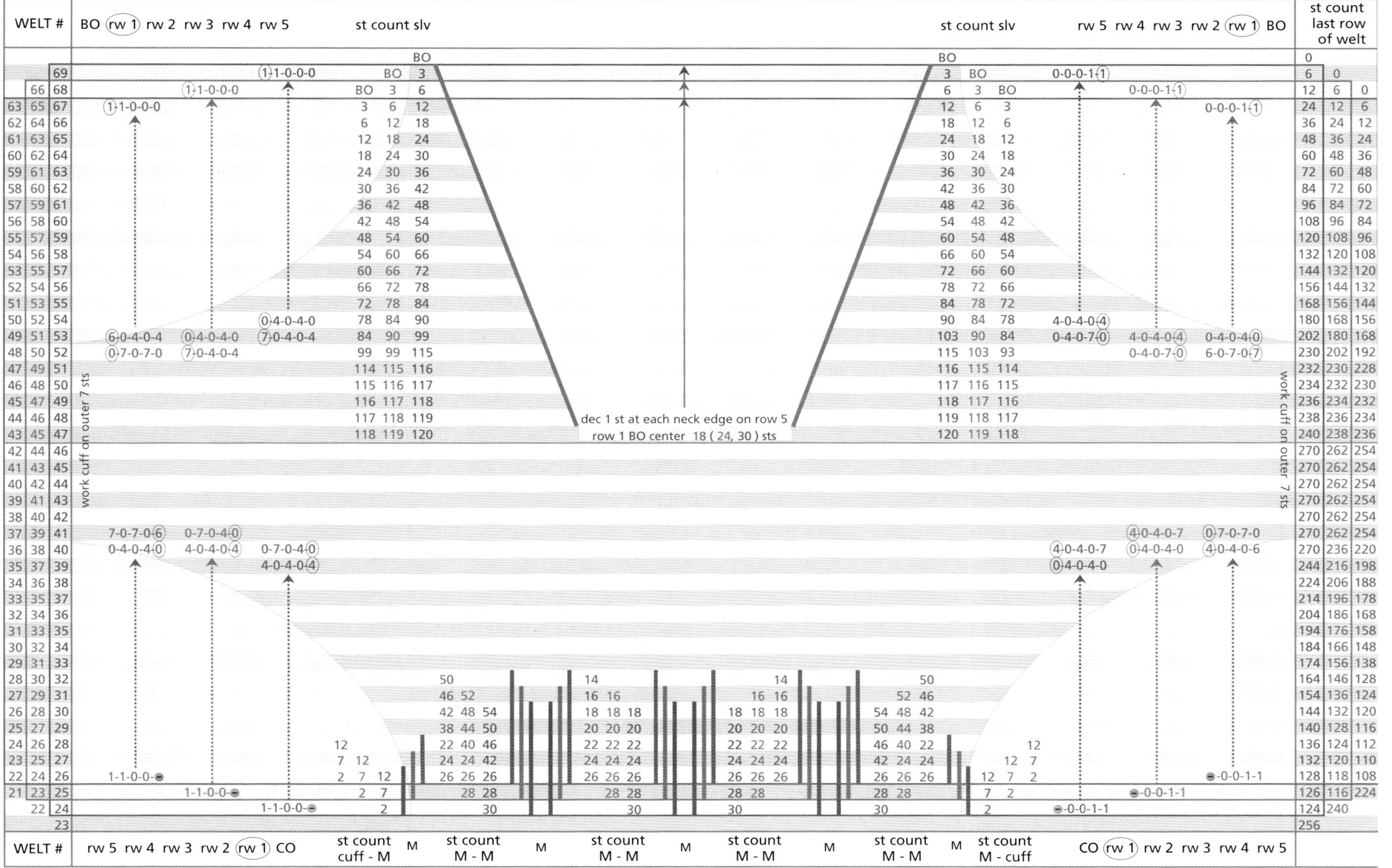

= size one
= size two
= size three
= all sizes

= Reverse Stockinette stitch welt, 5 rows
= Stockinette stitch welt, 5 rows

M = marker

= on row 1 use JSSBO to BO 112 (120, 128) sts, then work 112 (120, 128) sts; bodice worked on remaining sts

= decrease 1 stitch per welt 2 stitches out from marker on last row of welt

= decrease at neck edge as directed above

= work as directed to this point

= increase 1 st at sleeve edge each row (below center line); decrease 1 st at sleeve edge each row (above center line)

Note: All stitch counts refer to the number of stitches at completion of the last row of the welt

going green

Light seems to play with this fabric as it rolls over high and low relief, peeks through, then disappears into rows of delicate eyelets, while gently illuminating the soft halo offered by the oh-so-tender blend of cashmere and merino. Generous ease around the yoke provides deep dolman sleeves that slowly taper to narrow cuffs and a wide flowing swing of rhythmic fabric that swirls around the torso. Going Green is lush, light and luxuriant. Beware—once on, you won't want to take it off!

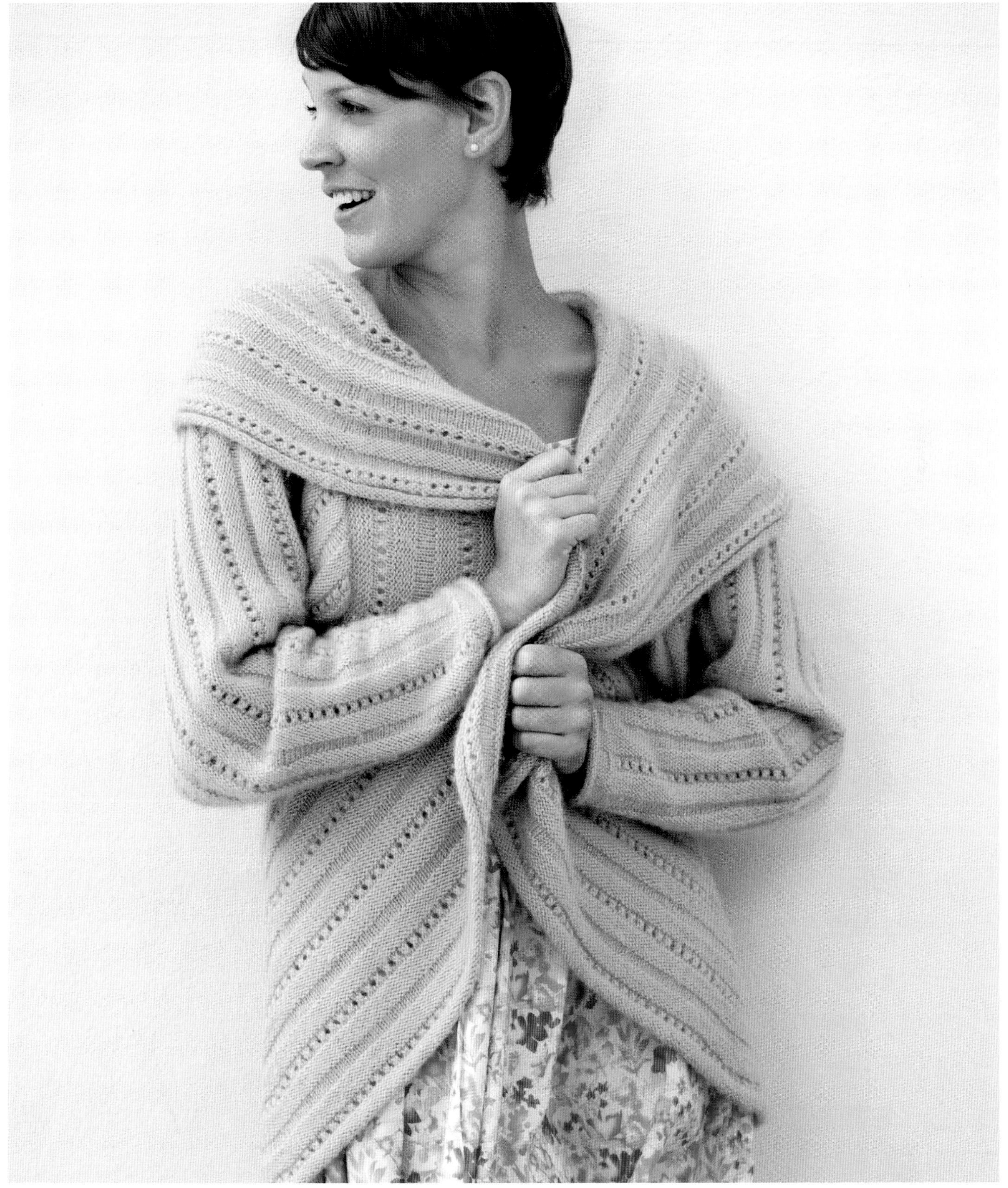

Sizes
One (Two, Three); shown here in Size One.

Knitted Measurements
Collar: 13 (14, 15)"/33 (36, 38)cm
Center Back: 30¾ (32¼, 33¾)"/78 (82, 86)cm
Center Back Neck to Cuff: 28¼ (29¼, 30)"/72 (74, 76)cm

Approximate As-Worn Measurements
Collar: 10½ (11½, 12½)"/27 (29, 32)cm
Center Back: 31 (32½, 34)"/79 (83, 86)cm
Center Back Neck to Cuff: 32½ (33½, 34½)"/83 (85, 88)cm

Materials
Single-ply, DK weight cashmere/merino blend yarn, 1555 (1716, 1866) yd/1422 (1569, 1706)m. As shown, 10 (11, 12) balls Karabella Boise (50% cashmere/50% merino, 1¾ oz/50g, 163 yd/149m) in color #69.

One 32 (32, 40)" size 5 (3.75mm) circular needle or size required to obtain gauge.

Gauge
24 stitches and 30 rows = 4"/10cm

Before beginning, please review Chapter One, ***Silhouettes and Sizing*** and Chapter Two, ***Tips and Techniques***.

STITCH PATTERN: WELTED STRIPES WITH ALTERNATING EYELETS

Continuous, alternating welts of Reverse Stockinette stitch and Stockinette stitch with eyelets worked every other Stockinette stitch welt.

Welts 1 and 3—Reverse Stockinette Stitch, 6 rows
When working in the round: (RS) Purl all rows.
When working flat: Purl on RS rows, knit on WS rows.
Welt 2—Stockinette Stitch with Eyelets, 5 rows
When working in the round: (RS) Knit all rows, working eyelet row on row 3.
When working flat: Knit on RS rows, purl on WS rows, working eyelet row on row 3.
Eyelet Row: On RS rows, *k2 tog, YO; repeat from * across entire row.
Welt 4—Stockinette Stitch, 5 rows
When working in the round: (RS) Knit all rows.
When working flat: Knit on RS rows, purl on WS rows.
Repeat welts 1-4.

OUTER CIRCLE

Use a long-tail or double method to cast on 641 (673, 705) stitches, placing a marker in between the following 8 sections of 80 (84, 88) stitches each, with 1 stitch after the last marker. Use a different color marker for the last marker to denote the beginning and end of each row.

Welt 1, Reverse Stockinette Stitch (Note: This outer welt has 8 rows instead of the normal 6 rows. The first 3 rows are worked flat before joining the work into a circle. It is important to the directional integrity of the pattern that the circle be joined at the completion of the third row as instructed.) Row 1: (RS) Purl. Row 2: Knit. Row 3: Purl to last stitch, slip 1. Adjust work to ensure that cast-on edge is not twisted around needle. (See *No Twist Join*, Chapter Two.) Join work into a circle by placing the last, slipped stitch from row 3 back onto the left needle. Two stitches are now on the left needle before the marker. Purl these two stitches together. Continue next rows in the round. Rows 4-8: Purl. 640 (672, 704) stitches.

Welt 2, Stockinette Stitch with Eyelets Rows 1-4: Work first 4 rows of Stockinette stitch with eyelets. Row 5: *K2, k2tog, knit to within 4 stitches of next marker, k2tog, k2, slip marker; repeat from * across entire row. 624 (656, 688) stitches.

Welt 3, Reverse Stockinette Stitch Rows 1-5: Purl. Row 6: *P2, p2tog, purl to within 4 stitches of next marker, p2tog, p2, slip marker; repeat from * across entire row. 608 (640, 672) stitches.

Welts 4 - 19 (20, 21) (Note: Continue in Welted Stripes with Alternating Eyelets stitch pattern throughout remainder of garment.) Continue decreases at markers in last row of each welt as established. 352 (368, 384) stitches.

BACK BODICE AND SLEEVES

After the collar and lapels are completed and bound off, the bodice is worked flat on the remaining live stitches in the center of the garment. Change to the working-flat version of Welted Stripes with Alternating Eyelets stitch pattern after row 2 of next welt.

Welt 20 (21, 22) Row 1: Work first 176 (184, 192) stitches, then use Jeny's Surprisingly Stretchy Bind Off method to bind off remaining 176 (184, 192) stitches. Row 2: Work even. Row 3: Change to working-flat version of Welted Stripes with Alternating Eyelets stitch pattern. Work even. (Note for Sizes 2 and 3: In order to continue to work eyelets on RS row for remainder of garment, break yarn, slide stitches to other side of needle to reposition beginning of row. Rejoin yarn.) Row(s) 4 (4-5, 4): Increase 1 stitch at beginning and end of each row. Row 5 (6, 5): Increase 1 stitch at beginning and end of row and continue decreases in established manner at 3 remaining markers. 6 decreases worked/welt. 174 (184, 190) stitches.

Welts 21 (22, 23) – 24 (25, 26) Continue to increase 1 stitch at beginning and end of each row and to decrease in established manner at markers in last row of each welt. 6 decreases worked/welt. 194 (204, 210) stitches.

Welts 25 (26, 27) – 34 (35, 36) No further marker decreases; remove all stitch markers. Continue to increase 1 stitch at beginning and end of each row. 304 (314, 320) stitches.

Welt 35 (36, 37) Cast on 1 stitch at the beginning of each row. (Note: To achieve desired sleeve length, add or subtract 5 stitches for each inch, distributed across all rows in this and the next welt.) 310 (319, 326) stitches.

Welt 36 (37, 38) Rows 1-3 (4, 3): Cast on 1 stitch at beginning of row. Row 4 (5, 4): Cast on 7 (7, 9) stitches at beginning of row. Row 5 (6, 5): Cast on 6 (6, 8) stitches at beginning of row. 326 (336, 346) stitches.

Cuffs

Welts 37 (38, 39) – 42 (44, 46) Place markers 6 stitches in from each end of sleeves to indicate cuff stitches. Work the stitches between the markers even, in the established pattern, and, at the same time, work the cuff stitches in Reverse Stockinette stitch only. 326 (336, 346) stitches.

Neck, Front Bodice and Sleeves

In the next welt, stitches in the center of the row are bound off to create the back neck and begin shaping the two front bodice panels. Continue to work cuff stitches in Reverse Stockinette stitch and the stitches between the markers in the established Welted Stripes with Alternating Eyelets pattern.

Welt 43 (45, 47) Row 1: Work 143 (147, 151) stitches, use basic method to bind off center 40 (42, 44) stitches, work remaining 143 (147, 151) stitches. Row 2: Work in established pattern to the second neck edge, add a second ball of yarn and continue row. Rows 3-6: Work even. 143 (147, 151) stitches/sleeve.

Welts 44 (46, 48) – 48 (51, 53) Work in established pattern, decreasing 1 stitch at each neck edge on row 1 of each welt. 138 (141, 145) stitches/sleeve.

Welt 49, Size One Apply in reverse order any sleeve length changes made in welts 35-36 in this and the next welt. Continue to decrease 1 stitch at each neck edge on row 1. Row 1: Bind off 6 stitches at beginning (sleeve end) of row. Row 2: Bind off 7 stitches at beginning (sleeve end) of row. Rows 3-6: Bind off 1 stitch at beginning of row. 128/129 stitches/sleeve.

Welt 54, Size Three Work in established pattern, decreasing 1 stitch at each neck edge *every other* row. 142 stitches/sleeve.

Welt 52 (55), Sizes Two and Three Apply in reverse order any sleeve length changes made in welts 36-37 (37-38) in this and the next welt. Decrease 1 stitch at each neck edge *every other* row. Row 1: Bind off 6 (8) stitches at beginning (sleeve end) of row. Row 2: Bind off 7 (9) stitches at beginning (sleeve end) of row. Rows 3-5 (3-6): Bind off 1 stitch at beginning of row. 130 (129/128) stitches/sleeve.

Welt 50 (53, 56) Work decreases at neck edges *every other* row. Bind off 1 stitch at beginning of each row. 123 (124, 124) stitches/sleeve.

Welts 51 (54, 57) - 64 (67, 70) Continue to work decreases at neck edges as established and, at the same time, decrease 1 stitch at each sleeve edge each row. 8 (9, 8) stitches/sleeve.

Welt 65 (68, 71) Continue to work decreases at neck edges as established. Rows 1-2 (1-3, 1-2): Decrease 1 stitch at each sleeve edge each row. Row(s) 3-6 (4-5, 3-6): Work even at sleeve edges. Bind off remaining 3 stitches/sleeve.

Finishing

Use cast-on yarn tail to sew first rows on Welt 1 together. Weave in ends. Block. With tapestry needle and matching yarn, sew neck/front bodice edge to bound-off inner collar edge. Sew underarm seam so that the finished seam is outside on the sleeves and inside on the cuffs. Tack cuffs to reinforce rolled shape.

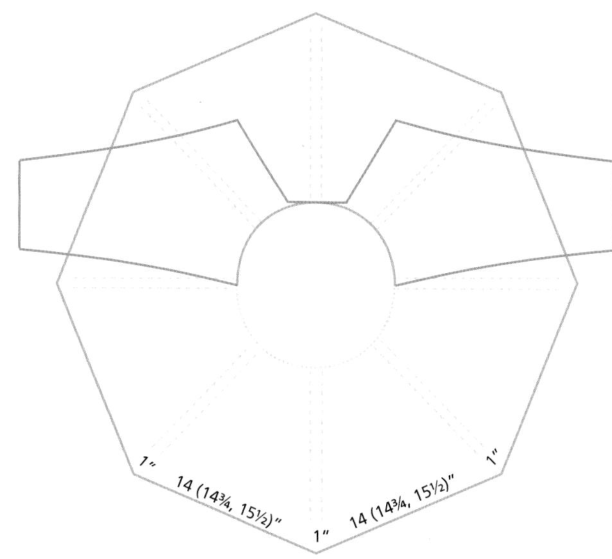
1"
14 (14¾, 15½)"
1"
14 (14¾, 15½)"
1"

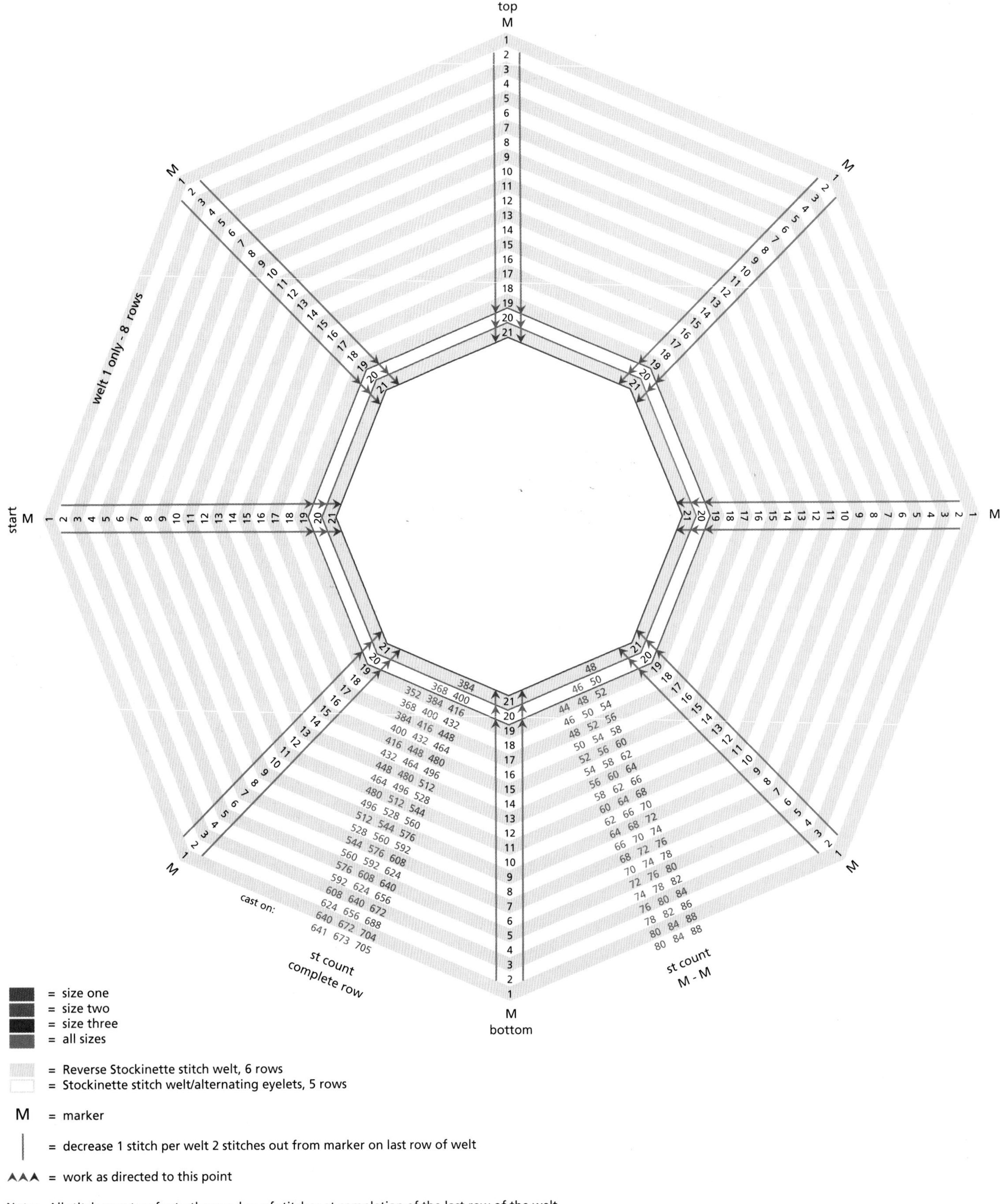

top
M
start
M
bottom
welt 1 only - 8 rows
cast on:
st count
complete row
384
368 400
352 384 416
368 400 432
384 416 448
400 432 464
416 448 480
432 464 496
448 480 512
464 496 528
480 512 544
496 528 560
512 544 576
528 560 592
544 576 608
560 592 624
576 608 640
592 624 656
608 640 672
624 656 688
640 672 704
641 673 705
st count
M - M
48
46 50
44 48 52
46 50 54
48 52 56
50 54 58
52 56 60
54 58 62
56 60 64
58 62 66
60 64 68
62 66 70
64 68 72
66 70 74
68 72 76
70 74 78
72 76 80
74 78 82
76 80 84
78 82 86
80 84 88
80 84 88
= size one
= size two
= size three
= all sizes
= Reverse Stockinette stitch welt, 6 rows
= Stockinette stitch welt/alternating eyelets, 5 rows
M = marker
= decrease 1 stitch per welt 2 stitches out from marker on last row of welt
= work as directed to this point
Note: All stitch counts refer to the number of stitches at completion of the last row of the welt

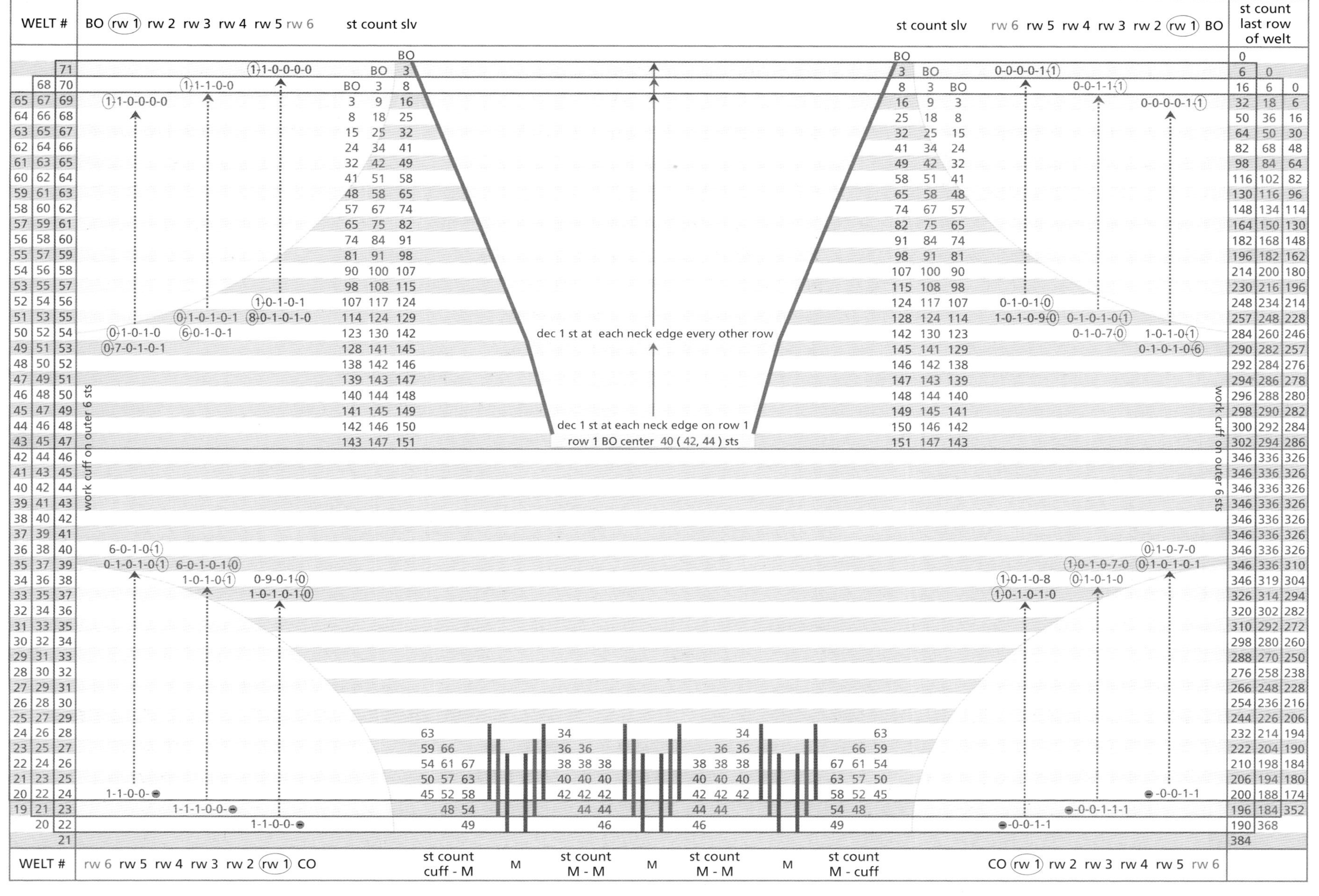

= size one
= size two
= size three
= all sizes

= Reverse Stockinette stitch welt, 6 rows
= Stockinette stitch welt/alternating eyelets, 5 rows

M = marker

● ● ● = on row 1 work 176 (184, 192) sts, then use JSSBO to BO 176 (184, 192) sts; bodice worked on rem sts; see pattern note row 3

| | | = decrease 1 st per welt 2 sts out from marker on last row of welt | = decrease at neck edge as directed above

▲ ▲ ▲ = work as directed to this point

⋮ ⋮ ⋮ = increase 1 st at sleeve edge each row (below center line); decrease 1 st at sleeve edge each row (above center line)

Note: All stitch counts refer to the number of stitches at completion of the last row of the welt

mink in motion

The swooning begins just rows into knitting this uniquely luxurious creation. The yarn begins to bloom and you begin to develop a tendency to sit mindlessly stroking the glorious fabric that falls from your needles. Yes, this is knitting heaven—and it is guilt free! The minks that are the source of this remarkable handspun yarn are sheared once a year and live the healthy, stress-free lives necessary for them to produce thick, lustrous coats year after year. The resulting fabric is reminiscent of fur, but is finer, softer, lighter and uniquely malleable in a way that invites the wearer to explore its vast styling potential. So go ahead, knit yourself a mink!

Sizes
One (Two, Three); shown here in Size Two.

Knitted Measurements
Collar: 12½ (13, 13½)"/32 (33, 34)cm
Center Back: 28 (29½, 31)"/71 (75, 79)cm
Center Back Neck to Cuff: 25¾ (26½, 27¼)"/65 (67, 69)cm

Approximate As-Worn Measurements
Collar: 10½ (11, 11½)"/27 (28, 29)cm
Center Back: 29½ (31, 32½)"/75 (79, 83)cm
Center Back Neck to Cuff: 32¾ (33¾, 34¾)"/83 (86, 88)cm

Materials
Four-ply, DK weight mink/cashmere blend, 1304 (1449, 1606) yd/1192 (1325, 1469)m (A); and 501 (575, 615) yd/458 (526, 562)m in contrasting color (B). As shown, 6 (7, 7) skeins Great Northern Yarns Mink Cashmere (70% mink/30% cashmere, 2 oz/56g, 230 yd/210m) in color Jet Black (A); and 3 (3, 3) skeins of the same yarn in color Natural (B).

One 32 (32, 40)" size 5 (3.75mm) circular needle or size required to obtain gauge.

Gauge
24 stitches and 32 rows = 4"/10cm

Before beginning, please review Chapter One, ***Silhouettes and Sizing*** and Chapter Two, ***Tips and Techniques***.

STITCH PATTERN: WELTED STRIPES
Continuous, alternating welts of Stockinette stitch in yarns A and B, and Reverse Stockinette stitch in yarn A.

Welt 1—Stockinette Stitch, 6 rows, yarns A and B
Work all even rows in A, odd rows in B.
When working in the round: (RS) Knit all rows.
When working flat: Knit on RS rows, purl on WS rows.
Welt 2—Reverse Stockinette Stitch, 5 rows, yarn A
When working in the round: (RS) Purl all rows.
When working flat: Purl on RS rows, knit on WS rows.
Repeat welts 1 and 2.

OUTER CIRCLE
With A, use a long-tail or double method to cast on 593 (625, 657) stitches, placing a marker in between the following 8 sections of 74 (78, 82) stitches each, with 1 stitch after the last marker. Use a different color marker for the last marker to denote the beginning and end of each row.

Welt 1, Stockinette Stitch (Note: The first 3 rows of this welt are worked flat before joining the work into a circle. It is important to the directional integrity of the pattern that the circle be joined at the completion of the third row as instructed.) Row 1: (RS) With B, knit. Break yarn. Row 2: With A, purl. Row 3: With B, knit to last stitch, slip 1. Adjust work to ensure that cast-on edge is not twisted around needle. (See *No Twist Join*, Chapter Two.) Join work into a circle by placing the last, slipped stitch from row 3 back onto the left needle. Two stitches are now on the left needle before the marker. Knit these two stitches together. Continue next rows in the round. Row 4: With A, knit. Row 5: With B, knit. Row 6: With A, knit. 592 (624, 656) stitches.

Welt 2, Reverse Stockinette Stitch Rows 1-4: With A, purl. Row 5: *P2, p2tog, purl to within 4 stitches of next marker, p2tog, p2, slip marker; repeat from * across entire row. 576 (608, 640) stitches.

Welt 3, Stockinette Stitch Rows 1-5: Starting with B, and alternating colors each row, knit. Row 6: With A, *K2, k2tog, knit to within 4 stitches of next marker, k2tog, k2, slip marker; repeat from * across entire row. 560 (592, 624) stitches.

Welts 4 - 19 (20, 21) (Note: Continue in Welted Stripes stitch pattern throughout remainder of garment.) Continue decreases at markers in last row of each welt as established. 304 (320, 336) stitches.

BACK BODICE AND SLEEVES
After the collar and lapels are completed and bound off, the bodice is worked flat on the remaining live stitches in the center of the garment. Change to the working-flat version of Welted Stripes stitch pattern after row 1 of next welt.

Welt 20 (21, 22) Row 1: Use Jeny's Surprisingly Stretchy Bind Off method to bind off first 152 (160, 168) stitches, then work remaining 152 (160, 168) stitches. Rows 2-3: Change to working-flat version of Welted Stripes stitch pattern. Work even. Row(s) 4 (4-5, 4): Increase 1 stitch at beginning and end of each row. Row 5 (6, 5): Increase 1 stitch at beginning and end of row and continue decreases in established manner at 3 remaining markers. 6 decreases worked/welt. 150 (160, 166) stitches.

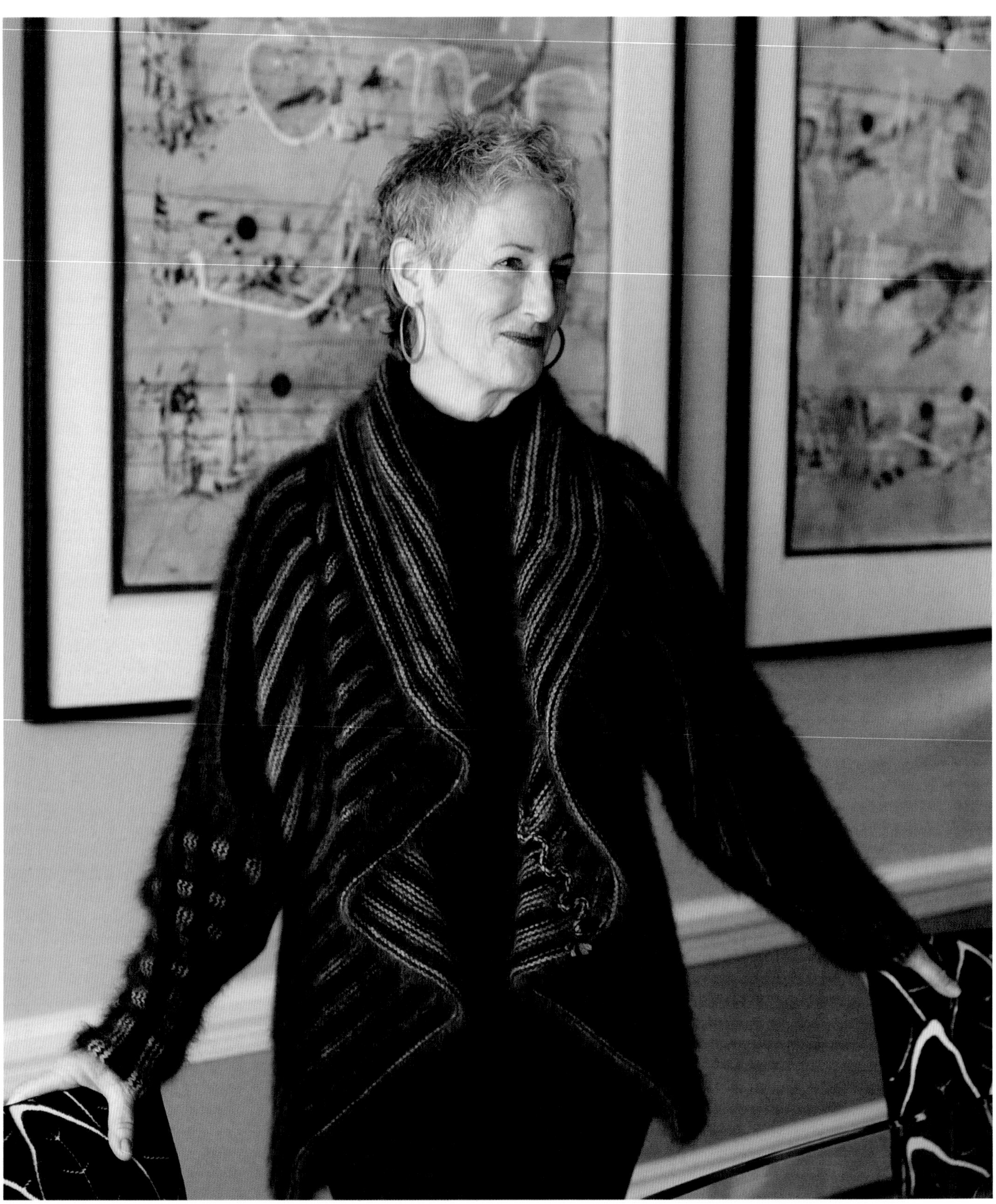

Welts 21 (22, 23) – 25 (26, 27) Continue to increase 1 stitch at beginning and end of each row and to decrease in established manner at markers in last row of each welt. 6 decreases worked/welt. 176 (184, 192) stitches.

Welts 26 (27, 28) – 34 (36, 37) No further marker decreases; remove all stitch markers. Continue to increase 1 stitch at beginning and end of each row. 274 (294, 302) stitches.

Welt 35 (37, 38) Cast on 1 stitch at the beginning of each row. (Note: To achieve desired sleeve length, add or subtract 4-5 stitches for each inch, distributed across all rows in this and the next welt.) 280 (300, 307) stitches.

Welt 36 (38, 39) Rows 1-3: Cast on 1 stitch at beginning of each row. Row 4: Cast on 7 (1, 1) stitches at beginning of row. Row 5: Cast on 6 (0, 2) stitches at beginning of row. Row 6, Size Three only: Cast on 1 stitch at beginning of row. 296 (304, 314) stitches.

Cuffs

Welts 37 (39, 40) – 41 (43, 45) Place markers 7 stitches in from each end of sleeves to indicate cuff stitches. Work the stitches between the markers even, in the established pattern. At the same time, work the cuff stitches in Stockinette stitch only, alternating colors as established. 296 (304, 314) stitches.

Neck, Front Bodice and Sleeves

In the next welt, stitches in the center of the row are bound off to create the back neck and begin shaping the two front bodice panels. Add a second ball of each yarn as necessary to work both sleeves at the same time. Continue to work cuff stitches

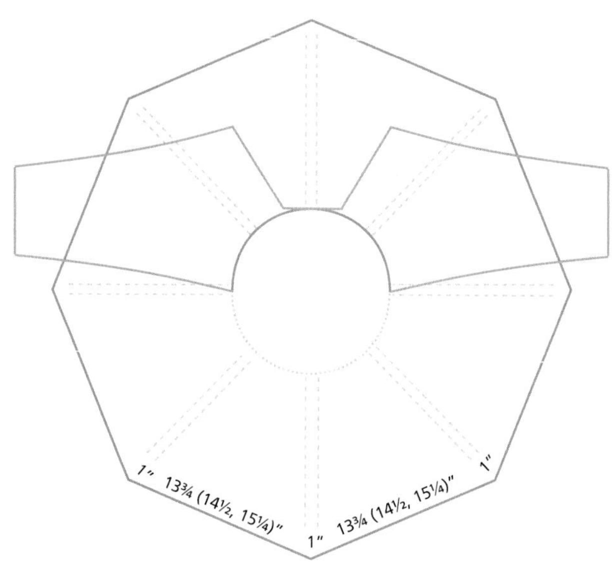

in Stockinette stitch and the stitches between the markers in the established Welted Stripes pattern.

Welt 42 (44, 46) Row 1: Work 129 (132, 136) stitches, use basic method to bind off center 38 (40, 42) stitches, work remaining 129 (132, 136) stitches. Row 2: Work in established pattern to the second neck edge, add a second ball of yarn and continue row. Rows 3-5: Work even. 129 (132, 136) stitches/sleeve.

Welts 43 (45, 47) – 46 (48, 51) Work in established pattern, decreasing 1 stitch at each neck edge on row 1 of each welt. 125 (128, 131) stitches/sleeve.

Welt 47 (49, 52) Apply in reverse order any sleeve length changes made in welts 35-36 (37-38, 38-39) in this and the next welt. Continue decreasing at neck edges on row 1. Row 1: Bind off 6 (0, 1) stitches at beginning (sleeve end) of row and 1 stitch at each neck edge. Row 2: Bind off 7 (1, 2) stitches at beginning (sleeve end) of row. Rows 3-6 (3-6, 3-5): Bind off 1 stitch at beginning of each row. 115/116 (124/125, 127) stitches/sleeve.

Welt 48 (50, 53) Continue to work decreases at neck edges as established and, at the same time, bind off 1 stitch at beginning of each row. 112 (121, 123) stitches/sleeve.

Welts 49 (51, 54) – 54 (56, 58) Continue to work decreases at neck edges as established and, at the same time, decrease 1 stitch at each sleeve edge each row. 73 (82, 91) stitches/sleeve.

Welts 55 (57, 59) – 62 (65, 68) Decrease 1 stitch at each neck edge *every other* row and, at the same time, decrease 1 stitch at each sleeve edge each row. 7 (7, 8) stitches/sleeve.

Welt 63 (66, 69) Continue to work decreases at neck edges every other row. Rows 1-2: Decrease 1 stitch at each sleeve edge each row. Row 3: Decrease 0 (0, 1) stitches at each sleeve edge. Rows 4-6 (4-5, 4-6): Work even at sleeve edges. Bind off remaining 2 stitches/sleeve.

Finishing

Use cast-on yarn tail to sew first rows on Welt 1 together. Weave in ends. Block. With tapestry needle and matching yarn, sew neck/front bodice edge to bound-off inner collar edge. Sew underarm seams. Tack cuffs to reinforce rolled shape.

To create the braid trim, cut five 40"/102cm lengths of yarn (3 of A and 2 of B) and thread together through a tapestry needle. With the public side of the lapel facing you, locate the top of welt 10 (11, 12) at the point where rows begin and end. Thread the yarn through the fabric so that the needle enters 1 stitch to the right and exits 1 stitch to the left of the start-of-row line. Remove the needle and adjust the strands of yarn so that all are of equal length and divided into 5 groups: two outer groups of 2 strands A each, two inner groups of 2 strands B each, and a center group of two strands A. Hold two groups in one hand and three in the other.

*Braid, moving the outermost of the three groups held in one hand to the center and adding it to the groups held with the other hand. Repeat from * until braid measures approximately 10 (11, 12)"/25.5 (28, 30.5)cm. Tie a simple overhand knot at the end. Arrange in a loose zigzag pattern approximately ¾"/2cm wide and tack to lapel, following the start-of-row line toward welt 1. Adjust location of the knot so that it sits adjacent to the last row of welt 1. Trim yarn strands even beneath knot.

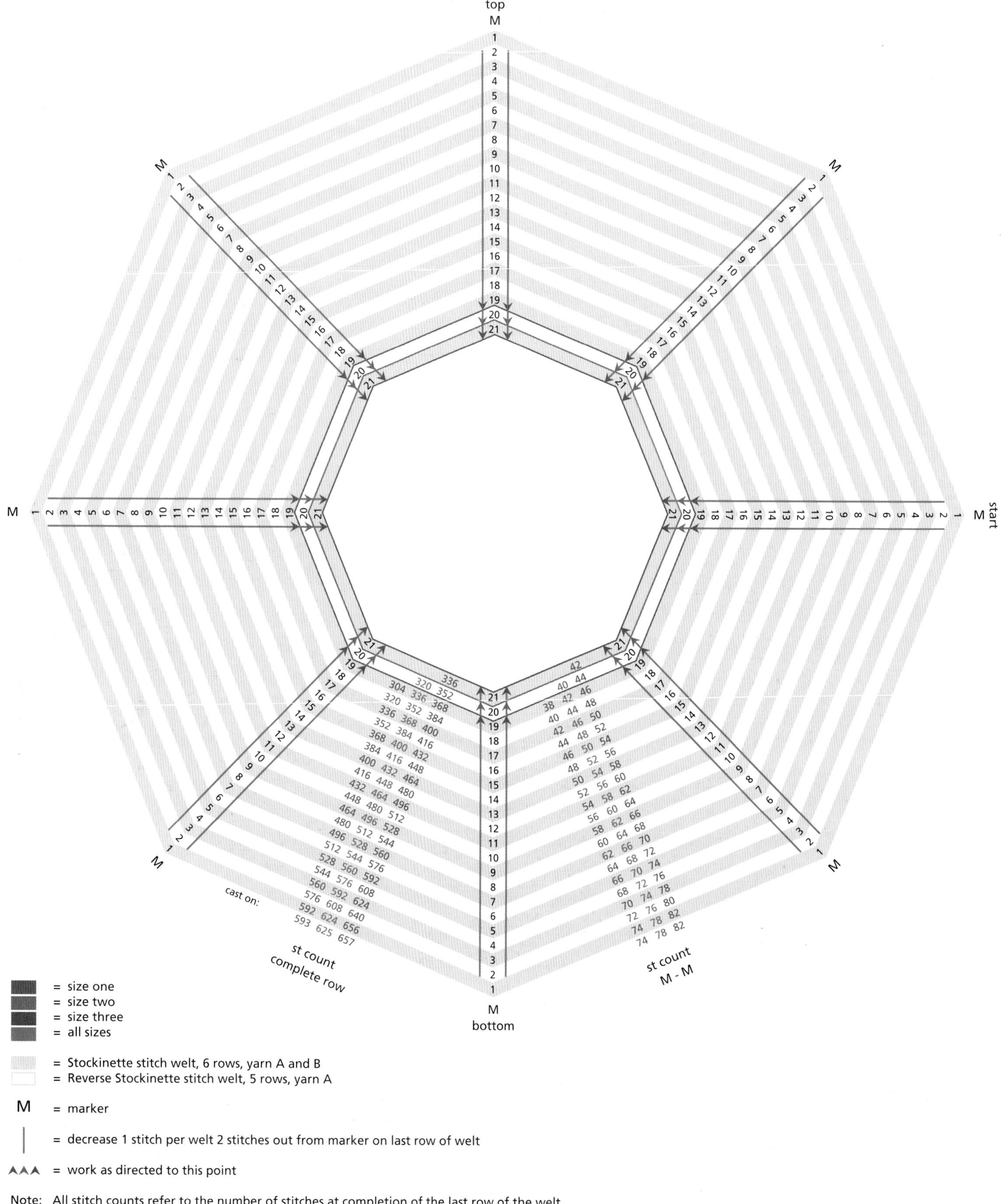
top
M
M
M
M
start
M
M
M
bottom
cast on:
st count
complete row
336
320 352
304 336 368
320 352 384
336 368 400
352 384 416
368 400 432
384 416 448
400 432 464
416 448 480
432 464 496
448 480 512
464 496 528
480 512 544
496 528 560
512 544 576
528 560 592
544 576 608
560 592 624
576 608 640
592 624 656
593 625 657
st count
M - M
42
40 44
38 42 46
40 44 48
42 46 50
44 48 52
46 50 54
48 52 56
50 54 58
52 56 60
54 58 62
56 60 64
58 62 66
60 64 68
62 66 70
64 68 72
66 70 74
68 72 76
70 74 78
72 76 80
74 78 82
74 78 82
= size one
= size two
= size three
= all sizes
= Stockinette stitch welt, 6 rows, yarn A and B
= Reverse Stockinette stitch welt, 5 rows, yarn A
M = marker
= decrease 1 stitch per welt 2 stitches out from marker on last row of welt
= work as directed to this point
Note: All stitch counts refer to the number of stitches at completion of the last row of the welt

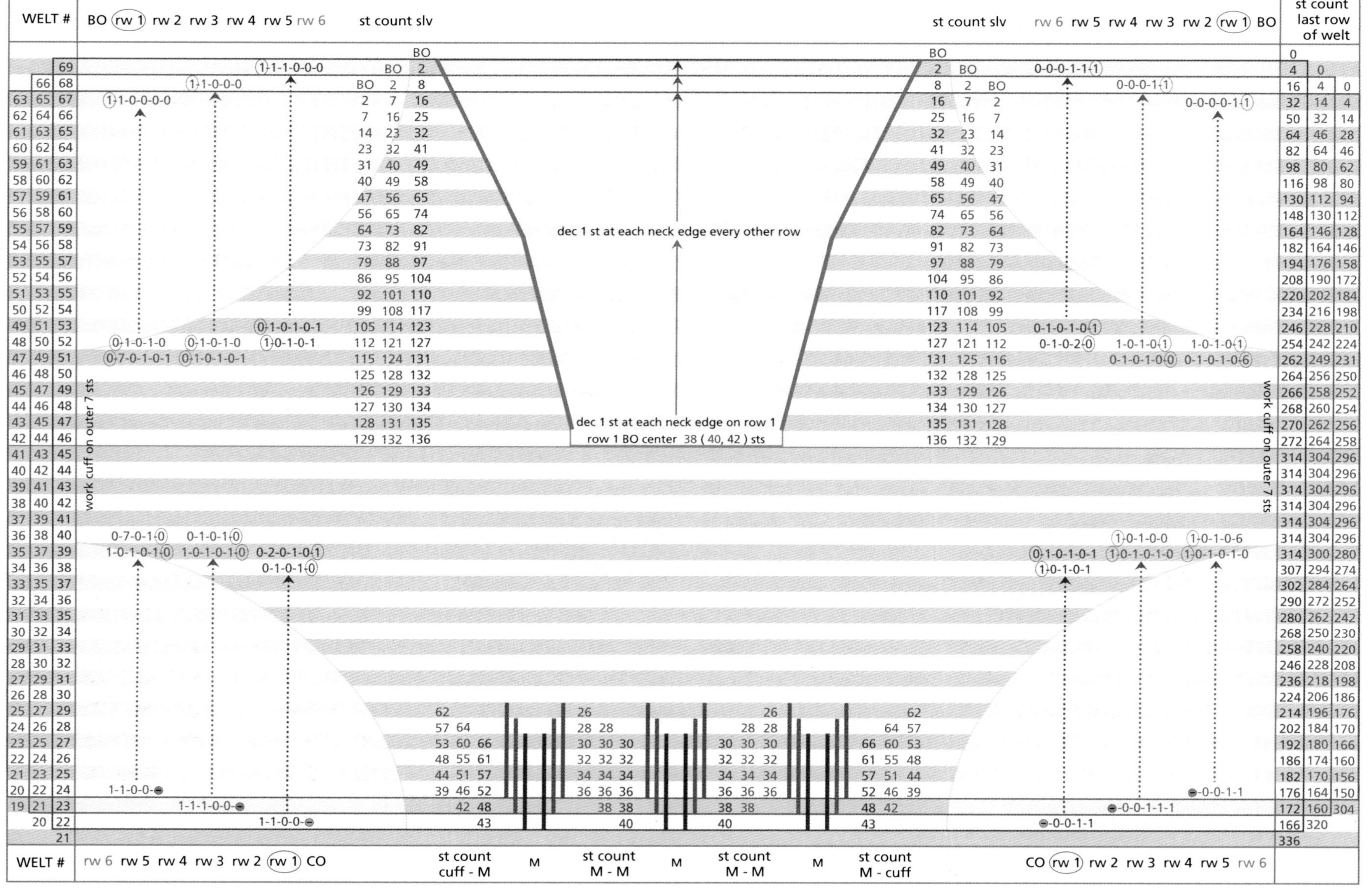

= size one
= size two
= size three
= all sizes

= Stockinette stitch welt, 6 rows
= Reverse Stockinette stitch welt, 5 rows

M = marker

= on row use JSSBO to BO 152 (160, 168) sts, then work 152 (160, 168) sts; bodice worked on remaining sts

= decrease 1 stitch per welt 2 stitches out from marker on last row of welt

= decrease at neck edge as directed above

= work as directed to this point

= increase 1 st at sleeve edge each row (below center line); decrease 1 st at sleeve edge each row (above center line)

Note: All stitch counts refer to the number of stitches at completion of the last row of the welt

tangerine rose

In Tangerine Rose, a single track of silk ribbon weaves its way through and around a deep collar and wide border rich in texture and pattern before ending its journey in the rosette corsage that blooms on one lapel. Intricacy gives way to elegant simplicity in the slim, fitted back, allowing the pure beauty of the fine hand-dyed silk and merino yarn to take center stage. Slender sleeves taper to split cuffs that recall the roll of the welts above. Feel free to dress up or dress down—this jacket can go a long way with you in either direction.

Sizes
One (Two, Three); shown here in Size One.

Knitted Measurements
Collar: 11½ (12, 12½)"/29 (31, 32)cm
Center Back: 30¾ (32, 33½)"/78 (81, 85)cm
Center Back Neck to Cuff: 30¼ (31, 31¾)"/77 (79, 81)cm

Approximate As-Worn Measurements
Collar: 10¼ (10¾, 11¼)"/26 (27, 29)cm
Center Back: 30 (31¼, 32½)"/76 (79, 83)cm
Center Back Neck to Cuff: 33¼ (34, 34¾)"/84 (86, 88)cm

Materials
Single-ply, worsted weight silk/merino blend yarn, 1477 (1633, 1807) yd/1351 (1493, 1652)m; and silk ribbon, 4 yd/3.7m. As shown, 8 (9, 10) skeins Sundara Yarns Aran Silky Merino (50% silk/50% merino, 3½ oz/100g, 200 yd/183m) in color Spiced; and 4 yd/3.7m Hanah Silk ribbon in color Tuscany.

One 32 (32, 40)" size 7 (4.5mm) circular needle and one 32 (32, 40)" size 15 (10.0mm) circular needle or sizes required to obtain gauge.

Gauge
18 stitches and 25 rows = 4"/10cm

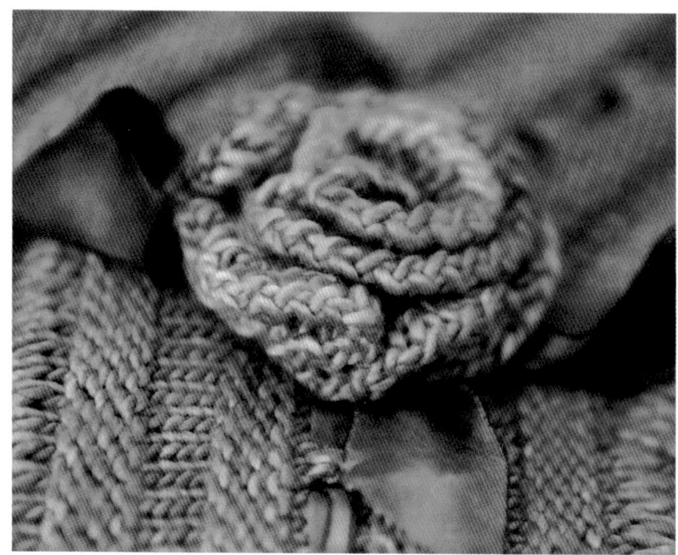

Before beginning, please review Chapter One, ***Silhouettes and Sizing*** and Chapter Two, ***Tips and Techniques***.

STITCH PATTERNS: WELTED STRIPES WITH EYELETS AND CONDO ROW

Continuous, alternating welts of Reverse Stockinette stitch and Stockinette stitch. In outer circle, Stockinette stitch welts are at times worked in one of two alternate patterns.

Welt 1—Reverse Stockinette Stitch, 4 rows
When working in the round: (RS) Purl all rows.
When working flat: Purl on RS rows, knit on WS rows.
Welt 2—Stockinette Stitch, 5 rows
When working in the round: (RS) Knit all rows.
When working flat: Knit on RS rows, purl on WS rows.
Repeat welts 1 and 2.

Welt 2 alternate—Stockinette Stitch with Eyelets, 5 rows
Working in the round: (RS) Knit all rows, working eyelet row on row 3.
Eyelet row: *K2tog, YO; repeat from * across entire row.
Welt 2 alternate—Stockinette Stitch with Condo Row, 4 rows
Knit rows 1, 3, 4 with smaller needle, row 2 with larger needle (condo row).
Working in the round: Knit all rows.

OUTER CIRCLE

Use a long-tail or double method to cast on 529 (561, 593) stitches, placing a marker in between the following 8 sections of 66 (70, 74) stitches each, with 1 stitch after the last marker. Use a different color marker for the last marker to denote the beginning and end of each row.

Welt 1, Reverse Stockinette Stitch (Note: This outer welt has 6 rows instead of the normal 4 rows. The first 3 rows are worked flat before joining the work into a circle. It is important to the directional integrity of the pattern that the circle be joined at the completion of the third row as instructed.) Row 1: (RS) Purl. Row 2: Knit. Row 3: Purl to last stitch, slip 1. Adjust work to ensure that cast-on edge is not twisted around needle. (See *No Twist Join*, Chapter Two.) Join work into a circle by placing the last, slipped stitch from row 3 back onto the left needle. Two stitches are now on the left needle before the marker. Purl these two stitches together. Continue next rows in the round. Rows 4-6: Purl. 528 (560, 592) stitches.

Welt 2, Stockinette Stitch with Eyelets Rows 1-4: Work first 4 rows of Stockinette stitch with eyelets. Row 5: *K2, k2tog, knit to within 4 stitches of next marker, k2tog, k2, slip marker; repeat from * across entire row. 512 (544, 576) stitches.

Welt 3, Reverse Stockinette Stitch Rows 1-3: Purl. Row 4: *P2, p2tog, purl to within 4 stitches of next marker, p2tog, p2, slip marker; repeat from * across entire row. 496 (528, 560) stitches.

Welts 4 - 20 (21, 22) (Note: Continue in Welted Stripes stitch pattern throughout remainder of garment substituting Stockinette stitch with condo row on welts 6 and 14 and Stockinette stitch with eyelets on welts 10 and 18.) Continue decreases in last row of each welt as established. 224 (240, 256) stitches.

BACK BODICE AND SLEEVES

After the collar and lapels are completed and bound off, the bodice is worked flat on the remaining live stitches in the center of the garment. No further use of alternate Stockinette

stitch patterns. Change to the working-flat version of Welted Stripes stitch pattern after row 1 of next welt.

Welt 21 (22, 23) Row 1: Use Jeny's Surprisingly Stretchy Bind Off method to bind off first 112 (120, 128) stitches, then work remaining 112 (120, 128) stitches. Rows 2-3: Change to working-flat version of Welted Stripes stitch pattern. Work even. Row 4, Size Two only: Increase 1 stitch at beginning and end of row. Row 4 (5, 4): Increase 1 stitch at beginning and end of row and continue decreases in established manner at 3 remaining markers. 6 decreases worked/welt. 108 (118, 124) stitches.

Welts 22 (23, 24) - 23 (24, 25) Continue to increase 1 stitch at beginning and end of each row and to decrease in established manner at markers in last row of each welt. 6 decreases worked/welt. 114 (124, 130) stitches.

Welts 24 (25, 26) - 34 (35, 36) No further marker decreases; remove all stitch markers. Continue to increase 1 stitch at beginning and end of each row. 214 (222, 230) stitches.

Welt 35 (36, 37) Rows 1 and 3: Cast on 4 stitches at beginning of row. Rows 2 and 4: Cast on 6 stitches at beginning of row. Row 5, Size Two only: Cast on 5 stitches at beginning of row. (Note: To achieve desired sleeve length, add or subtract 4 stitches for each inch, distributed across all rows in this and the next welt.) 234 (247, 250) stitches.

Welt 36 (37, 38) Row 1: Cast on 5 (6, 5) stitches at beginning of row. Row 2: Cast on 7 (5, 6) stitches at beginning of row. Row 3: Cast on 6 (10, 5) stitches at beginning of row. Row(s) 4-5 (4, 4-5): Cast on 10 stitches at beginning of (each) row. 272 (278, 286) stitches.

Cuffs

Welts 37 (38, 39) - 42 (44, 46) Place markers 10 stitches in from each sleeve end to indicate cuff stitches. Row 1: K6, p2, k2, slip marker, work in established pattern to next marker, slip marker, k2, p2, k6. Row 2: P6, k2, p2, slip marker, work in established pattern to next marker, slip marker, p2, k2, p6. Subsequent rows: Work the stitches between the markers even in the established pattern and, at the same time, work the cuff stitches even, repeating the cuff pattern in rows 1 and 2 above. 272 (278, 286) stitches.

Neck, Front Bodice and Sleeves

In the next welt, stitches in the center of the row are bound off to create the back neck and begin shaping the two front bodice panels. Continue to work cuff stitches in established cuff pattern and the stitches between the markers in the established Welted Stripes pattern.

Welt 43 (45, 47) Row 1: Work 117 (118, 121) stitches, use basic method to bind off center 38 (42, 44) stitches, work remaining 117 (118, 121) stitches. Row 2: Work in established patterns to the second neck edge, add a second ball of yarn and continue row. Rows 3-4: Work even. 117 (118, 121) stitches/sleeve.

Welts 44 (46, 48) - 48 (51, 54) Work in established pattern, decreasing 1 stitch at each neck edge on row 1 of each welt. 112 (112, 114) stitches/sleeve.

Welt 49 (52, 55) Apply in reverse order any sleeve length changes made in welts 35-36 (36-37, 37-38) in this and the next welt. Continue decreasing at neck edges on row 1. Rows 1-2: Bind off 10 stitches at beginning (sleeve end) of each row. Row 3: Bind off 6 (5, 5) stitches at beginning of row. Row 4: Bind off 7 (6, 6) stitches at beginning of row. Row 5, Size Two only: Bind off 5 stitches at beginning of row. 94/95 (91/95, 97/98) stitches/sleeve.

Welt 50 (53, 56) Continue to work decreases at neck edges as established. Row 1: Bind off 5 (6, 5) stitches at beginning of row. Row 2: Bind off 6 (4, 6) stitches at beginning of row. Row 3: Bind off 4 (6, 4) stitches at beginning of row. Row 4: Bind off 6 (4, 6) stitches at beginning of row. Row 5, Sizes One and Three only: Bind off 4 stitches at beginning of row. 81 (82, 84) stitches/sleeve.

Welts 51 (54, 57) - 61 (63, 65) Continue to work decreases at neck edges as established and, at the same time, decrease 1 stitch at each sleeve edge each row. 21 (27, 35) stitches/sleeve.

Welts 62 (64, 66) - 63 (66, 69) Decrease 1 stitch at each neck edge *every other* row and, at the same time, decrease 1 stitch at each sleeve edge each row. 7 (6, 8) stitches/sleeve.

Welt 64 (67, 70) Continue to work decreases at neck edges every other row. Row 1: Decrease 1 stitch at each sleeve edge. Row 2: Decrease 1 (0, 1) stitch at each sleeve edge. Row(s) 3-5 (3-4, 3-5): Work even at sleeve edges. Row(s) 4-5 (4, 4-5): Work even at sleeve edges. Bind off remaining 3 stitches/sleeve.

Finishing

Use cast-on yarn tail to sew first rows on Welt 1 together. Weave in ends. Block. With tapestry needle and matching yarn, sew neck/front bodice edge to bound-off inner collar edge. Sew underarm seam from wrist to wrist, leaving the cuffs open. Reinforce seam at each end. (Note: Tangerine Rose, as shown, was sewn together so that the "wrong side"

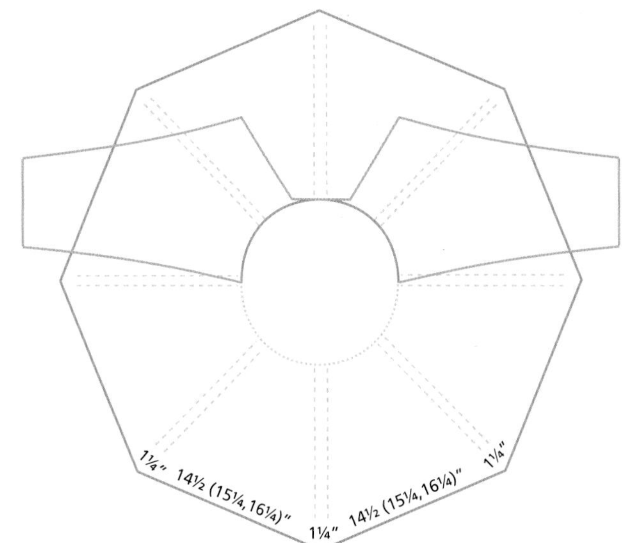

is seen in the torso and sleeves and the "right side" in the collar and lapels.)

With a tapestry needle threaded with ribbon, loosely weave ribbon in and out of the middle row of eyelets starting and ending with eyelets at the start-of-row point. Check to see that the ribbon length is sufficient to allow some stretch of the knitted fabric. Tie ends in simple bow and trim ends.

To create the rosette, start with enough yarn to leave a 12" tail and cast on 16 stitches. Row 1: (RS) Knit. Row 2 and all even rows: Purl. Rows 3, 5, 7: *Knit into front and back of stitch; repeat from * to end of row. Row 9: Bind off all stitches, preserving a tail of 12". With both yarn tails held together with two fingers, loosely wrap the bound off edge around and around to form a rosette. Use a tapestry needle and one yarn tail to sew the rosette together. Center the rosette over the silk ribbon bow and sew on using remaining yarn tail. Weave in any remaining ends.

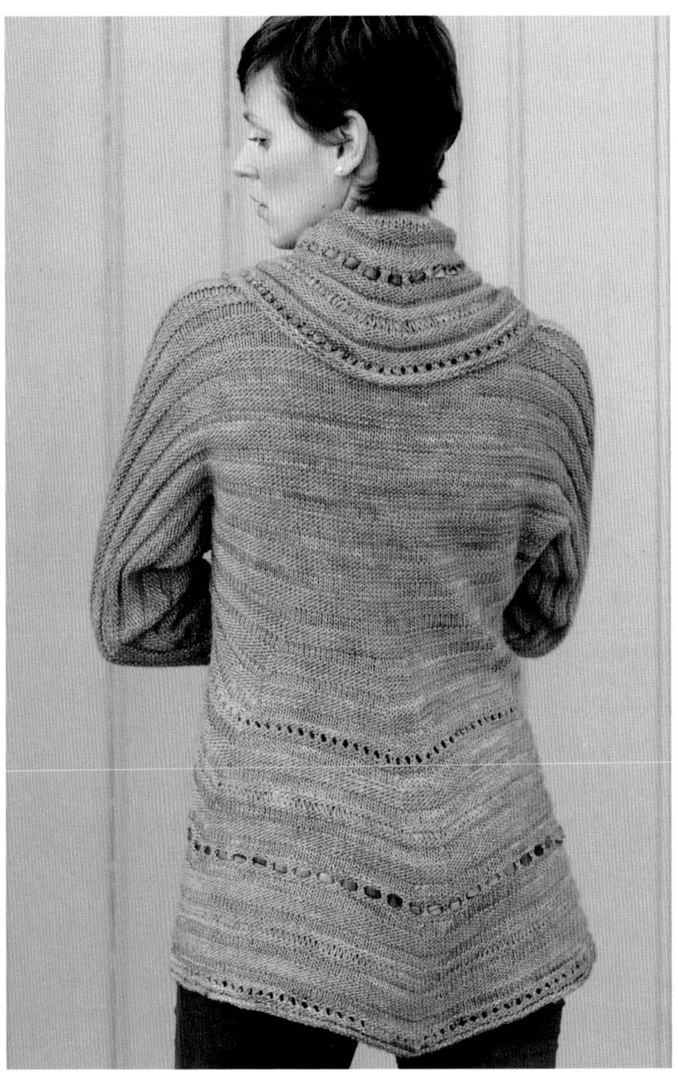

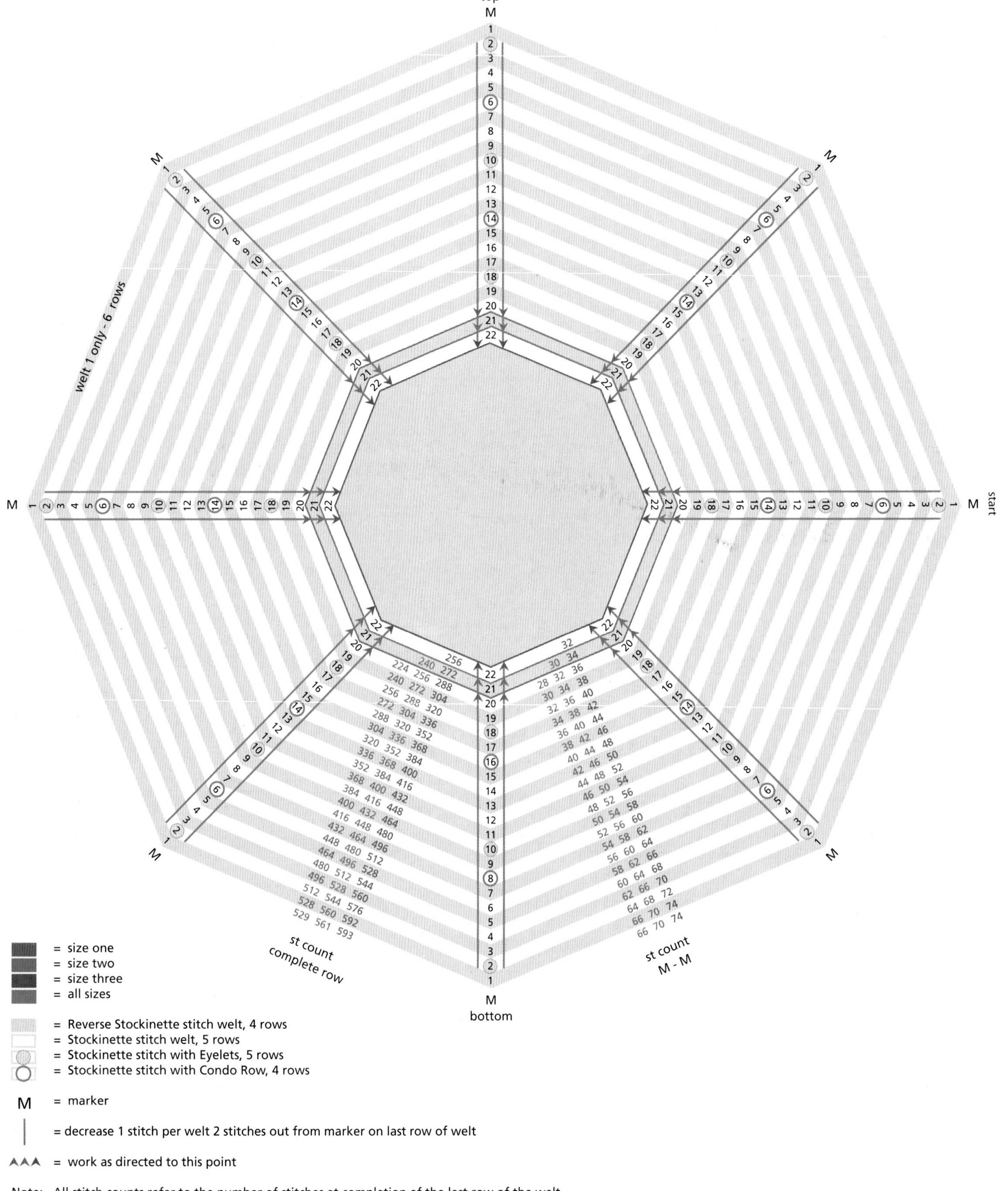
top
M
bottom
start
welt 1 only - 6 rows
st count
complete row
256
240 272
224 256 288
240 272 304
256 288 320
272 304 336
288 320 352
304 336 368
320 352 384
336 368 400
352 384 416
368 400 432
384 416 448
400 432 464
416 448 480
432 464 496
448 480 512
464 496 528
480 512 544
496 528 560
512 544 576
528 560 592
529 561 593
st count
M - M
32
30 34
28 32 36
30 34 38
32 36 40
34 38 42
36 40 44
38 42 46
40 44 48
42 46 50
44 48 52
46 50 54
48 52 56
50 54 58
52 56 60
54 58 62
56 60 64
58 62 66
60 64 68
62 66 70
64 68 72
66 70 74
66 70 74
= size one
= size two
= size three
= all sizes
= Reverse Stockinette stitch welt, 4 rows
= Stockinette stitch welt, 5 rows
= Stockinette stitch with Eyelets, 5 rows
= Stockinette stitch with Condo Row, 4 rows
M = marker
= decrease 1 stitch per welt 2 stitches out from marker on last row of welt
= work as directed to this point
Note: All stitch counts refer to the number of stitches at completion of the last row of the welt

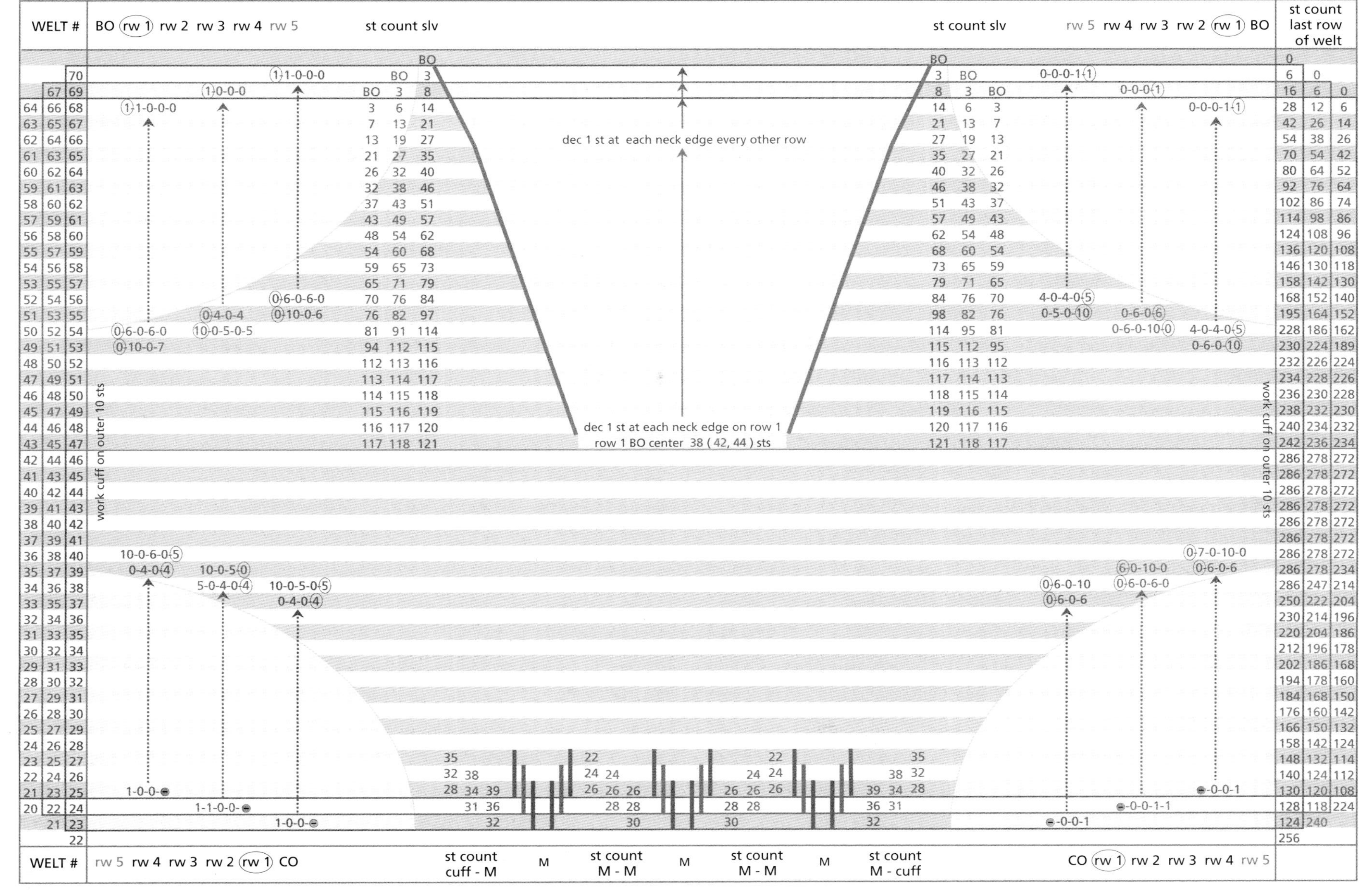

= size one
= size two
= size three
= all sizes

= Reverse Stockinette stitch welt, 4 rows
= Stockinette stitch welt, 5 rows

M = marker

= on row use JSSBO to BO 112 (120, 128) sts, then work 112 (120, 128) sts; bodice worked on remaining sts

= decrease 1 stitch per welt 2 stitches out from marker on last row of welt

= decrease at neck edge as directed above

= work as directed to this point

= increase 1 st at sleeve edge each row (below center line); decrease 1 st at sleeve edge each row (above center line)

Note: All stitch counts refer to the number of stitches at completion of the last row of the welt

depth of field

A rich mix of tone-on-tone textures are at play here. Nubby, distressed merino twists around a thick sleek strand of shining silk to form the chunky yarn used to create a series of deep, rounded welts that are the supporting structure of this garment. In contrast, an ethereal web of mohair and silk peeks out between the heavy welts, creating bands of transparency that assure the finished jacket will be lightweight and supple with elegant drape. Wide gussets at the bust provide extra ease and broad lapels that can be encouraged to cascade or gathered and pinned to show off the cape-like collar.

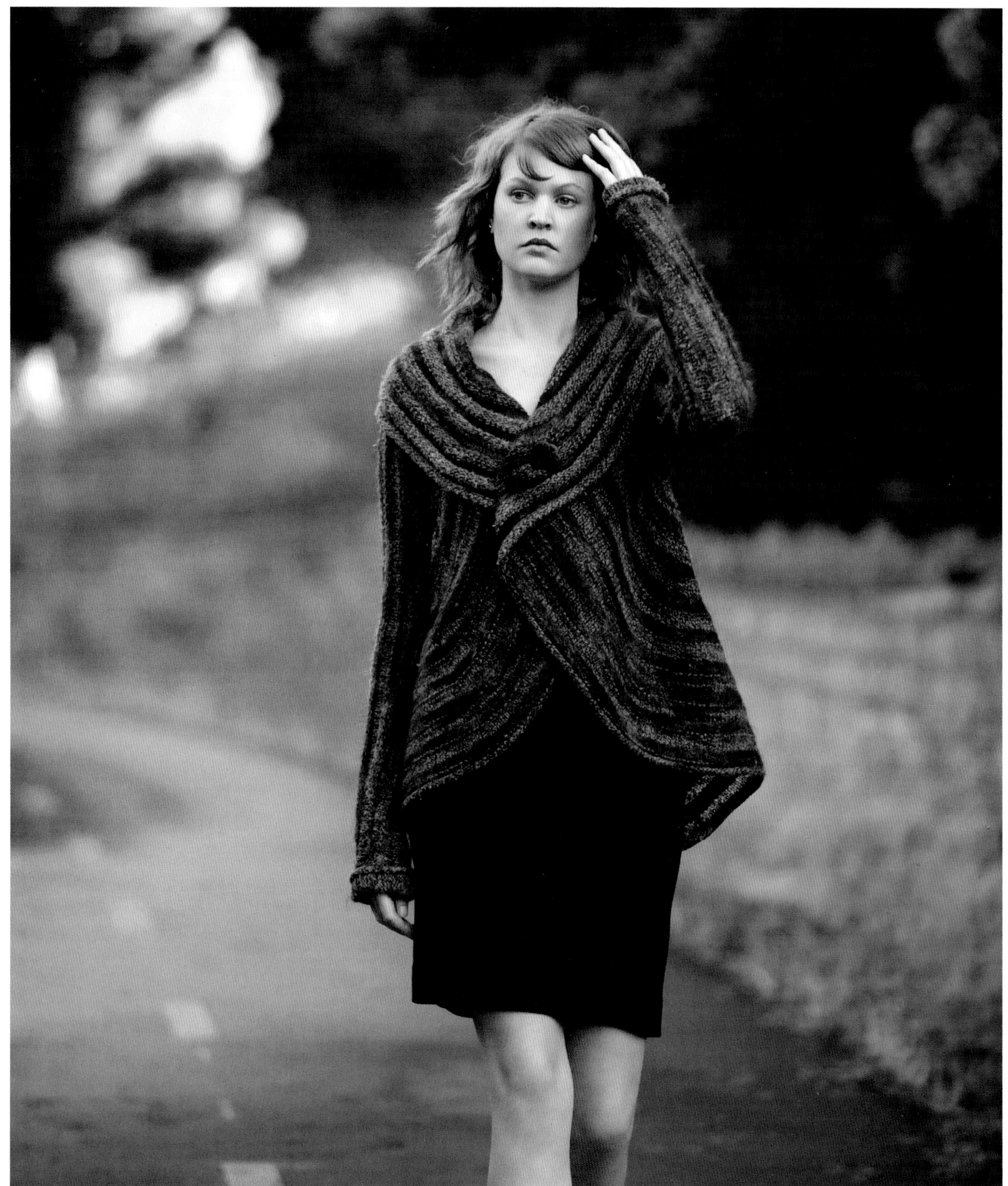

Sizes
One (Two, Three); shown here in Size Two.

Knitted Measurements
Collar: 16 (17, 18)"/41 (43, 46)cm
Center Back: 32 (34, 36)"/81 (86, 91)cm
Center Back Neck to Cuff: 26½ (27¼, 27¾)"/67 (69, 70)cm

Approximate As-Worn Measurements
Collar: 13 (14, 15)"/33 (36, 38)cm
Center Back: 32 (34, 36)"/81 (86, 91)cm
Center Back Neck to Cuff: 32¾ (33¾, 34½)"/83 (86, 88)cm

Materials
Two-ply, chunky weight silk/wool blend yarn, 771 (860, 976) yd/705 (786, 892)m (A); and two-ply, lace weight brushed mohair blend yarn, 1047 (1210, 1339) yd/957 (1106, 1224) m in coordinating color (B). (Note: Yarn B is held double throughout.) As shown, 9 (10, 12) skeins Alchemy Wabi-Sabi (66% silk/34% wool, 1¾ oz/50g, 86 yd/78.6m) in colorway #12w-Ocean Floor (A); and 4 (4, 5) skeins Alchemy Haiku (60% mohair/40% silk, 1 oz/25g, 325 yd/297m) in same colorway (B).

One 40 (40, 47)" size 10 (6.0mm) circular needle or size required to obtain gauge.

Gauge
16 stitches and 18 rows = 4"/10cm

Before beginning, please review Chapter One, ***Silhouettes and Sizing*** and Chapter Two, ***Tips and Techniques***.

STITCH PATTERN: WELTED STRIPES

Continuous, alternating welts of Reverse Stockinette stitch in yarn A and Stockinette stitch in yarn B.

Welt 1— Reverse Stockinette Stitch, 5 Rows, yarn A
When working in the round: (RS) Purl all rows.
When working flat: Purl on RS rows, knit on WS rows.
Welt 2—Stockinette Stitch, 4 Rows, yarn B (2 strands)
When working in the round: (RS) Knit all rows.
When working flat: Knit on RS rows, purl on WS rows.
Repeat welts 1 and 2.

OUTER CIRCLE

With A, use a long-tail or double method to cast on 473 (505, 537) stitches, placing a marker in between the following 8 sections of 59 (63, 67) stitches each, with 1 stitch after the last marker. Use a different color marker for the last marker to denote the beginning and end of each row.

Welt 1, Reverse Stockinette Stitch (Note: This outer welt has 7 rows instead of the normal 5 rows. The first 3 rows are worked flat before joining the work into a circle. It is important to the directional integrity of the pattern that the circle be joined at the completion of the third row as instructed.) Row 1: (RS) With A, purl. Row 2: Knit. Row 3: Purl to last stitch, slip 1. Adjust work to ensure that cast-on edge is not twisted around needle. (See No Twist Join, Chapter Two.) Join work into a circle by placing the last, slipped stitch from row 3 back onto the left needle. Two stitches are now on the left needle before the marker. Purl these two stitches together. Continue next rows in the round. Rows 4-7: Purl. 472 (504, 536) stitches.

Welt 2, Stockinette Stitch Rows 1-3: With two strands of B held together, knit. Row 4: *K2, k2tog, knit to within 4 stitches of next marker, k2tog, k2, slip marker; repeat from * across entire row. 456 (488, 520) stitches.

Welt 3, Reverse Stockinette Stitch Rows 1-4: With A, purl. Row 5: *P2, p2tog, purl to within 4 stitches of next marker, p2tog, p2, slip marker; repeat from * across entire row. 440 (472, 504) stitches.

Welts 4 - 17 (18, 19) (Note: Continue in Welted Stripes stitch pattern throughout remainder of garment.) Continue decreases at marker in last row of each welt as established. 216 (232, 248) stitches.

BACK BODICE AND SLEEVES

After the collar and lapels are completed and bound off, the bodice is worked flat on the remaining live stitches in the center of the garment. Change to the working-flat version of Welted Stripes stitch pattern after row 1 of next welt.

Welt 18 (19, 20) Row 1: Break yarn and slip the last 12 stitches just worked back onto the left needle to reposition beginning of row. Using Jeny's Surprisingly Stretchy Bind Off method, rejoin yarn and bind off 132 (140, 148) stitches; work remaining 84 (92, 100) stitches. Rows 2-3: Change to working-flat version of Welted Stripes stitch pattern. Work even. Row 4, Size Two only: Increase 1 stitch at beginning and end of row. Row 4 (5, 4): Increase 1 stitch at beginning and end of row and continue decreases in established manner at 3 remaining markers. 6 decreases worked/welt. 80 (90, 96) stitches.

Welts 19 (20, 21) – 21 (22, 23) Continue to increase 1 stitch at beginning and end of each row and to decrease in established manner at markers in last row of each welt. 6 decreases worked/welt. 90 (98, 106) stitches.

Welts 22 (23, 24) – 24 (25, 26) No further marker decreases; remove all stitch markers. Continue to increase 1 stitch at beginning and end of each row. 116 (126, 132) stitches.

Welt 25 (26, 27) Rows 1-4: Cast on 8 stitches at beginning of each row. Row 5, Sizes One and Three only: Cast on 6 (4) stitches at beginning of row. (Note: To achieve desired sleeve length, add or subtract 2-3 stitches for each inch, distributed across all rows in this and the next welt.) 154 (158, 168) stitches.

Welt 26 (27, 28) Row 1: Cast on 11 (5, 8) stitches at beginning of row. Row 2: Cast on 5 (9, 4) stitches at beginning of row. Row 3: Cast on 14 (4, 14) stitches at beginning of row. Row 4: Cast on 14 stitches at beginning of row. Row 5, Size Two only: Cast on 14 stitches at beginning of row. 198 (204, 208) stitches.

Cuffs

Welts 27 (28, 29) – 32 (34, 36) Place markers 14 stitches in from each end of sleeves to indicate cuff stitches. Work the stitches between the markers even, in the established pattern. At the same time, work the cuff stitches in Reverse Stockinette stitch only and in yarn A only, adding a small bobbin of A at each cuff as necessary. 198 (204, 208) stitches.

Neck, Front Bodice and Sleeves

In the next welt, stitches in the center of the row are bound off to create the back neck and begin shaping the two front bodice panels. Add a second ball of each yarn as necessary to work both sleeves at the same time. Continue to work cuff stitches in Reverse Stockinette stitch and the stitches between the markers in the established Welted Stripes pattern.

Welt 33 (35, 37) Row 1: Work 87 (89, 90) stitches, use basic method to bind off center 24 (26, 28) stitches, work remaining 87 (89, 90) stitches. Row 2: Work in established pattern to the second neck edge, add a second ball of yarn and continue row. Row 3-5: Work even. 87 (89, 90) stitches/sleeve.

Welts 34 (36, 38) – 38 (41, 44) Work in established pattern, decreasing 1 stitch at each neck edge on row 1 of each welt. 82 (83, 83) stitches/sleeve.

Welt 39 (42), Sizes One And Two Apply in reverse order any sleeve length changes made in welts 25-26 (26-27) in this and the next welt. Continue decreasing at neck edges on row 1. Rows 1-2: Bind off 14 stitches at beginning (sleeve end) of each row. Row 3: Bind off 5 (4) stitches at beginning of row. Row 4: Bind off 11 (9) stitches at beginning of row. Row 5, Size One only: Bind off 6 stitches at beginning of row. 56 (59/64) stitches/sleeve.

Welt 40, Size One Continue to work decreases at neck edges as established, and, at the same time, bind off 8 stitches at beginning of each row. 39 stitches/sleeve.

Welt 45, Size Three Apply in reverse order any sleeve length changes made in welts 27-28 in this and the next welt. No

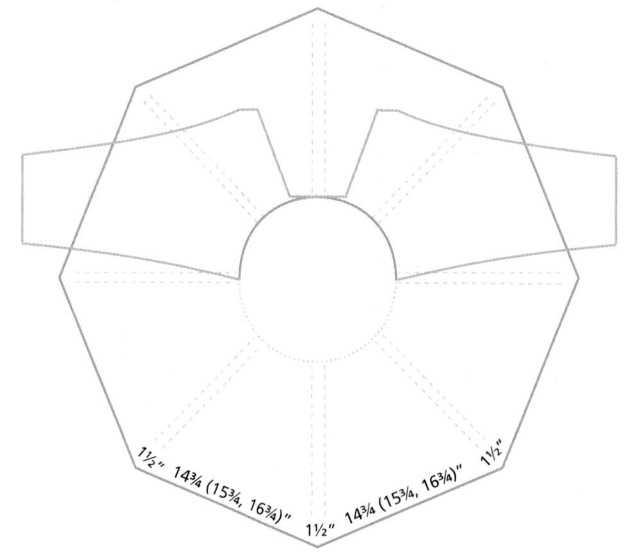

decreases at neck edges in this welt. Rows 1-2: Bind off 14 stitches at beginning (sleeve end) of each row. Rows 3 and 5: Bind off 4 stitches at beginning of row. Row 4: Bind off 8 stitches at beginning of row. 61 stitches/sleeve.

Welt 43 (46), Sizes Two And Three No decreases at neck edges in this welt. Row 1: Bind off 5 (8) stitches at beginning of row. Rows 2-5 (2-4): Bind off 8 stitches at beginning of each row. 43 (45) stitches/sleeve.

Welts 41 (44, 47) - 46 (49, 51) No decreases at neck edges in this group of welts. Decrease 1 stitch at each sleeve edge each row. 12 (16, 22) stitches/sleeve.

Welt 47, Size One No decreases at neck edges this welt. Rows 1-3: Decrease 1 stitch at each sleeve edge each row. Rows 4-5: Work even. Bind off remaining 9 stitches/sleeve.

Welt 50, Size Two Decrease 1 stitch at each neck edge *every other* row, and, at the same time, decrease 1 stitch at each sleeve edge each row. Bind off remaining 10 stitches/sleeve.

Welt 52, Size Three Decrease 1 stitch at each neck edge *every other* row, and, at the same time, decrease 1 stitch at each sleeve edge each row. 16 stitches/sleeve.

Welt 53, Size Three Continue to decrease 1 stitch at each neck edge every other row. Rows 1-3: Decrease 1 stitch at each sleeve edge each row. Rows 4-5: Work even at sleeve edges. Bind off remaining 10 stitches/sleeve.

Finishing

Use cast-on yarn tail to sew first rows on Welt 1 together. Weave in ends. Block. With tapestry needle and matching yarn, sew neck/front bodice edge to bound-off inner collar edge so that the "wrong side" is seen in the torso and sleeves and the "right side" in the collar and lapels. Sew underarm seams so that the finished seam is outside on the sleeves and inside on the cuffs with the exception of the 2 outer edge cuff stitches where the finished seam is once again outside. Fold cuff back and tack to hold in place at the seam, allowing the last two stitches to curl forward at the top.

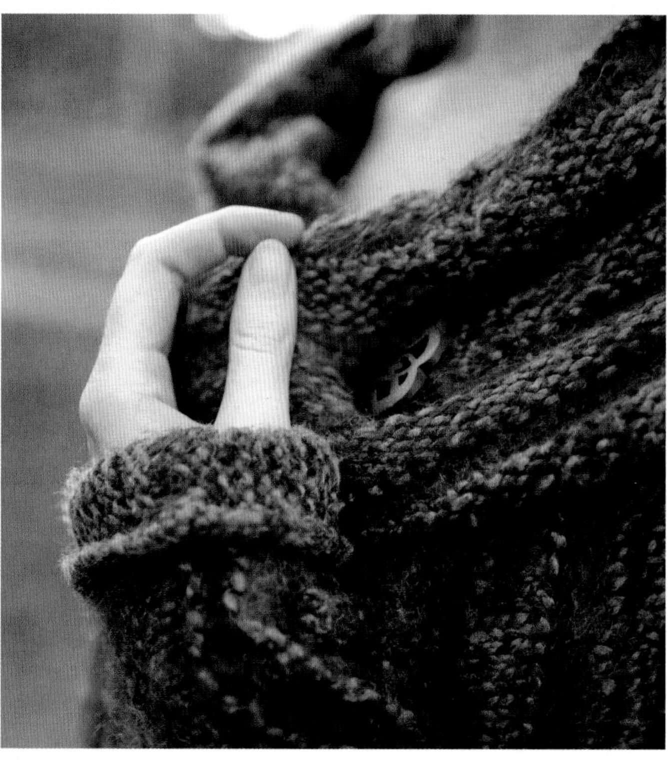

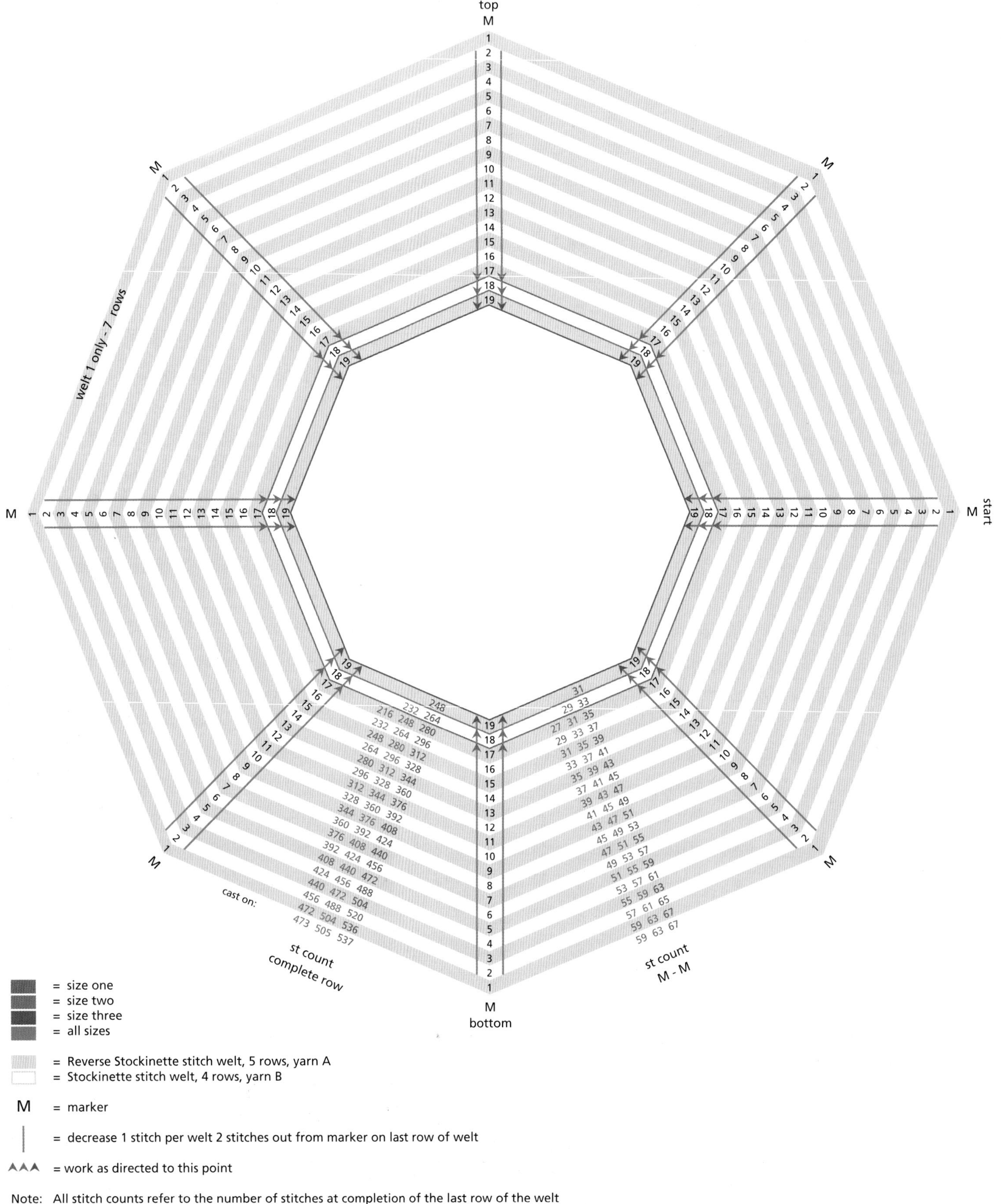

top
M
M
M
welt 1 only - 7 rows
M
start
M
M
M
bottom
M
248
232 264
216 248 280
232 264 296
248 280 312
264 296 328
280 312 344
296 328 360
312 344 376
328 360 392
344 376 408
360 392 424
376 408 440
392 424 456
408 440 472
424 456 488
440 472 504
456 488 520
472 504 536
473 505 537
cast on:
st count
complete row
31
29 33
27 31 35
29 33 37
31 35 39
33 37 41
35 39 43
37 41 45
39 43 47
41 45 49
43 47 51
45 49 53
47 51 55
49 53 57
51 55 59
53 57 61
55 59 63
57 61 65
59 63 67
59 63 67
st count
M - M
= size one
= size two
= size three
= all sizes
= Reverse Stockinette stitch welt, 5 rows, yarn A
= Stockinette stitch welt, 4 rows, yarn B
M = marker
= decrease 1 stitch per welt 2 stitches out from marker on last row of welt
= work as directed to this point
Note: All stitch counts refer to the number of stitches at completion of the last row of the welt

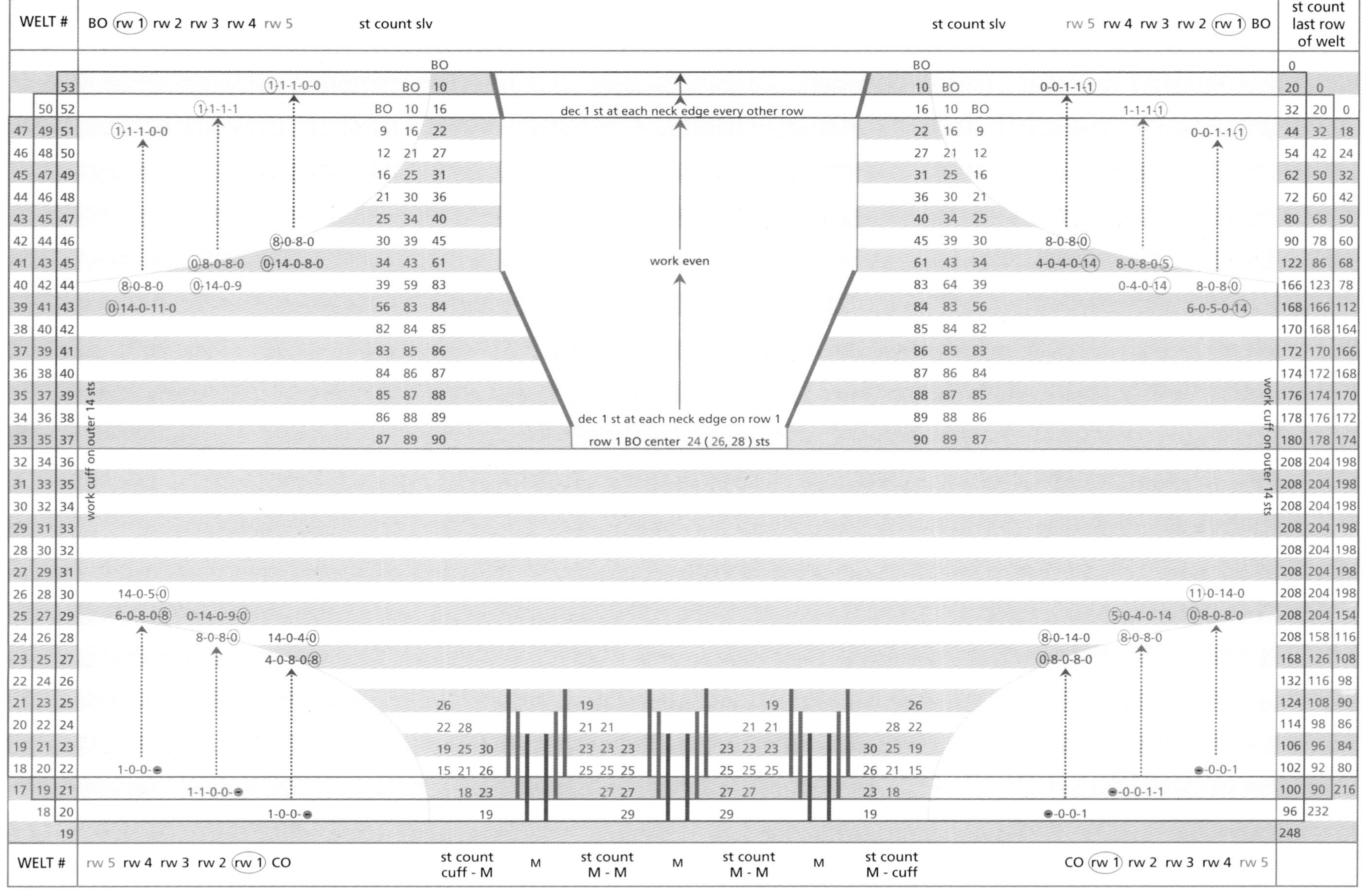

= size one
= size two
= size three
= all sizes

= Reverse Stockinette stitch welt, 5 rows
= Stockinette stitch welt, 4 rows

M = marker

● ● ● = row 1, break yarn, slip last 12 sts worked to left needle, rejoin yarn, use JSSBO to BO 132 (140, 148) sts , then work 84 (92, 100) sts; bodice worked on remaining sts

| | | = decrease 1 stitch per welt 2 stitches out from marker on last row of welt | = decrease at neck edge as directed above

▲ ▲ ▲ = work as directed to this point

⋮ ⋮ ⋮ = increase 1 st at sleeve edge each row (below center line); decrease 1 st at sleeve edge each row (above center line)

Note: All stitch counts refer to the number of stitches at completion of the last row of the welt

Forest Fiesta

Lavishly proportioned at the front, sleekly tapered in the back, Forest Fiesta provides a generous canvas across which lively bands of color gaily swirl. An expansive collar, broad lapels and wide gussets at the bust line combine to offer extra ease and coverage across the front bodice. Thick, pleated cuffs complete a strong statement. This jacket is at once big and bold, light and springy, thanks to an artful blend of silk, mohair and wool. Wear it hooded, wrap it double across the chest for extra warmth, or let it swing wide, free and utterly full of fun.

Sizes
One (Two, Three); shown here in Size Two.

Knitted Measurements
Collar: 15 (15¾, 17)"/38 (40, 43)cm
Center Back: 29 (30¾, 32½)"/74 (78, 82)cm
Center Back Neck to Cuff: 26 (26½, 27)"/66 (67, 69)cm

Approximate As-Worn Measurements
Collar: 12½ (13, 13½)"/32 (33, 34)cm
Center Back: 29¾ (31½, 33¼)"/75 (80, 84)cm
Center Back Neck to Cuff: 33 (34, 34¾)"/84 (86, 88)cm

Materials
Two-ply, DK weight silk/mohair blend yarn with long color repeat, 1475 (1645, 1835) yd/1349 (1505, 1678)m. As shown, 11 (13, 14) skeins Noro Silk Garden Lite (45% silk/45% kid mohair/10% lamb's wool, 1¾ oz/50g, 137 yd/125m) in color #2015. Color discontinued. Suggested substitution: 11 (13, 14) skeins Freia Fine Handpaints (100% wool, 1¾ oz/50g, 145 yd/133m) in color Metal Earth.

One 40 (40, 47)" size 7 (4.5mm) circular needle or size required to obtain gauge.

Gauge
21 stitches and 25 rows = 4"/10cm

Before beginning, please review Chapter One, ***Silhouettes and Sizing*** and Chapter Two, ***Tips and Techniques***.

STITCH PATTERN: WELTED STRIPES
Continuous, alternating welts of Reverse Stockinette stitch and Stockinette stitch.

Welt 1— Reverse Stockinette Stitch, 6 rows
When working in the round: (RS) Purl all rows.
When working flat: Purl on RS rows, knit on WS rows.
Welt 2—Stockinette Stitch, 5 rows
When working in the round: (RS) Knit all rows.
When working flat: Knit on RS rows, purl on WS rows.
Repeat welts 1 and 2.

OUTER CIRCLE
Use a long-tail or double method to cast on 513 (545, 577) stitches, placing a marker in between the following 8 sections of 64 (68, 72) stitches each, with 1 stitch after the last marker. Use a different color marker for the last marker to denote the beginning and end of each row.

Welt 1, Reverse Stockinette Stitch (Note: This outer welt has 8 rows instead of the normal 6 rows. The first 3 rows are worked flat before joining the work into a circle. It is important to the directional integrity of the pattern that the circle be joined at the completion of the third row as instructed.) Row 1: (RS) Purl. Row 2: Knit. Row 3: Purl to last stitch, slip 1. Adjust work to ensure that cast-on edge is not twisted around needle. (See *No Twist Join*, Chapter Two.) Join work into a circle by placing the last, slipped stitch from row 3 back onto the left needle. Two stitches are now on the left needle before the marker. Purl these two stitches together. Continue next rows in the round. Rows 4-8: Purl. 512 (544, 576) stitches.

Welt 2, Stockinette Stitch Rows 1-4: Knit. Row 5: *K2, k2 tog, knit to within 4 stitches of next marker, k2tog, k2, slip marker; repeat from * across entire row. 496 (528, 560) stitches.

Welt 3, Reverse Stockinette Stitch Rows 1-5: Purl. Row 6: *P2, p2tog, purl to within 4 stitches of next marker, p2tog, p2, slip marker; repeat from * across entire row. 480 (512, 544) stitches.

Welts 4 - 18 (19, 20) (Note: Continue in Welted Stripes stitch pattern throughout remainder of garment.) Continue decreases at markers in last row of each welt as established. 240 (256,272) stitches.

BACK BODICE AND SLEEVES
After the collar and lapels are completed and bound off, the bodice is worked flat on the remaining live stitches in the center of the garment. Change to the working-flat version of Welted Stripes stitch pattern after row 1 of next welt.

Welt 19 (20, 21) Row 1: Break yarn and slip the last 12 (14, 16) stitches just worked back onto the left needle to reposition beginning of row. Using Jeny's Surprisingly Stretchy Bind Off method, rejoin yarn and bind off 144 (156, 168) stitches; work remaining 96 (100, 104) stitches. Rows 2-3: Change to working-flat version of Welted Stripes stitch pattern. Work even. Row(s) 4-5 (4, 4-5): Increase 1 stitch at beginning and end of each row. Row 6 (5, 6): Increase 1 stitch at beginning and end of row and continue decreases in established manner at 3 remaining markers. 6 decreases worked/welt. 96 (98, 104) stitches.

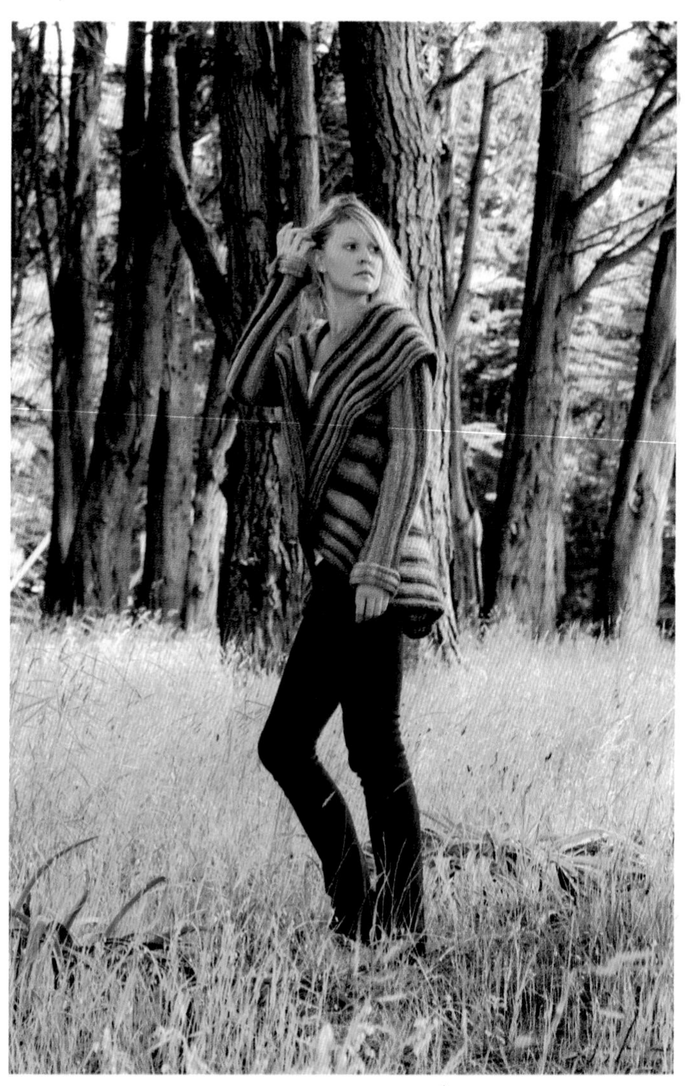

Welts 20 (21, 22) – 21 (22, 23) Continue to increase 1 stitch at beginning and end of each row and to decrease in established manner at markers in last row of each welt. 6 decreases worked/welt. 106 (108, 114) stitches.

Welts 22 (23, 24) – 25 (26, 27) No further marker decreases; remove all stitch markers. Continue to increase 1 stitch at beginning and end of each row. 150 (152, 158) stitches.

Welt 26 (27, 28) Cast on 8 stitches at beginning of each row. (Note: To achieve desired sleeve length, add or subtract 3-4 stitches for each inch, distributed across all rows in this and the next welt.) 190 (200, 198) stitches.

Welt 27 (28, 29) Row 1: Cast on 8 (6, 8) stitches at beginning of row. Row 2: Cast on 5 (11, 6) stitches at beginning of row. Row 3: Cast on 9 (5, 11) stitches at beginning of row. Row 4: Cast on 4 (28, 5) stitches at beginning of row. Row(s) 5-6 (5, 5-6): Cast on 28 stitches at beginning of each row. 272 (278, 284) stitches.

Cuffs

Welts 28 (30) – 33 (37), Sizes One and Three Place markers 28 stitches in from each sleeve end to indicate cuff stitches. Row 1: K6, (p6, k5) twice, slip marker, work in established pattern to next marker, slip marker, (k5, p6) twice, k6. Row 2: P6, (k6, p5) twice, slip marker, work in established pattern to next marker, slip marker, (p5, k6) twice, p6. Subsequent rows: Work the stitches between the markers even in the established pattern, and, at the same time, work the cuff stitches even, repeating the cuff pattern in rows 1 and 2 above. 272 (284) stitches.

Welts 29 – 35, Size Two Place markers 28 stitches in from each sleeve end to indicate cuff stitches. Row 1: P6, (k6, p5) twice, slip marker, work in established pattern to next marker, slip marker, (p5, k6) twice, p6. Row 2: K6, (p6, k5) twice, slip marker, work in established pattern to next marker, slip marker, (k5, p6) twice, k6. Subsequent rows: Work the stitches between the markers even in the established pattern and, at the same time, work the cuff stitches even, repeating the cuff pattern in rows 1 and 2 above. 278 stitches.

Neck, Front Bodice and Sleeves

In the next welt, stitches in the center of the row are bound off to create the back neck and begin shaping the two front bodice panels. Continue to work cuff stitches in the established cuff stitch pattern and the stitches between the markers in the established Welted Stripes pattern.

Welt 34 (36, 38) Row 1: Work 121 (123, 125) stitches, use basic method to bind off center 30 (32, 34) stitches, work remaining 121 (123, 125) stitches. Row 2: Work in established patterns to the second neck edge, add a second ball of yarn and continue row. (Note: If working with a yarn with broad sections of color repeats such as the yarn shown, it is important that the second ball of yarn begin with the same color as is currently working in opposite sleeve.) Row 3-5: Work even. 121 (123, 125) stitches/sleeve.

Welts 35 (37, 39) – 39 (42, 45) Work in established patterns, decreasing 1 stitch at each neck edge on row 1 of each welt. 116 (117, 118) stitches/sleeve.

Welt 40 (43, 46) Apply in reverse order any sleeve length changes made in welts 26-27 (27-28, 28-29) in this and the next welt. Continue decreasing at neck edges on row 1. Rows 1-2: Bind off 28 stitches at beginning (sleeve end) of each row. Row 3: Bind off 4 (5, 5) stitches at beginning of row. Row 4: Bind off 9 (11, 11) stitches at beginning (sleeve end) of row. Row 5: Bind off 5 (6, 6) stitches at beginning of row. Row 6, Size Two only: Bind off 8 stitches at beginning of row. 78 (69/77, 78) stitches/sleeve.

Welt 41 (44, 47) Continue to work decreases at neck edges as established. Bind off 8 stitches at beginning of each row. 53 (52, 53) stitches/sleeve.

Welt(s) 42-44 (45-46, 48) Continue to work decreases at neck edges as established and, at the same time, decrease 1 stitch at each sleeve edge each row. 34 (39, 47) stitches/sleeve.

Welts 45 (47, 49) - 47 (50, 53) No decreases at neck edges in this group of welts. Decrease 1 stitch at each sleeve edge each row. 17 (17, 19) stitches/sleeve.

Welt 48 (51, 54) Decrease 1 stitch at each neck edge *every other* row. Rows 1-2: Decrease 1 stitch at each sleeve edge each row. Row 3: Decrease 1 (0, 1) stitch each sleeve edge. Rows 4-5 (4-6, 4-5): Work even at sleeve edges. Bind off remaining 11 (12, 13) stitches/sleeve.

Finishing

Use cast-on yarn tail to sew first rows on Welt 1 together. Weave in ends. Block. With tapestry needle and matching yarn, sew neck edge to bound-off inner collar edge. Sew underarm seams.

Complete pleated cuffs by securing yarn on the inside of the seam at the bottom of rib 1 (see illustration). Working from

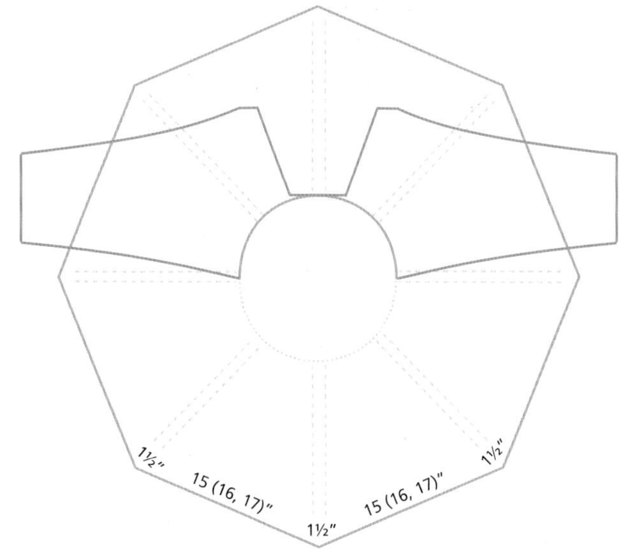

the outside, bring threaded needle from back to front through the center of the stitch in the bottom row of rib 1 immediately to the right of the seam. Insert the threaded needle from front to back in the center of the next stitch to the right. *Working from the bottom to the top of the cuff and following the same row of stitches, bring needle from back to front immediately above the top of rib 1; insert needle from front to back just below the bottom of rib 2; bring needle from back to front immediately above the top of rib 2; insert needle from front to back just below the bottom of rib 3; bring needle from back to front immediately above the top of rib 3. Insert the threaded needle from front to back one stitch to the right. Working from the top to the bottom of the cuff, repeat, threading the needle through in the same manner and at the same points. Repeat from * around full width of cuff, gently pulling the yarn thread after each round to pleat the cuffs to the extent that the stockinette ribs almost touch but allow a glimpse of the stranded yarn that lies between. Secure and weave in end.

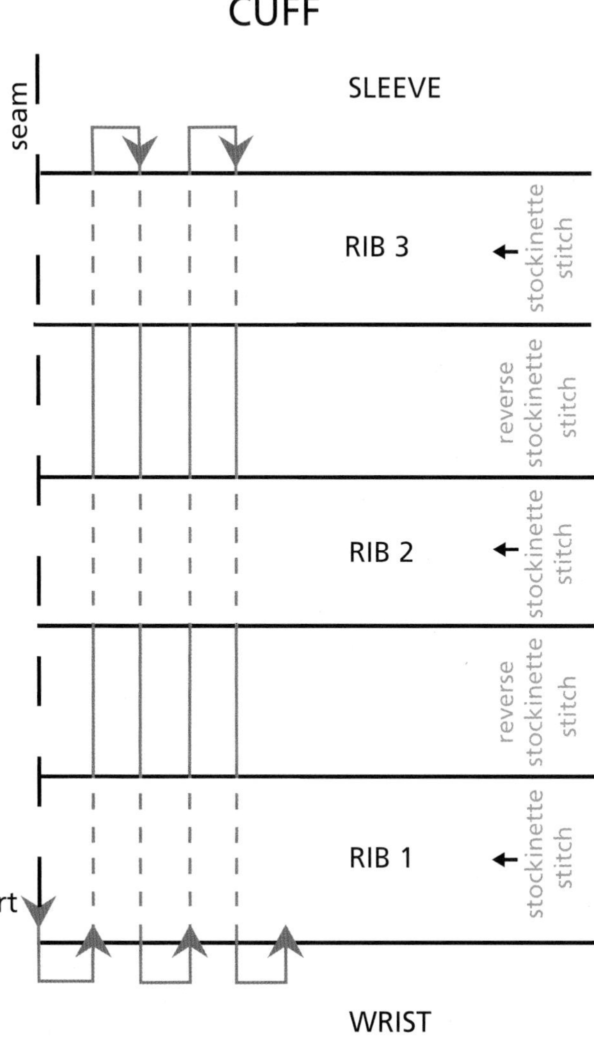

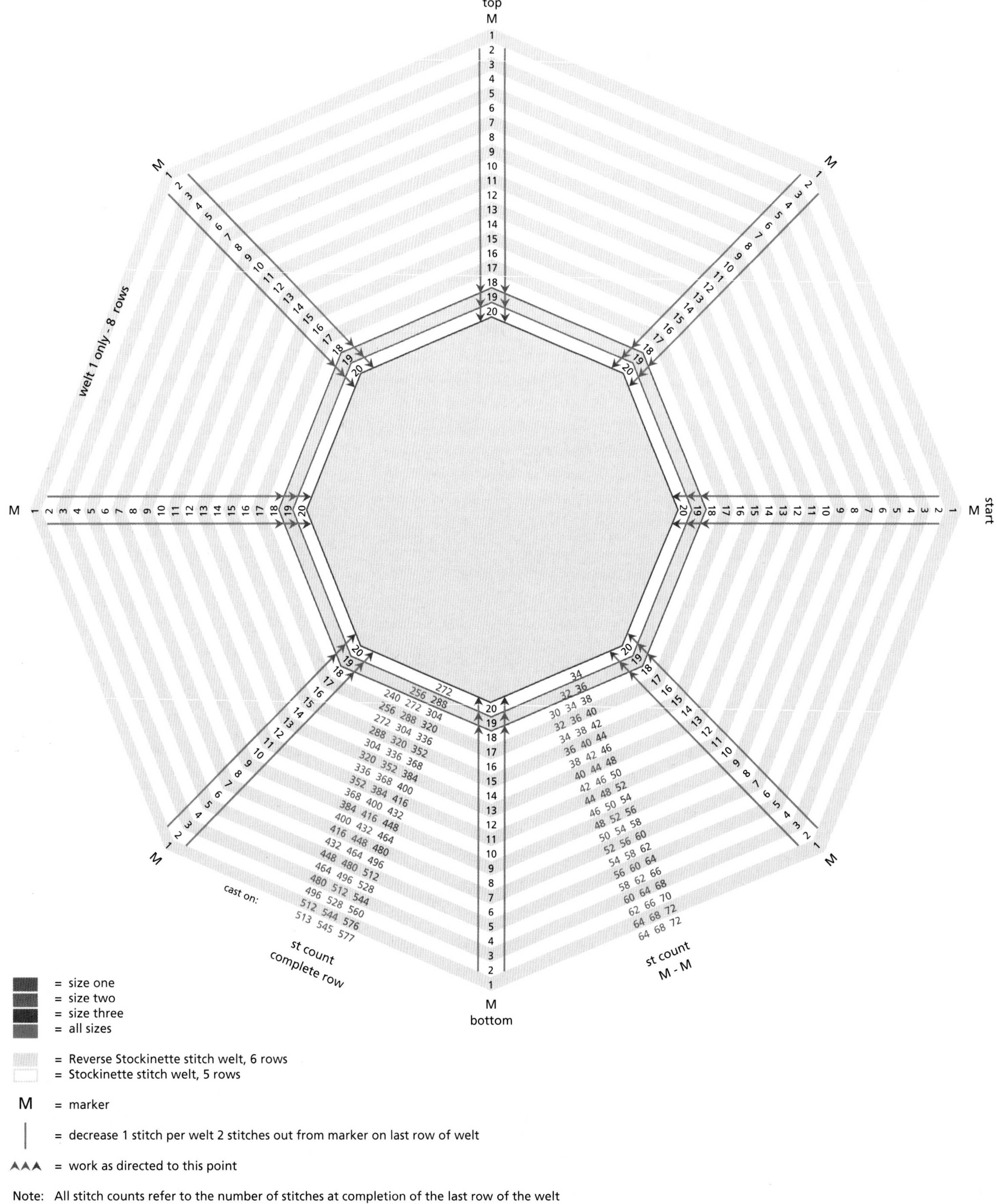

top
M
bottom
start
welt 1 only - 8 rows
cast on:
st count
complete row
st count
M - M
272
256 288
240 272 304
256 288 320
272 304 336
288 320 352
304 336 368
320 352 384
336 368 400
352 384 416
368 400 432
384 416 448
400 432 464
416 448 480
432 464 496
448 480 512
464 496 528
480 512 544
496 528 560
512 544 576
513 545 577
34
32 36
30 34 38
32 36 40
34 38 42
36 40 44
38 42 46
40 44 48
42 46 50
44 48 52
46 50 54
48 52 56
50 54 58
52 56 60
54 58 62
56 60 64
58 62 66
60 64 68
62 66 70
64 68 72
64 68 72
= size one
= size two
= size three
= all sizes
= Reverse Stockinette stitch welt, 6 rows
= Stockinette stitch welt, 5 rows
M = marker
= decrease 1 stitch per welt 2 stitches out from marker on last row of welt
= work as directed to this point
Note: All stitch counts refer to the number of stitches at completion of the last row of the welt

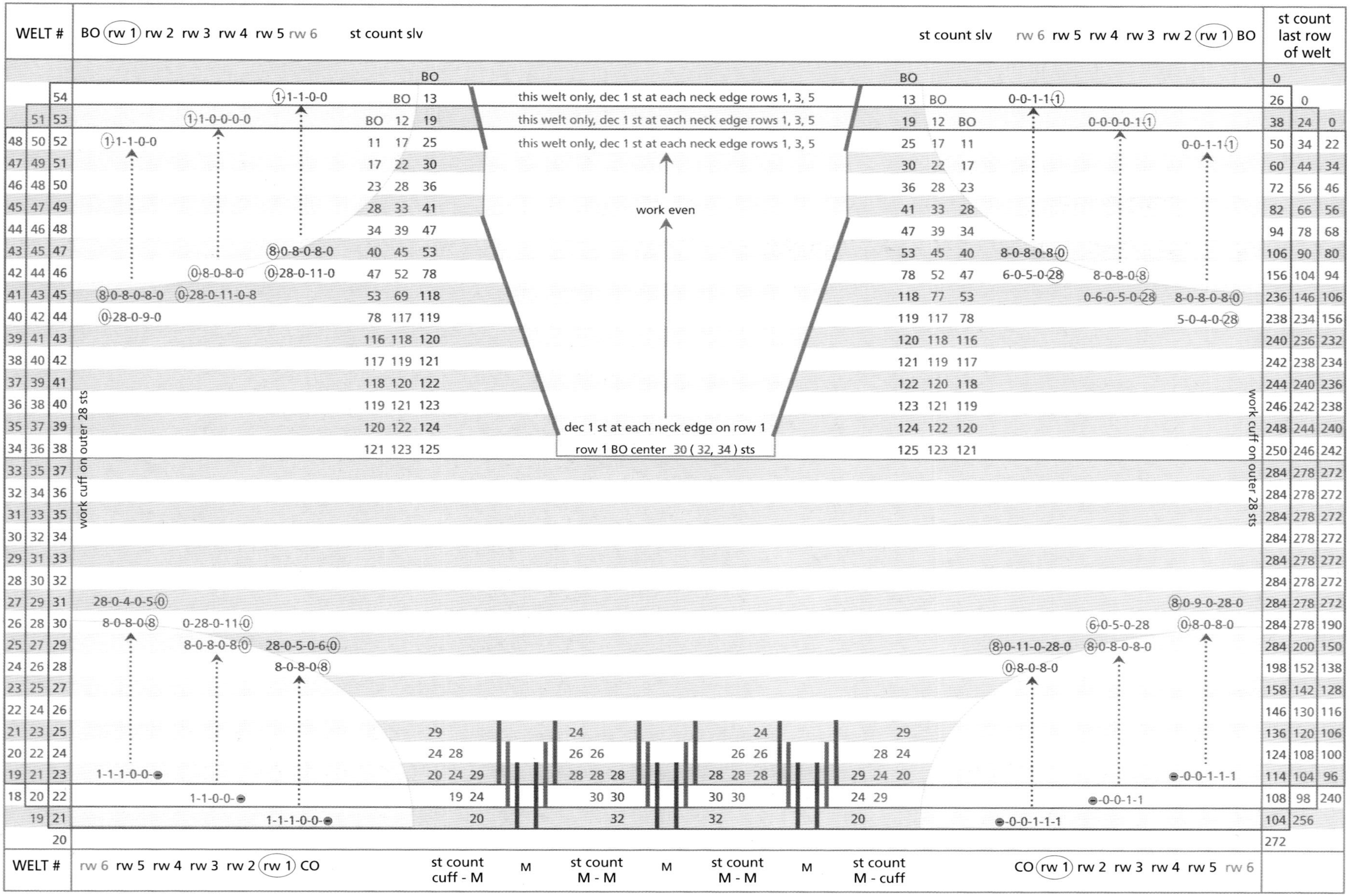

WELT #	BO (rw 1) rw 2 rw 3 rw 4 rw 5 rw 6	st count slv		st count slv	rw 6 rw 5 rw 4 rw 3 rw 2 (rw 1) BO	st count last row of welt
		BO		BO		0
54	(1)-1-1-0-0	BO 13	this welt only, dec 1 st at each neck edge rows 1, 3, 5	13 BO	0-0-1-1-(1)	26 0
51 53	(1)-1-0-0-0-0	BO 12 19	this welt only, dec 1 st at each neck edge rows 1, 3, 5	19 12 BO	0-0-0-0-1-(1)	38 24 0
48 50 52	(1)-1-1-0-0	11 17 25	this welt only, dec 1 st at each neck edge rows 1, 3, 5	25 17 11	0-0-1-1-(1)	50 34 22
47 49 51		17 22 30		30 22 17		60 44 34
46 48 50		23 28 36		36 28 23		72 56 46
45 47 49		28 33 41	work even	41 33 28		82 66 56
44 46 48		34 39 47		47 39 34		94 78 68
43 45 47	(8)-0-8-0-8-0	40 45 53		53 45 40	8-0-8-0-8-(0)	106 90 80
42 44 46	(0)-8-0-8-0 (0)-28-0-11-0	47 52 78		78 52 47	6-0-5-0-(28) 8-0-8-0-(8)	156 104 94
41 43 45	(8)-0-8-0-8-0 (0)-28-0-11-0-8	53 69 118		118 77 53	0-6-0-5-0-(28) 8-0-8-0-8-(0)	236 146 106
40 42 44	(0)-28-0-9-0	78 117 119		119 117 78	5-0-4-0-(28)	238 234 156
39 41 43		116 118 120		120 118 116		240 236 232
38 40 42		117 119 121		121 119 117		242 238 234
37 39 41		118 120 122		122 120 118		244 240 236
36 38 40	work cuff on outer 28 sts	119 121 123		123 121 119	work cuff on outer 28 sts	246 242 238
35 37 39		120 122 124	dec 1 st at each neck edge on row 1	124 122 120		248 244 240
34 36 38		121 123 125	row 1 BO center 30 (32, 34) sts	125 123 121		250 246 242
33 35 37						284 278 272
32 34 36						284 278 272
31 33 35						284 278 272
30 32 34						284 278 272
29 31 33						284 278 272
28 30 32						284 278 272
27 29 31	28-0-4-0-5-(0)				(8)-0-9-0-28-0	284 278 272
26 28 30	8-0-8-0-(8) 0-28-0-11-(0)				(6)-0-5-0-28 (0)-8-0-8-0	284 278 190
25 27 29	8-0-8-0-8-(0) 28-0-5-0-6-(0)				(8)-0-11-0-28-0 (8)-0-8-0-8-0	284 200 150
24 26 28	8-0-8-0-(8)				(0)-8-0-8-0	198 152 138
23 25 27						158 142 128
22 24 26						146 130 116
21 23 25			29 | 24 | 24 | 29			136 120 106
20 22 24			24 28 | 26 26 | 26 26 | 28 24			124 108 100
19 21 23	1-1-1-0-0-●		20 24 29 | 28 28 28 | 28 28 28 | 29 24 20		●-0-0-1-1-1	114 104 96
18 20 22	1-1-0-0-●		19 24 | 30 30 | 30 30 | 24 29		●-0-0-1-1	108 98 240
19 21	1-1-1-0-0-●		20 | 32 | 32 | 20		●-0-0-1-1-1	104 256
20						272
WELT #	rw 6 rw 5 rw 4 rw 3 rw 2 (rw 1) CO		st count cuff - M | M | st count M - M | M | st count M - M | M | st count M - cuff		CO (rw 1) rw 2 rw 3 rw 4 rw 5 rw 6	

= size one
= size two
= size three
= all sizes

= Reverse Stockinette stitch welt, 6 rows
= Stockinette stitch welt, 5 rows

M = marker

● ● ● = row 1, break yarn, slip last 12 (14, 16) sts worked to left needle, rejoin yarn, use JSSBO to BO 144 (156, 168) sts, then work 96 (100, 104) sts; bodice worked on remaining sts

| | | = decrease 1 st per welt 2 sts out from marker on last row of welt | = decrease at neck edge as directed above

⋏ ⋏ ⋏ = work as directed to this point

⋮ ⋮ ⋮ = increase 1 st at sleeve edge each row (below center line); decrease 1 st at sleeve edge each row (above center line)

Note: All stitch counts refer to the number of stitches at completion of the last row of the welt

CHAPTER FOUR *centered ovals*

RUBIES AND RIBBONS

COPPER COLLAGE

SOPHIE'S SWIRL

GOLDEN GLOW

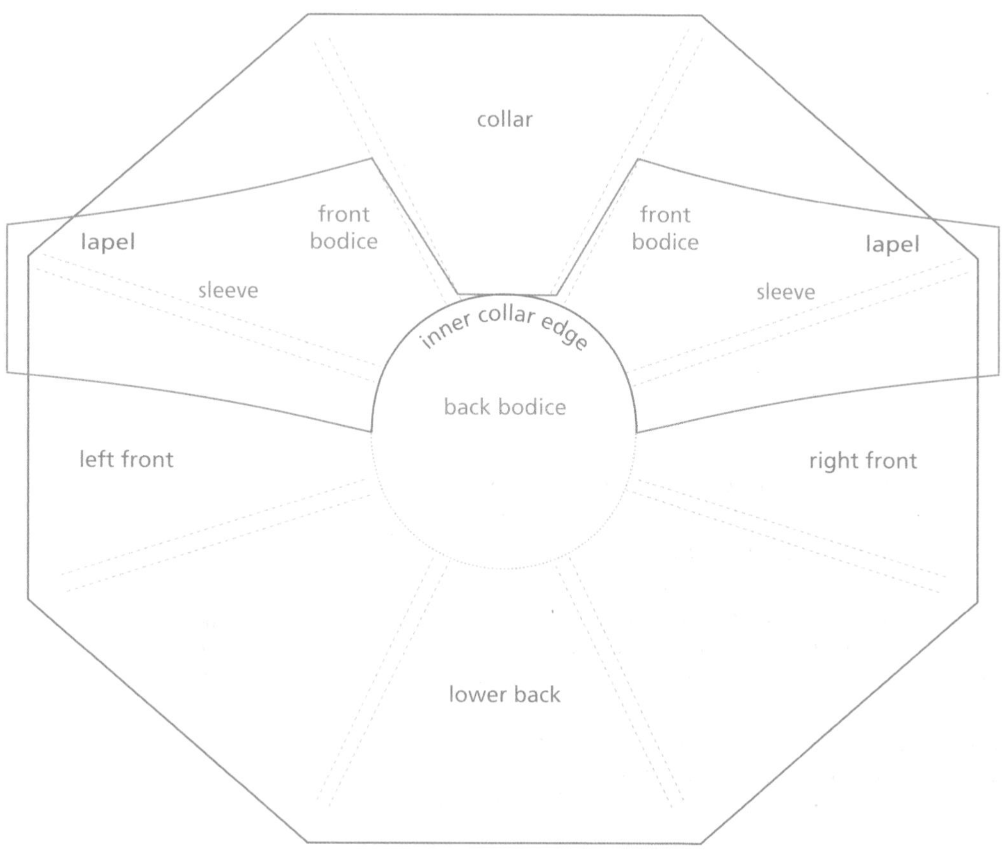

The ***centered oval silhouette*** offers a variety of choices in length, style and fit. *Centered ovals* all have deep collars and are gently sculpted with horizontal welts and straight edges across the back. From there the styles and fit diverge. Some are long with expansive shawl collars, sweeping front panels and more ease in the bodice and sleeves. Some are short and more fitted throughout, with subtle draping at the front and collars that hug the edge of the shoulder. Looking for something in between? Adjust your size accordingly.

rubies and ribbons

That color—that dive-in, deep, luscious, ruby red—just steals the show. But there's more. Ruffled bands of ribbons swirl around the expansive shawl collar and across the lower back before ending in a tumble of bows down the front. The shimmer of the sheer silk welts contrasts with the soft halo and denser weave of the merino and silk blend welts on either side. This semi-fitted Swirl offers broad lapels to wrap and style according to whim, but its fine, light fabric is perhaps at its most beautiful when simply left open and allowed to flutter and ripple on the move.

Sizes
One (Two, Three); shown here in Size Two.

Knitted Measurements
Collar: 11½ (12, 13)"/29 (30, 33)cm
Center Back: 26 (27¼, 28½)"/66 (69, 72)cm
Center Back Neck to Cuff: 23 (23¾, 24½)"/58 (60, 62)cm

Approximate As-Worn Measurements
Collar: 9½ (10, 11)"/24 (25, 28)cm
Center Back: 27½ (28¾, 30¼)"/70 (73, 77)cm
Center Back Neck to Cuff: 33 (33¾, 34¾)"/84 (86, 88)cm

Materials
Three-ply, fingering weight silk/merino blend yarn, 962 (1063, 1156) yd/880 (972, 1057)m (A); two-ply, lace weight silk yarn, 906 (987, 1000) yd/828 (903, 914)m in coordinating color (B); and 10½ (12½, 14½) yd/9.6 (11.4, 13.3)m ribbon yarn. As shown, 2 (3, 3) skeins Sundara Yarn Fingering Silky Merino (50% silk/50% merino, 5¼ oz/150g, 500 yd/457m) in colorway Ruby Port (A); 1 (1, 1) skein Sundara Yarn Silk Lace (100% silk, 3½ oz/100g, 1000 yd/914m) in colorway Ruby Port (B); and 10½ (12½, 14½) yd/9.6 (11.4, 13.3)m Habu Textiles Fringe Tape Ribbon A-67 in color #4 Red.

One 32 (32, 40)" size 5 (3.75mm) circular needle or size required to obtain gauge.

Gauge
29 stitches and 36 rows = 4"/10cm

Before beginning, please review Chapter One, ***Silhouettes and Sizing*** and Chapter Two, ***Tips and Techniques***.

STITCH PATTERN: WELTED STRIPES WITH EYELETS
Continuous, alternating welts of Reverse Stockinette stitch in yarn A, and Stockinette stitch in yarn B. In outer oval, Stockinette stitch welts are worked in Stockinette Stitch with Eyelets in welts 4, 12 and 20.

Welt 1—Reverse Stockinette Stitch, 5 rows, yarn A
When working in the round: (RS) Purl all rows.
When working flat: Purl on RS rows, knit on WS rows.
Welt 2—Stockinette Stitch, 5 rows, yarn B
When working in the round: (RS) Knit all rows.
When working flat: Knit on RS rows, purl on WS rows.
Repeat welts 1 and 2.

Welt 2 alternate—Stockinette Stitch with Eyelets, 5 rows, yarn B
Working in the round: (RS) Knit all rows, working eyelet row on row 3.
Eyelet row: *K2tog, YO; repeat from * across entire row.

OUTER OVAL
With A, use a long-tail or double method to cast on 657 (697, 737) stitches, placing a marker in between each of the following 8 sections: Two sections of 72 (76, 80) stitches, 112 (120, 128) stitches, three sections of 72 (76, 80) stitches, 112 (120, 128), 72 (76, 80) stitches, with 1 stitch after the last marker. Use a different color marker for the last marker to denote the beginning and end of each row.

Welt 1, Reverse Stockinette Stitch (Note: This outer welt has 7 rows instead of the normal 5 rows. The first 3 rows of this welt are worked flat before joining the work into an oval. It is important to the directional integrity of the pattern that the oval be joined at the completion of the third row as instructed.) Row 1: (RS) With A, purl. Row 2: Knit. Row 3: Purl to last stitch, slip 1. Adjust work to ensure that cast-on edge is not twisted around needle. (See *No Twist Join*, Chapter Two.) Join work into an oval by placing the last, slipped stitch from row 3 back onto the left needle. Two stitches are now on the left needle before the marker. Purl these two stitches together. Continue next rows in the round. Rows 4-7: Purl. 656 (696, 736) stitches.

Welt 2, Stockinette Stitch Rows 1- 4: With B, knit. Row 5: *K2, k2tog, knit to within 4 stitches of next marker, k2tog, k2, slip marker; repeat from * across entire row. 640 (680, 720) stitches.

Welt 3, Reverse Stockinette Stitch Rows 1-4: With A, purl. Row 5: *P2, p2tog, purl to within 4 stitches of next marker, p2tog, p2, slip marker; repeat from * across entire row. 624 (664, 704) stitches.

Welts 4-22 (23, 24) (Note: Continue in Welted Stripes stitch pattern throughout remainder of garment, substituting Stockinette stitch with eyelets in welts 4, 12 and 20.) Continue decreases at markers in last row of each welt as established. 320, (344, 368) stitches.

BACK BODICE AND SLEEVES
After the collar and lapels are completed and bound off, the bodice is worked flat on the remaining live stitches in the center of the garment. Change to the working-flat version of Welted Stripes stitch pattern after row 1 of next welt.

Welt 23 (24, 25) Row 1: Work first 145 (156, 167) stitches*, then use Jeny's Surprisingly Stretchy Bind Off method to bind off 160 (172, 184) stitches; complete the first row of the welt by working the remaining 15 (16, 17) stitches. Slip stitches just worked back to left needle, break yarn and rejoin at * to reposition beginning of row. Rows 2-3: Change to working-flat version of Welted Stripes stitch pattern. Work even. Row 4: Increase 1 stitch at beginning and end of row. Row 5: Increase 1 stitch at beginning and end of row and continue decreases in established manner at 4 remaining markers. 8 decreases worked/welt. 156 (168, 180) stitches.

Welts 24 (25, 26) - 28 (29, 30) Continue to increase 1 stitch at beginning and end of each row and to decrease in established manner at markers in last row of each welt. 8 decreases worked/welt. 166 (178, 190) stitches.

Welts 29 (30, 31) – 33 (34, 35) No further marker decreases; remove all stitch markers. Continue to increase 1 stitch at beginning and end of each row. 216 (228, 240) stitches.

Welt 34 (35, 36) Rows 1 and 3: Cast on 3 (2, 2) stitches at beginning of row. Row 2: Cast on 5 (3, 3) stitches at beginning of row. Row 4: Cast on 4 (4, 3) stitches at beginning of row. Row 5: Cast on 3 (3, 2) stitches at the beginning of row. (Note: To achieve desired sleeve length, add or subtract 5 stitches for each inch, distributed across all rows in this and the next 6 welts.) 234 (242, 252) stitches.

Welts 35 (36, 37) - 40 (41, 42) Cast on 3 stitches at beginning of each row. 324 (332, 342) stitches.

Cuffs

Welts 41 (42, 43) – 47 (49, 51) Place markers 6 stitches in from each end of sleeves to indicate cuff stitches. Work the stitches between the markers even, in the established pattern. At the same time, work the cuff stitches in Stockinette stitch only and in yarn A only, adding a small bobbin of A at each cuff as necessary. 324 (332, 342) stitches.

Neck, Front Bodice and Sleeves

In the next welt, stitches in the center of the row are bound off to create the back neck and begin shaping the two front bodice panels. Add a second ball of each yarn as necessary to work both sleeves at the same time. Continue to work cuff stitches in Stockinette stitch and the stitches between the markers in the established Welted Stripes pattern.

Welt 48 (50, 52) Row 1: Work 138 (138, 140) stitches, bind off center 48 (56, 62) stitches, work remaining 138 (138, 140) stitches. Row 2: Work in established pattern to the second neck edge, add a second ball of yarn and continue row. Rows 3-5: Work even. 138 (138, 140) stitches/sleeve.

Welts 49 (51, 53) – 54 (57, 60) Work in established pattern, decreasing 1 stitch at each neck edge on row 1 of each welt. 132 (131, 132) stitches/sleeve.

Welts 55 (58, 61) - 60 (63, 66) Apply in reverse order any sleeve length changes made in welts 34-40 (35-41, 36-42) in these and the following welt. Continue decreasing at neck edges on row 1 and, at the same time, bind off 3 stitches at the beginning (sleeve end) of each row. 81 (80, 81) stitches/sleeve.

Welt 61 (64, 67) Continue to work decreases at neck edges as established. Row 1: Bind off 3 (3, 2) stitches at beginning

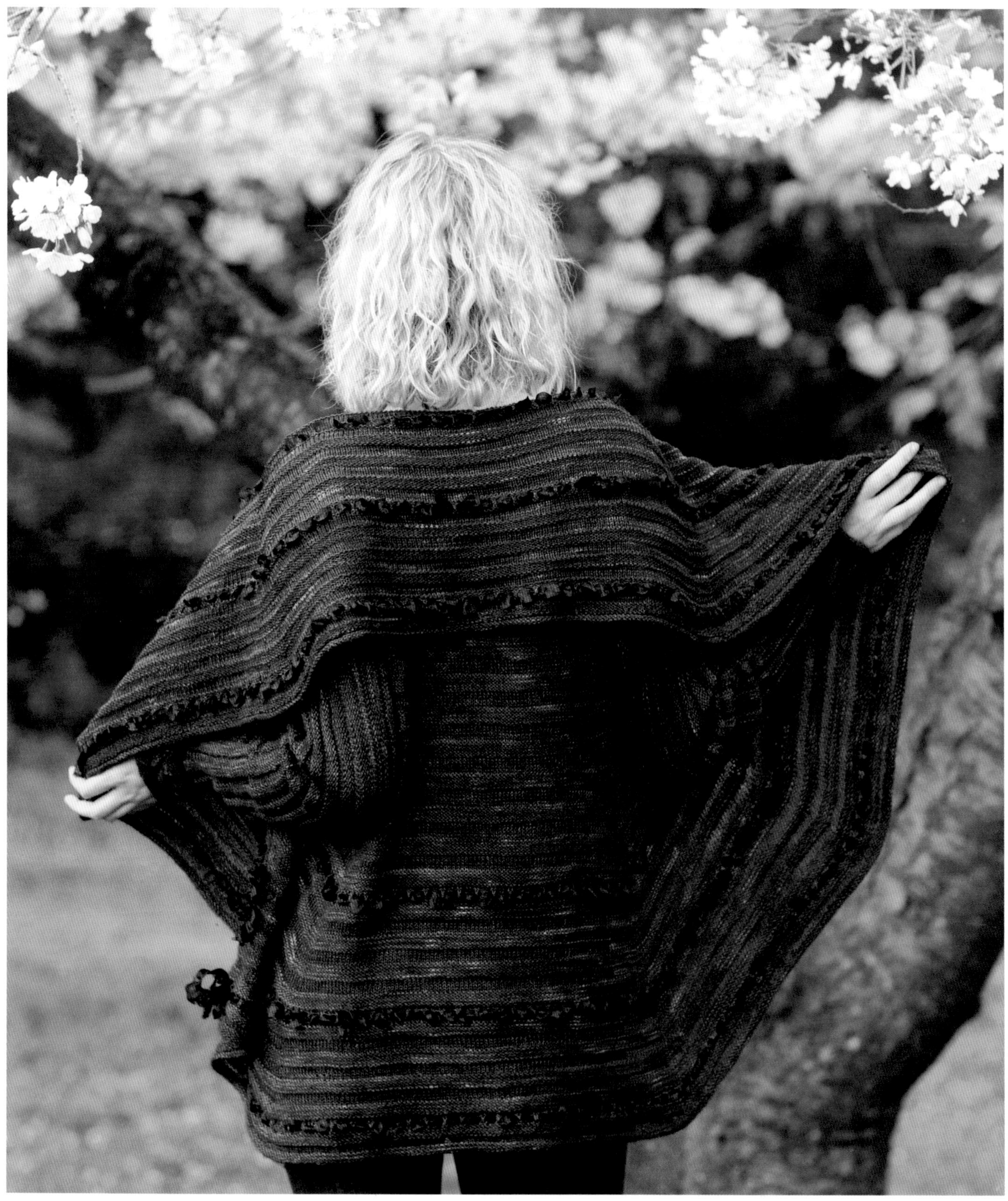

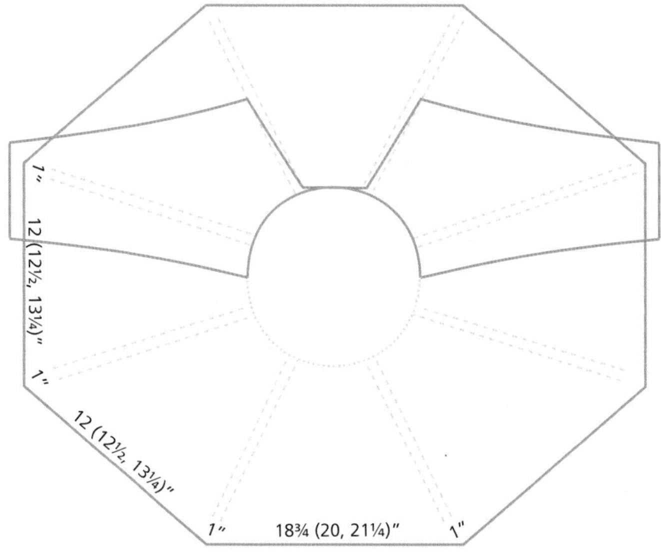

of row. Row 2: Bind off 4 (4, 3) stitches at beginning of row. Rows 3 and 5: Bind off 3 (2, 2) stitches at beginning of row. Row 4: Bind off 5 (3, 3) stitches at beginning of row. 71 (72, 74) stitches/sleeve.

Welts 62 (65, 68) – 69 (71, 73) Continue to work decreases at neck edges as established and, at the same time, decrease 1 stitch at each sleeve edge each row. 23 (30, 38) stitches/sleeve.

Welts 70 (72, 74) – 71 (74, 77) Decrease 1 stitch at each neck edge *every other* row and, at the same time, decrease 1 stitch at each sleeve edge each row. 8 (7, 8) stitches/sleeve.

Welt 72 (75, 78) Continue to work decreases at neck edges as established. Rows 1-2: Decrease 1 stitch at each sleeve edge each row. Rows 3-5: Work even at sleeve edges. Bind off remaining 3 stitches/sleeve.

Finishing

Use cast-on yarn tail to sew first rows on Welt 1 together. Weave in ends. Block. With tapestry needle and matching yarn, sew neck/front bodice edge to bound-off inner collar edge. Sew underarm seams.

With a tapestry needle threaded with ribbon, loosely weave ribbon in and out of an eyelet row, starting and ending with eyelets at the start-of-row point. Check to see that the ribbon length is sufficient to allow some stretch of the knitted fabric with approximately 7" extra on each end. Cut ribbon and repeat in remaining eyelet rows. Adjust ribbon so it is not twisted and ruffled edges are at bottom and visible between eyelets. Tie ends in simple bows and tie a knot at the edge of each of the ribbon ends. Tack cuffs to reinforce rolled shape.

top

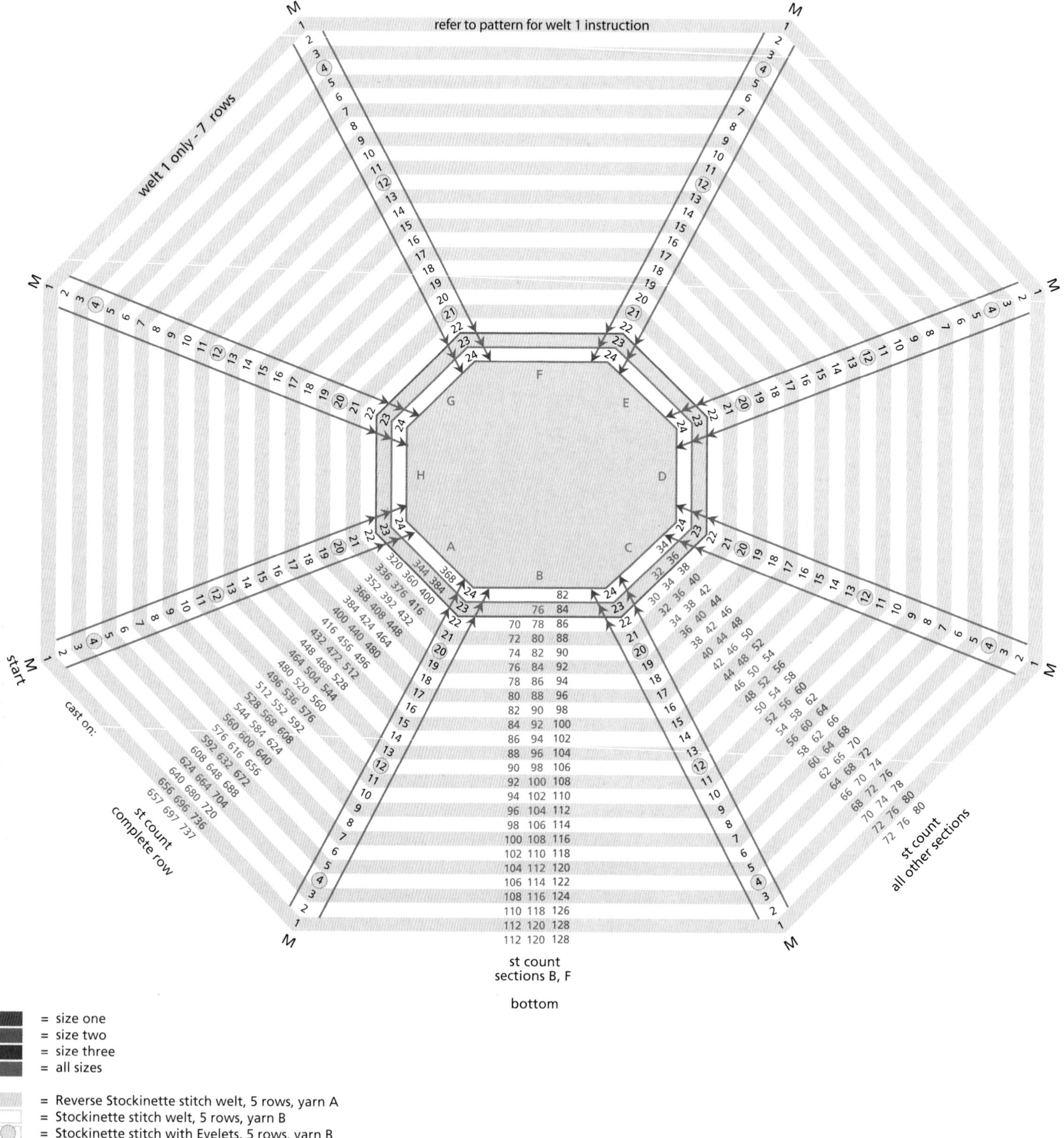

bottom

= size one
= size two
= size three
= all sizes

= Reverse Stockinette stitch welt, 5 rows, yarn A
= Stockinette stitch welt, 5 rows, yarn B
= Stockinette stitch with Eyelets, 5 rows, yarn B

M = marker

| = decrease 1 stitch per welt 2 stitches out from marker on last row of welt

▲▲▲ = work as directed to this point

Note: All stitch counts refer to the number of stitches at completion of the last row of the welt

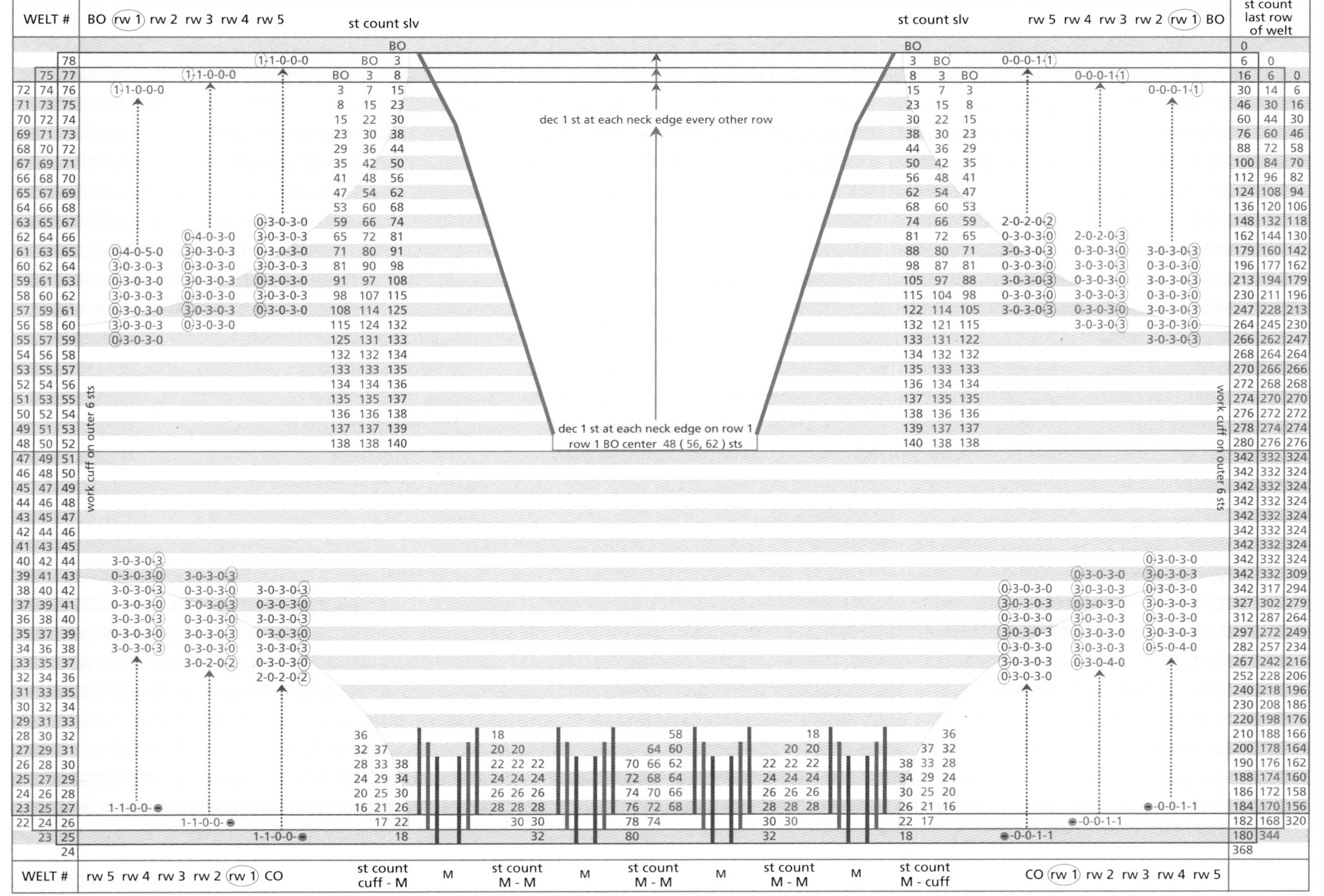

= size one
= size two
= size three
= all sizes

= Reverse Stockinette stitch welt, 5 rows
= Stockinette stitch welt, 5 rows

M = marker

= rw 1 work 145 (156, 167) sts*, use JSSBO to BO 160 (172, 184) sts, work 15 (16, 17) sts; break yarn, rejoin at *; bodice worked on rem sts

= decrease 1 st per welt 2 sts out from marker on last row of welt

= decrease at neck edge as directed above

= work as directed to this point

= increase 1 st at sleeve edge each row (below center line); decrease 1 st at sleeve edge each row (above center line)

Note: All stitch counts refer to the number of stitches at completion of the last row of the welt

copper collage

One colorway, a subtle blend of the browns and greens found in weathered copper, and three yarns each different from the other in fiber, structure and gauge, intertwine in a fabric in which color, light and texture continuously ebb and flow. Pure silk and superfine Peruvian alpaca lend a supple resilience to this jacket's sweeping proportions that invites and encourages imaginative styling. A bit of fringe across the collar adds a final textural statement and offers the pure beauty of yarn in its simplest form.

Sizes
One (Two, Three); shown here in Size Two.

Knitted Measurements
Collar: 17½ (18, 19½)"/44 (46, 49)cm
Center Back: 31½ (33¼, 35)"/80 (84, 89)cm
Center Back Neck to Cuff: 24 (24½, 25¼)"/61 (62, 64)cm

Approximate As-Worn Measurements
Collar: 13 (13¾, 14½)"/33 (35, 37)cm
Center Back: 33 (35, 37)"/84 (89, 94)cm
Center Back Neck to Cuff: 33 (34, 34¾)"/84 (86, 88)cm

Materials
Single-ply, worsted weight silk 872 (1012, 1104) yd/797 (925, 1009)m (A); three-ply, DK weight alpaca 665 (738, 835) yd/608 (675, 764)m yarn (B); and small loop bouclé, heavy worsted weight mohair/wool 157 (172, 197) yd/144 (157, 180)m (C); all yarns in coordinating colorway. As shown, 4 (4, 5) skeins Curious Creek "Isalo" (100% silk, 3¼ oz/95g, 262 yd/238m) in colorway Savanna Grasses (A); 3 (3, 3) skeins Curious Creek "Gombe" (100% superfine alpaca, 3½ oz/100g, 293 yd/266m) in same colorway (B); and 2 (2, 3) skeins Curious Creek "Shira" (54% mohair/18% wool/5% nylon, 3¾ oz/50g, 86 yd/78m) in same colorway (C).

One 40 (40, 47)" size 8 (5.0mm) circular needle or size required to obtain gauge.

Gauge
22 stitches and 24 rows = 4"/10cm

Before beginning, please review Chapter One, ***Silhouettes and Sizing*** and Chapter Two, ***Tips and Techniques***.

STITCH PATTERN: WELTED STRIPES

Continuous, alternating welts of Reverse Stockinette stitch in yarn A, and Stockinette stitch in yarns B and C.

Welt 1—Reverse Stockinette Stitch, *5* rows, yarn A
When working in the round: (RS) Purl all rows.
When working flat: Purl on RS rows, knit on WS rows.
Welt 2—Stockinette Stitch, *5* rows, yarns B and C
Work rows 1, 2, 4, 5 in yarn B, row 3 in yarn C.
When working in the round: (RS) Knit all rows.
When working flat: Knit on RS rows, purl on WS rows.
Repeat welts 1 and 2.

OUTER OVAL

With A, use a long-tail or double method to cast on 593 (625, 657) stitches, placing a marker in between each of the following 8 sections: 110 (114, 118) stitches, 58 (62, 66) stitches, 70 (74, 78) stitches, 58 (62, 66) stitches, 110 (114, 118) stitches, 58 (62, 66) stitches, 70 (74, 78) stitches, 58 (62, 66) stitches, with 1 stitch after the last marker. Use a different color marker for the last marker to denote the beginning and end of each row.

Welt 1, Reverse Stockinette Stitch (Note: This outer welt has 7 rows instead of the normal 5 rows. The first 3 rows of this welt are worked flat before joining the work into an oval. It is important to the directional integrity of the pattern that the oval be joined at the completion of the third row as instructed.) Row 1: (RS) With A, purl. Row 2: Knit. Row 3: Purl to last stitch, slip 1. Adjust work to ensure that cast-on edge is not twisted around needle. (See *No Twist Join*, Chapter Two.) Join work into an oval by placing the last, slipped stitch from row 3 back onto the left needle. Two stitches are now on the left needle before the marker. Purl these two stitches together. Continue next rows in the round. Rows 4-7: Purl. 592 (624, 656) stitches.

Welt 2, Stockinette Stitch (Note: When changing yarns at the beginning and end of a row in this and all subsequent outer oval welts, leave approximately 5" (12.7cm) of yarn tail at back of work at each end. These strands will become the fringe across the collar.) Rows 1-2: With B, knit. Row 3: With C, knit. Row 4: With B, knit. Row 5: *K2, k2tog, knit to within 4 stitches of next marker, k2tog, k2, slip marker; repeat from * across entire row. 576 (608, 640) stitches.

Welt 3, Reverse Stockinette Stitch Rows 1-4: With A, purl. Row 5: *P2, p2tog, purl to within 4 stitches of next marker, p2tog, p2, slip marker; repeat from * across entire row. 560 (592, 624) stitches.

Welts 4 - 22 (23, 24) (Note: Continue in Welted Stripes stitch pattern throughout remainder of garment.) Continue decreases at markers in last row of each welt as established. 256, (272, 288) stitches.

BACK BODICE AND SLEEVES

After the collar and lapels are completed and bound off, the bodice is worked flat on the remaining live stitches in the center of the garment. Change to the working-flat version of Welted Stripes stitch pattern after row 1 of next welt.

Welt 23 (24, 25) Row 1: Use Jeny's Surprisingly Stretchy Bind Off method to bind off 30 (33, 36) stitches, work 128 (136, 144) stitches*; complete the first row of the welt by using

JSSBO to bind off remaining 98 (103, 108) stitches. Break yarn and rejoin at * to reposition beginning of row. Rows 2-3: Change to working-flat version of Welted Stripes stitch pattern. Work even. Row 4: Increase 1 stitch at beginning and end of row. Row 5: Increase 1 stitch at beginning and end of row and continue decreases in established manner at 4 remaining markers. 8 decreases worked/welt. 124 (132, 140) stitches.

Welts 24 (25, 26) - 26 (27, 28) Continue to increase 1 stitch at beginning and end of each row and to decrease in established manner at markers in first row of each welt. 8 decreases worked/welt. 130 (138, 146) stitches.

Welts 27 (28, 29) – 28 (29, 30) Continue to decrease in established manner at markers in first row of each welt and, at the same time, cast on 5 stitches at beginning of each row. (Note: To achieve desired sleeve length, add or subtract 4 stitches for each inch, distributed across all rows in these and the next 4 welts.) 8 decreases worked/welt. 164 (172, 180) stitches.

Welts 29 (30, 31) – 31 (32, 33) No further marker decreases; remove all stitch markers. Cast on 5 stitches at beginning of each row. 239 (247, 255) stitches.

Welt 32 (33, 34) Row 1: Cast on 5 stitches at beginning of row. Rows 2-3: Cast on 3 (2, 2) stitches at beginning of row. Rows 4-5: Cast on 7 stitches at beginning of each row. 264 (270, 278) stitches.

Cuffs

Welts 33 (34, 35) – 38 (40, 42) Place markers 7 stitches in from each end of sleeves to indicate cuff stitches. Work the stitches between the markers even, in the established pattern. At the same time, work the cuff stitches in Reverse Stockinette stitch only and in yarn C only, adding a small bobbin of C at each cuff as necessary. 264 (270, 278) stitches.

Neck, Front Bodice and Sleeves

In the next welt, stitches in the center of the row are bound off to create the back neck and begin shaping the two front bodice panels. Add a second ball of each yarn as necessary to work both sleeves at the same time. Continue to work cuff stitches in Reverse Stockinette stitch and the stitches between the markers in the established Welted Stripes pattern.

Welt 39 (41, 43) Row 1: Work 110 (112, 114) stitches, use basic method to bind off center 44 (46, 50) stitches, work remaining 110 (112, 114) stitches. Row 2: Work in established pattern to the second neck edge, add a second ball of yarn and continue row. Rows 3-5: Work even. 110 (112, 114) stitches/sleeve.

Welts 40 (42, 44) – 44 (47, 50) Work in established pattern, decreasing 1 stitch at each neck edge on row 1 of each welt. 105 (106, 107) stitches/sleeve.

Welt 45 (48, 51) Apply in reverse order any sleeve length changes made in welts 27-32 (28-33, 29-34) in this and the next 5 welts. Continue decreasing at neck edges on row 1. Rows 1-2: Bind off 7 stitches at beginning (sleeve end) of each row. Rows 3-4: Bind off 3 (2, 2) stitches at beginning of each row. Row 5: Bind off 5 stitches at beginning of row. 94/89 (96/91, 97/92) stitches/sleeve.

Welts 46 (49, 52) – 50 (53, 56) Continue to work decreases at neck edges as established and, at the same time, bind off 5 stitches at beginning of each row. 24 (26, 27) stitches/sleeve.

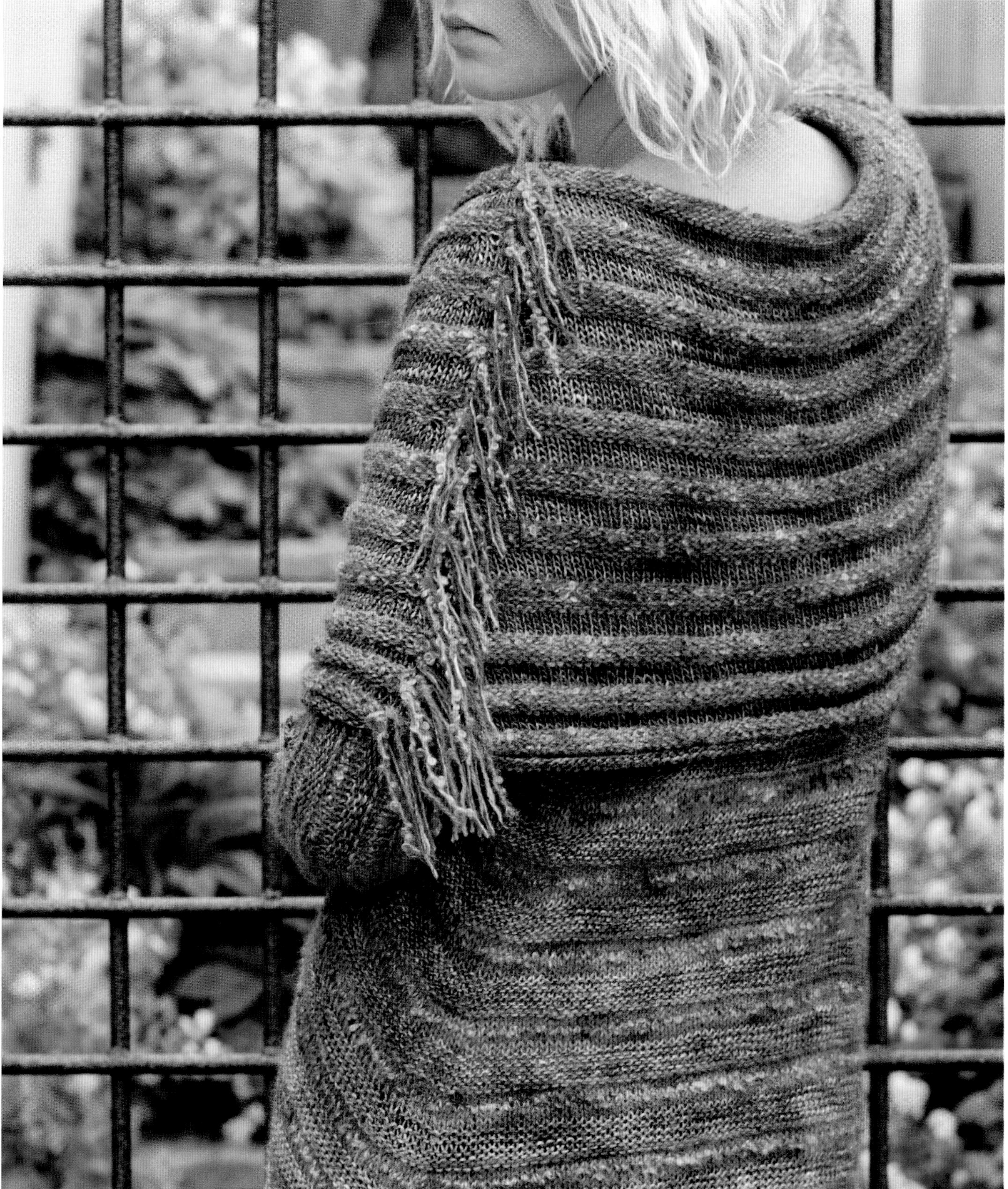

Welts 51 (54, 57) – 53 (56, 58) Continue to work decreases at neck edges as established and, at the same time, decrease 1 stitch at each sleeve edge each row. 6 (8, 15) stitches/sleeve.

Welt 54, Size One Continue to work decreases at neck edges as established. Rows 1-2: Decrease 1 stitch at each sleeve edge each row. Rows 3-5: Work even at sleeve edges. Bind off remaining 3 stitches/sleeve.

Welt 59, Size Three Decrease 1 stitch at each neck edge *every other* row and, at the same time, decrease 1 stitch at each sleeve edge each row. 7 stitches/sleeve.

Welt 57 (60), Sizes Two and Three Decrease 1 stitch at each neck edge *every other* row. Rows 1-2: Decrease 1 stitch at each sleeve edge each row. Rows 3-5: Work even at sleeve edges. Bind off remaining 3 stitches/sleeve.

Finishing

Use cast-on yarn tail to sew first rows on Welt 1 together. Weave in ends with the exception of those that will be incorporated into the fringe across the collar. Block. With tapestry needle and matching yarn, sew neck/front bodice edge to bound-off inner collar edge. Sew underarm seams so that finished seam is on the outside on the sleeves and inside on the cuffs.

Complete the fringe on the collar by tying neighboring groups of 2-3 strands together with double overhand knots positioned close against the knitted fabric. Trim each section of fringe even, at approximately 4" (10.2 cm). Tack cuffs to reinforce rolled shape.

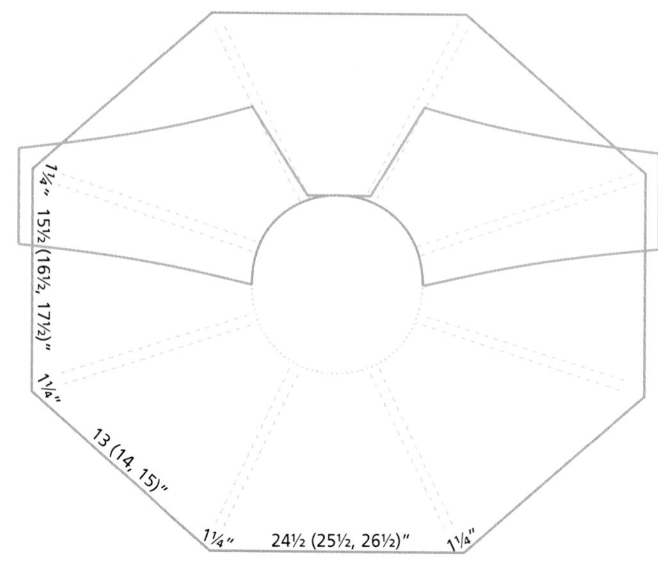
1¼"
15½ (16½, 17½)"
1¼"
13 (14, 15)"
1¼"
24½ (25½, 26½)"
1¼"

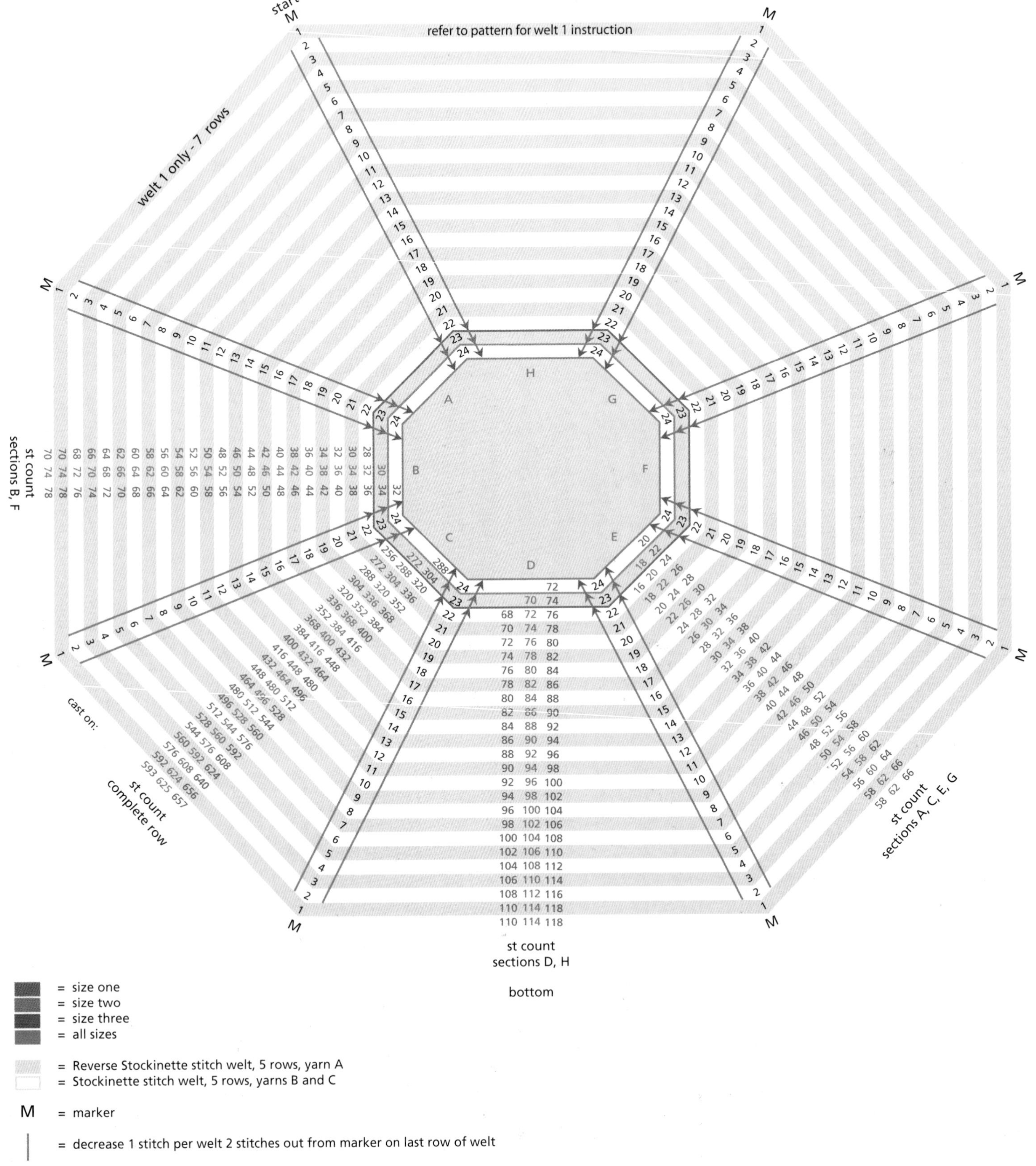

Note: All stitch counts refer to the number of stitches at completion of the last row of the welt

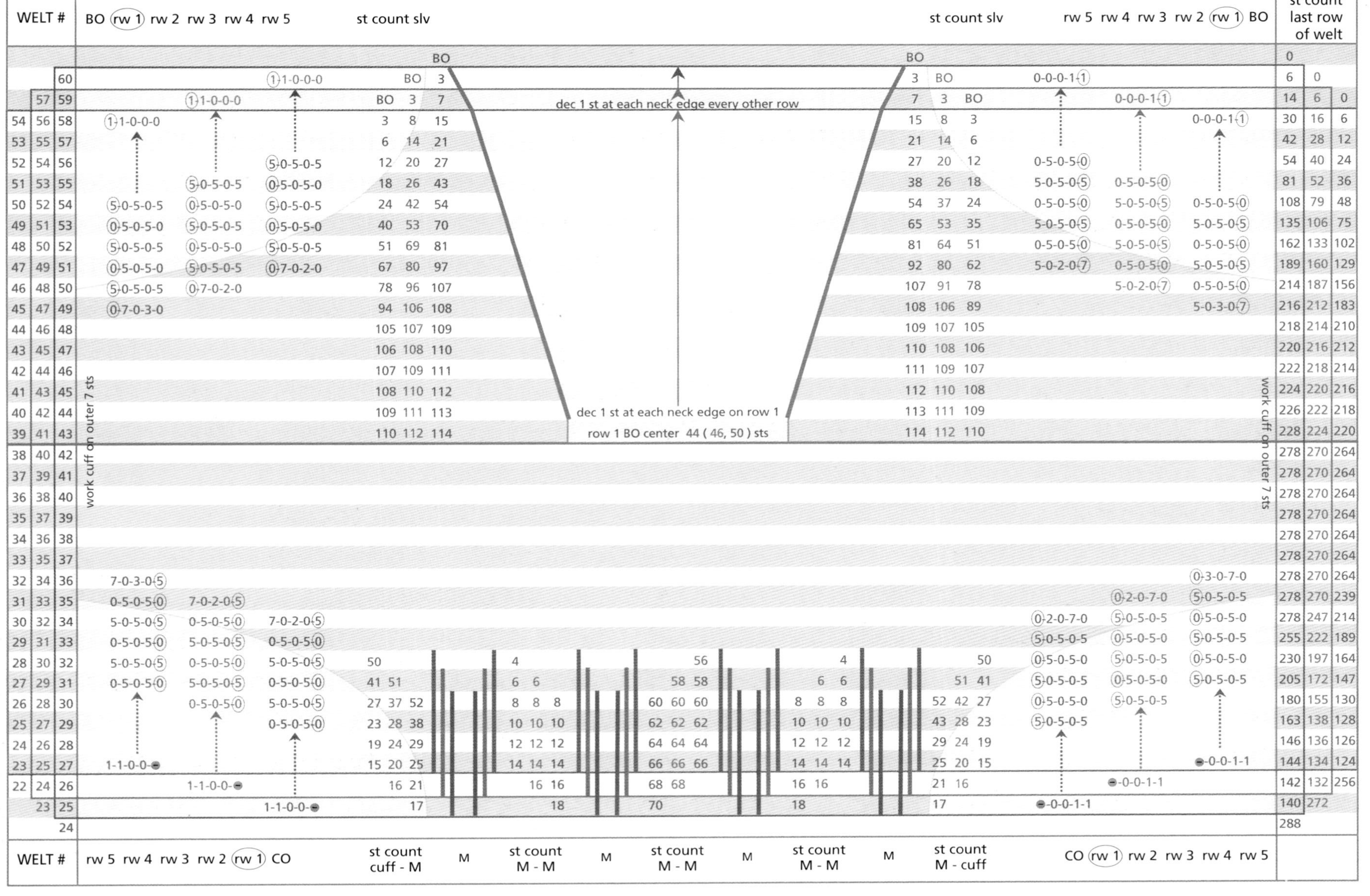

= size one
= size two
= size three
= all sizes

= Reverse Stockinette stitch welt, 5 rows
= Stockinette stitch welt, 5 rows

M = marker

= rw 1 use JSSBO to BO 30 (33, 36) sts, work 128 (136, 144) sts*, BO 98 (103, 108) sts; break yarn, rejoin at *; bodice worked on rem sts

= decrease 1 stitch per welt 2 stitches out from marker on last row of welt

= decrease at neck edge as directed above

= work as directed to this point

= increase 1 st at sleeve edge each row (below center line); decrease 1 st at sleeve edge each row (above center line)

Note: All stitch counts refer to the number of stitches at completion of the last row of the welt

sophie's swirl

Two manifestly different yarns come together in an energetic interplay of saturated color and contrasting texture. One side of the resulting fabric is rough hewn with loops of chunky multihued bouclé defining the terrain. On the flip side, silken rivers of fine, caressingly soft baby alpaca swirl and hold sway. This lightly structured short jacket can be worn double-breasted and closely fitted, or open and gently flared around the torso. Ornamental knots surround the cuffs, while a tier of nubby fringe highlights the waist. Taken altogether, Sophie's Swirl is a treat for the senses.

Sizes

One (Two, Three); shown here in Size One.

Knitted Measurements

Collar: 13 (13¾, 14½)"/33 (35, 37)cm
Center Back: 27 (28½, 30)"/69 (72, 76)cm
Center Back Neck to Cuff: 24¾ (25¼, 26)"/63 (64, 66)cm

Approximate As-Worn Measurements

Collar: 8 (8¾, 9½)"/20 (22, 24)cm
Center Back: 27 (28½, 30)"/69 (72, 76)cm
Center Back Neck to Cuff: 33¼ (34, 34¾)"/84 (86, 88)cm

Materials

Multiple-ply, DK weight alpaca yarn, 1306 (1453, 1609) yd/1194 (1329, 1471)m (A); and medium loop bouclé, bulky weight yarn, 138 (152, 171) yd/126 (139, 156)m (B). As shown, 6 (6, 7) skeins Shibui Baby Alpaca DK (100% baby alpaca, 3½ oz/100g, 255 yd/233m) in color Peony #220(A); and 3 (3, 4) skeins Noro Silk Mountain (65% wool/25% silk/10% kid mohair, 1¾ oz/50g, 55 yd/50m)in colorway #8 (B), discontinued. Suggested substitution: 1 (1, 1) skein Fleece Artist Baby Alpaca (4½ oz/125g, 180 yd/165m) in colorway Mahogany.

One 32 (32, 40)" size 7 (4.5mm) circular needle or size required to obtain gauge.

Gauge

24 stitches and 26 rows = 4"/10cm

Before beginning, please review Chapter One, ***Silhouettes and Sizing*** and Chapter Two, ***Tips and Techniques***.

Stitch Pattern: Welted Stripes

Continuous, alternating welts of Reverse Stockinette stitch in yarn A, and Stockinette stitch in yarns A and B.

Welt 1—Reverse Stockinette Stitch, 5 rows, yarn A
When working in the round: (RS) Purl all rows.
When working flat: Purl on RS rows, knit on WS rows.
Welt 2—Stockinette Stitch, 5 rows, yarns A and B
Work rows 1, 2, 4, 5 in yarn A, row 3 in yarn B.
When working in the round: (RS) Knit all rows.
When working flat: Knit on RS rows, purl on WS rows.
Repeat welts 1 and 2.

Outer Oval

With A, use a long-tail or double method to cast on 537 (569, 601) stitches, placing a marker in between each of the following 8 sections: Two sections of 54 (58, 62) stitches, 106 (110, 114) stitches, three sections of 54 (58, 62) stitches, 106 (110, 114) stitches, 54 (58, 62) stitches, with 1 stitch after the last marker. Use a different color marker for the last marker to denote the beginning and end of each row.

Welt 1, Reverse Stockinette Stitch (Note: This outer welt has 7 rows instead of the normal 5 rows. The first 3 rows of this welt are worked flat before joining the work into an oval. It is important to the directional integrity of the pattern that the oval be joined at the completion of the third row as instructed.) Row 1: (RS) With A, purl. Row 2: Knit. Row 3: Purl to last stitch, slip 1. Adjust work to ensure that cast-on edge is not twisted around needle. (See *No Twist Join*, Chapter Two.) Join work into an oval by placing the last, slipped stitch from row 3 back onto the left needle. Two stitches are now on the left needle before the marker. Purl these two stitches together. Continue next rows in the round. Rows 4-7: Purl. 536 (568, 600) stitches.

Welt 2, Stockinette Stitch Rows 1-2: With A, knit. Row 3: With B, knit, leaving approximately 6" (15.2cm) of yarn tail at back of work at beginning and end of row. These strands will become the knotted fringe at the lower right front. Row 4: With A, knit. Row 5: *K2, k2 tog, knit to within 4 stitches of next marker, k2tog, k2, slip marker; repeat from * across entire row. 520 (552, 584) stitches.

Welt 3, Reverse Stockinette Stitch Rows 1-4: With A, purl. Row 5: *P2, p2tog, purl to within 4 stitches of next marker, p2tog, p2, slip marker; repeat from * across entire row. 504 (536, 568) stitches.

Welts 4 - 18 (19, 20) (Note: Continue in Welted Stripes stitch pattern throughout remainder of garment.) Continue decreases at markers in last row of each welt as established, leaving yarn tails at each end of color B rows throughout this group of welts. 264 (280, 296) stitches.

Back Bodice and Sleeves

After the collar and lapels are completed and bound off, the bodice is worked flat on the remaining live stitches in the center of the garment. Change to the working-flat version of Welted Stripes stitch pattern after row 1 of next welt.

Welt 19 (20, 21) Row 1: Work first 122 (129, 136) stitches*, then use Jeny's Surprisingly Stretchy Bind Off method to bind off 132 (140, 148) stitches; complete the first row of the welt

by working the remaining 10 (11, 12) stitches. Slip stitches just worked back to left needle, break yarn and rejoin at * to reposition beginning of row. Rows 2-3: Change to working-flat version of Welted Stripes stitch pattern. Work even. Row 4: Increase 1 stitch at beginning and end of row. Row 5: Increase 1 stitch at beginning and end of row and continue decreases in established manner at 4 remaining markers. 8 decreases worked/welt. 128 (136, 144) stitches.

Welts 20 (21, 22) - 23 (24, 25) Continue to increase 1 stitch at beginning and end of every row and to decrease in established manner at markers in last row of each welt. 8 decreases worked/welt. 136 (144, 152) stitches.

Welts 24 (25, 26) Continue to decrease in established manner at markers in last row of each welt and, at the same time, cast on 6 stitches at the beginning of each row. (Note: To achieve desired sleeve length, add or subtract 4-5 stitches for each inch, distributed across all rows in this and the next 4 welts.) 8 decreases worked/welt. 158 (166, 174) stitches.

Welts 25 (26, 27) – 27 (28, 29) No further marker decreases; remove all stitch markers. Cast on 6 stitches at the beginning of each row. 248 (256, 264) stitches.

Welt 28 (29, 30) Row 1: Cast on 3 (2, 2) stitches at the beginning of row. Row 2: Cast on 5 (4, 4) stitches at the beginning of row. Row 3: Cast on 2 stitches at beginning of row. Rows 4-5: Cast on 7 stitches at beginning of each row. 272 (278, 286) stitches.

Cuffs

Welts 29 (30, 31) – 35 (37, 39) Place markers 7 stitches in from each end of sleeves to indicate cuff stitches. Work the stitches between the markers even, in the established pattern. At the same time, work the cuff stitches in Reverse Stockinette stitch only and in yarn A only, adding a small bobbin of A at each cuff as necessary. When working with yarn B, leave a yarn tail of approximately 5" (12.7cm) at back of work at the beginning and end of row. 272 (278, 286) stitches.

Neck, Front Bodice and Sleeves

In the next welt, stitches in the center of the row are bound off to create the back neck and begin shaping the two front bodice panels. Add a second ball of each yarn as necessary to work both sleeves at the same time. Continue to work cuff stitches in Reverse Stockinette stitch and the stitches between the markers in the established Welted Stripes pattern. When working yarn B rows, leave yarn tails at each sleeve end of row.

Welt 36 (38, 40) Row 1: Work 118 (119, 122) stitches, use basic method to bind off center 36 (40, 42) stitches, work remaining 118 (119, 122) stitches. Row 2: Work in established pattern to the second neck edge, add a second ball of yarn and continue row. Rows 3-5: Work even. 118 (119, 122) stitches/sleeve.

Welts 37 (39, 41) – 42 (45, 48) Work in established pattern, decreasing 1 stitch at each neck edge on row 1 of each welt. 112 (112, 114) stitches/sleeve.

Welt 43 (46, 49) Apply in reverse order any sleeve length changes made in welts 24-28 (25-29, 26-30) in this and the next 4 welts. Continue decreasing at neck edges on row 1. Rows 1-2: Bind off 7 stitches at beginning (sleeve end) of each row. Row 3: Bind off 2 stitches at beginning of row. Row 4: Bind off 5 (4, 4) stitches at beginning of row. Row 5: Bind off 3 (2, 2) stitches at beginning of row. 99 (100, 102) stitches/sleeve.

Welts 44 (47, 50) – 47 (50, 53) Continue to work decreases at neck edges as established and, at the same time bind off 6 stitches at beginning of each row. 35 (36, 38) stitches/sleeve.

Welts 48 (51, 54) – 50 (52, 54) Continue to work decreases at neck edges as established and, at the same time, decrease 1 stitch at each sleeve edge each row. 17 (24, 32) stitches/sleeve.

Welt(s) 51 (53, 55) – (54, 57) Decrease 1 stitch at each neck edge *every other* row and, at the same time, decrease 1 stitch at each sleeve edge each row. 9 stitches/sleeve.

Welt 52 (55, 58) Continue to decrease 1 stitch at each neck edge every other row. Rows 1-3: Decrease 1 stitch at each sleeve edge each row. Row 4: Decrease 1 (0, 1) stitch at each sleeve edge. Row 5: Work even at sleeve edges. Bind off remaining 3 stitches/sleeve.

FINISHING

Use cast-on yarn tail to sew first rows on Welt 1 together. Weave in ends with the exception of the yarn B tail ends in the outer oval and at cuffs. Block. With tapestry needle and matching yarn, sew neck/front bodice edge to bound-off inner collar edge so that the "wrong side" is seen in the torso and sleeves and the "right side" in the collar and lapels. Sew underarm seams so that the finished seam is outside on the sleeves and inside on the cuffs.

Complete the fringe on the lower right front by tying the two strands of yarn B in each welt together with a double overhand knot positioned close against the knitted fabric. Trim each section of fringe even at approximately 5" (12.7 cm).

Create the knotted trim at cuffs by loosely tying one yarn B tail end at a time in a simple overhand knot close against the knitted fabric, on the outside of the sleeve, just above the cuff. With the same tail end, tie a second overhand knot close against the first. Use a tapestry needle to thread the rest of the tail end back through the center of each of the two knots, anchoring them as one just above the cuff. Weave in end on inside of sleeve. Repeat around cuffs. Tack cuffs to reinforce.

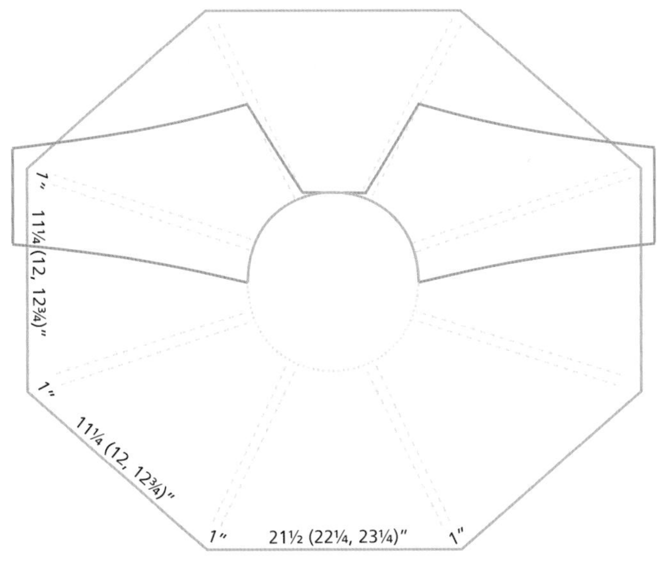
1"
11¼ (12, 12¾)"
1"
11¼ (12, 12¾)"
1"
21½ (22¼, 23¼)"
1"

top

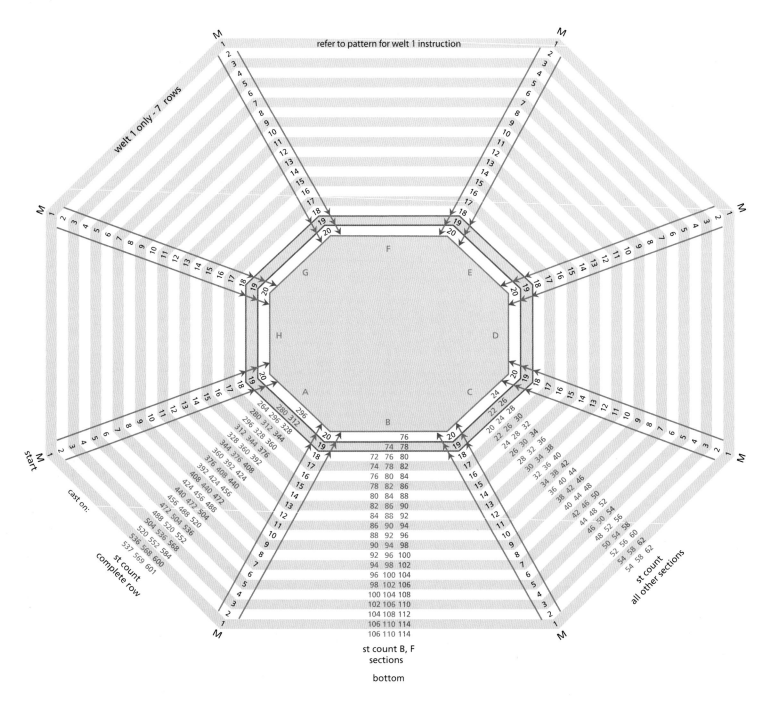

refer to pattern for welt 1 instruction

welt 1 only - 7 rows

M

1 2 3 4 5 6 7 8 9 10 11 12 13 14 15 16 17 18 19 20

F G H A B C D E

M start

bottom

welt	st count complete row (cast on:)	st count B, F sections	st count all other sections
20	296	76	24
19	280 312	74 78	22 26
18	264 296 328	72 76 80	20 24 28
17	280 312 344	74 78 82	22 26 30
16	296 328 360	76 80 84	24 28 32
15	312 344 376	78 82 86	26 30 34
14	328 360 392	80 84 88	28 32 36
13	344 376 408	82 86 90	30 34 38
12	360 392 424	84 88 92	32 36 40
11	376 408 440	86 90 94	34 38 42
10	392 424 456	88 92 96	36 40 44
9	408 440 472	90 94 98	38 42 46
8	424 456 488	92 96 100	40 44 48
7	440 472 504	94 98 102	42 46 50
6	456 488 520	96 100 104	44 48 52
5	472 504 536	98 102 106	46 50 54
4	488 520 552	100 104 108	48 52 56
3	504 536 568	102 106 110	50 54 58
2	520 552 584	104 108 112	52 56 60
1	536 568 600	106 110 114	54 58 62
cast on	537 569 601	106 110 114	54 58 62

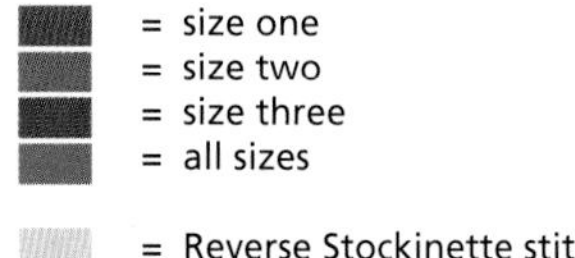

= size one
= size two
= size three
= all sizes

= Reverse Stockinette stitch welt, 5 rows, yarn A
= Stockinette stitch welt, 5 rows, yarns A and B

M = marker

| = decrease 1 stitch per welt 2 stitches out from marker on last row of welt

⋀⋀⋀ = work as directed to this point

Note: All stitch counts refer to the number of stitches at completion of the last row of the welt

WELT #			BO (rw 1) rw 2 rw 3 rw 4 rw 5			st count slv										st count slv			rw 5 rw 4 rw 3 rw 2 (rw 1) BO			st count last row of welt		
								BO								BO						0		
		58			①-1-1-1-0		BO	3								3	BO		0-1-1-1-①			6	0	
	55	57		①-1-1-0-0		BO	3	9								9	3	BO		0-0-1-1-①		18	6	0
52	54	56	①-1-1-1-0			3	9	17								17	9	3			0-1-1-1-①	34	18	6
51	53	55				9	16	24				dec 1 st at each neck edge every other row				24	16	9				48	32	18
50	52	54				17	24	32								32	24	17				64	48	34
49	51	53			⓪-6-0-6-0	23	30	38								38	30	23	6-0-6-0-⑥			76	60	46
48	50	52		⓪-6-0-6-0	⑥-0-6-0-6	29	36	51								57	36	29	0-6-0-6-⓪	6-0-6-0-⑥		108	72	58
47	49	51	⓪-6-0-6-0	⑥-0-6-0-6	⓪-6-0-6-0	35	49	70								70	55	35	6-0-6-0-⑥	0-6-0-6-⓪	6-0-6-0-⑥	140	104	70
46	48	50	⑥-0-6-0-6	⓪-6-0-6-0	⑥-0-6-0-6	48	68	83								89	68	54	0-6-0-6-⓪	6-0-6-0-⑥	0-6-0-6-⓪	172	136	102
45	47	49	⓪-6-0-6-0	⑥-0-6-0-6	⓪-7-0-4-0	67	81	102								102	87	67	2-0-2-0-⑦	0-6-0-6-⓪	6-0-6-0-⑥	204	168	134
44	46	48	⑥-0-6-0-6	⓪-7-0-4-0		80	100	114								114	100	86		2-0-2-0-⑦	0-6-0-6-⓪	228	200	166
43	45	47	⓪-7-0-5-0			99	112	115								115	112	99			3-0-2-0-⑦	230	224	198
42	44	46				112	113	116								116	113	112				232	226	224
41	43	45				113	114	117								117	114	113				234	228	226
40	42	44				114	115	118								118	115	114				236	230	228
39	41	43				115	116	119								119	116	115				238	232	230
38	40	42				116	117	120								120	117	116				240	234	232
37	39	41				117	118	121				dec 1 st at each neck edge on row 1				121	118	117				242	236	234
36	38	40	work cuff on outer 7 sts			118	119	122				row 1 BO center 36 (40, 42) sts				122	119	118			work cuff on outer 7 sts	244	238	236
35	37	39																				286	278	272
34	36	38																				286	278	272
33	35	37																				286	278	272
32	34	36																				286	278	272
31	33	35																				286	278	272
30	32	34																				286	278	272
29	31	33																				286	278	272
28	30	32	7-0-2-0-③																		⓪-5-0-7-0	286	278	272
27	29	31	0-6-0-6-⓪	7-0-2-0-②																⓪-4-0-7-0	⑥-0-6-0-6	286	278	248
26	28	30	6-0-6-0-⑥	0-6-0-6-⓪	7-0-2-0-②														⓪-4-0-7-0	⑥-0-6-0-6	⓪-6-0-6-0	286	256	218
25	27	29	0-6-0-6-⓪	6-0-6-0-⑥	0-6-0-6-⓪														⑥-0-6-0-6	⓪-6-0-6-0	⑥-0-6-0-6	264	226	188
24	26	28	6-0-6-0-⑥	0-6-0-6-⓪	6-0-6-0-⑥	44				8		60		8				38	⓪-6-0-6-0	⑥-0-6-0-6	⓪-6-0-6-0	234	196	158
23	25	27		6-0-6-0-⑥	0-6-0-6-⓪	27	45			10 10		62 62		10 10			39	27	⑥-0-6-0-6	⓪-6-0-6-0		204	166	136
22	24	26			6-0-6-0-⑥	23	28	46		12 12 12		64 64 64		12 12 12		40	28	23	⓪-6-0-6-0			174	144	134
21	23	25				19	24	29		14 14 14		66 66 66		14 14 14		29	24	19				152	142	132
20	22	24				15	20	25		16 16 16		68 68 68		16 16 16		25	20	15				150	140	130
19	21	23	1-1-0-0-●			11	16	21		18 18 18		70 70 70		18 18 18		21	16	11			●-0-0-1-1	148	138	128
18	20	22		1-1-0-0-●			12	17		20 20		72 72		20 20		17	12			●-0-0-1-1		146	136	264
	19	21			1-1-0-0-●			13		22		74		22		13			●-0-0-1-1			144	280	
		20																				296		
WELT #			rw 5 rw 4 rw 3 rw 2 (rw 1) CO			st count cuff - M			M	st count M - M	M	st count M - M	M	st count M - M	M	st count M - cuff			CO (rw 1) rw 2 rw 3 rw 4 rw 5					

= size one
= size two
= size three
= all sizes

= Reverse Stockinette stitch welt, 5 rows
= Stockinette stitch welt, 5 rows

M = marker

● ● ● = rw 1 work 122 (129, 136) sts*, use JSSBO to BO 132 (140, 148) sts, work 10 (11, 12) sts; break yarn, rejoin at *; bodice worked on rem sts

| | | = decrease 1 st per welt 2 sts out from marker on last row of welt | = decrease at neck edge as directed above

▲ ▲ ▲ = work as directed to this point

⋮ ⋮ ⋮ = increase 1 st at sleeve edge each row (below center line); decrease 1 st at sleeve edge each row (above center line)

Note: All stitch counts refer to the number of stitches at completion of the last row of the welt

golden glow

First it's the thick mane of golden fringe that demands your attention. Next your eye is drawn to the thin strands of pure silk ribbon scoring deep, open weave V's round and round before settling into dense, shimmering rows above and below. Velvety silk and merino welts unite all the elements into one stunning tone-on-tone textural delight. This short, fitted jacket is glitzy enough to wear over your little black dress in the evening, yet seems every bit as comfortable paired with jeans on an afternoon walk in the woods.

Sizes
One (Two, Three); shown here in Size One.

Knitted Measurements
Collar: 13 (13½, 14½)"/33 (34, 37)cm
Center Back: 27¾ (29, 30½)"/70 (74, 77)cm
Center Back Neck to Cuff: 27¾ (28½, 29¼)"/70 (72, 74)cm

Approximate As-Worn Measurements
Collar: 9½ (10, 11)"/24 (25, 28)cm
Center Back: 24 (25¼, 26¾)"/61 (64, 68)cm
Center Back Neck to Cuff: 33 (33¾, 34¾)"/84 (86, 88)cm

Materials
Single-ply, worsted weight silk/merino blend yarn, 899 (969, 1080) yd/822 (886, 988)m (A); and DK weight silk ribbon yarn, 792 (882, 944) yd/724 (807, 867)m in coordinating color (B). As shown, 9 (9, 10) skeins Alchemy Yarns Synchronicity (50% silk/50% merino, 1¾ oz/50g, 110 yd/101m) in colorway #35e-Fauna (A); and 4 (4, 4) skeins Alchemy Yarns Silken Straw (100% silk, 1½ oz/40g, 236 yd/216m) in same colorway (B).

One 32 (32, 40)" size 6 (4.0mm) and one 32 (32, 40)" size 13 (9.0mm) circular needle, three size 6 (4.0mm) double point needles, or sizes required to obtain gauge.

Gauge
24 stitches and 26 rows = 4"/10cm

Before beginning, please review Chapter One, ***Silhouettes and Sizing*** and Chapter Two, ***Tips and Techniques***.

Stitch Pattern: Welted Stripes with Alternating Condo Row

Continuous, alternating welts of Reverse Stockinette stitch in yarn A, and Stockinette stitch in yarn B. Stockinette stitch welts are worked in Stockinette stitch with condo row on every fourth welt.

Welts 1 and 3—Reverse Stockinette Stitch, 5 rows, yarn A
When working in the round: (RS) Purl all rows.
When working flat: Purl on RS rows, knit on WS rows.
Welt 2—Stockinette Stitch, 4 rows, yarn B
When working in the round: (RS) Knit all rows.
When working flat: Knit on RS rows, purl on WS rows.
Welt 4—Stockinette Stitch with Condo Row, 2 rows, yarn B
Work row 1 with smaller needle and row 2 with larger needle (condo row).
When working in the round: (RS) Knit all rows.
When working flat: Knit on RS rows, purl on WS rows.
Repeat welts 1-4.

Outer Oval

With A and smaller size circular needles, use a long-tail or double method to cast on 585 (617, 649) stitches, placing a marker in between each of the following 8 sections: 60 (64, 68) stitches, 112 (116, 120) stitches, three sections of 60 (64, 68) stitches, 112 (116, 120) stitches, two sections of 60 (64, 68), with 1 stitch after the last marker. Use a different color marker for the last marker to denote the beginning and end of each row.

Welt 1, Reverse Stockinette Stitch (Note: This outer welt has 7 rows instead of the normal 5 rows. The first 3 rows of this welt are worked flat before joining the work into an oval. It is important to the directional integrity of the pattern that the oval be joined at the completion of the third row as instructed.) Row 1: (RS) With A, purl. Row 2: Knit. Row 3: Purl to last stitch, slip 1. Adjust work to ensure that cast-on edge is not twisted around needle. (See *No Twist Join*, Chapter Two.) Join work into an oval by placing the last, slipped stitch from row 3 back onto the left needle. Two stitches are now on the left needle before the marker. Purl these two stitches together. Continue next rows in the round. Rows 4-7: Purl. 584 (616, 648) stitches.

Welt 2, Stockinette Stitch (Note: When changing yarns at the beginning and end of a row in this and all subsequent outer oval welts, leave approximately 7" (17.8cm) of yarn tail at back of work at each end. These strands will be incorporated into the fringe at the lapel.) Rows 1-3: With B, knit. Row 4: *K2, k2tog, knit to within 4 stitches of next marker, k2tog, k2, slip marker; repeat from * across entire row. 568 (600, 632) stitches.

Welt 3, Reverse Stockinette Stitch Rows 1-4: With A, purl. Row 5: *P2, p2tog, purl to within 4 stitches of next marker, p2tog, p2, slip marker; repeat from * across entire row. 552 (584, 616) stitches.

Welt 4, Stockinette Stitch with Condo Row Row 1: With B, knit. Row 2: With larger needles, *K2, k2tog, knit to within 4 stitches of next marker, k2tog, k2, slip marker; repeat from * across entire row. Change to smaller needles after completing row 2. 536 (568, 600) stitches.

Welt 5 - 20 (21, 22) (Note: Continue in Welted Stripes with Alternating Condo Row stitch pattern throughout remainder of garment.) Continue decreases in last row of each welt as established. 280 (296, 312) stitches.

Back Bodice and Sleeves

After the collar and lapels are completed and bound off, the bodice is worked flat on the remaining live stitches in the center of the garment. Change to the working-flat version of Welted Stripes with Alternating Condo Row stitch pattern after row 1 of next welt.

Welt 21 (22, 23) Row 1: Use Jeny's Surprisingly Stretchy Bind Off method to bind off 11 (12, 13) stitches, work 140 (148, 156) stitches*; complete the first row of the welt by using JSSBO to bind off remaining 129 (136, 143) stitches. Break yarn and rejoin at * to reposition beginning of row. Rows 2-3: Change to working-flat version of Welted Stripes with Alternating Condo Row stitch pattern. Work even. Row 4, Sizes One and Three only: Increase 1 stitch at beginning and end of row. Row 5 (4, 5): Increase 1 stitch at beginning and end of row and continue decreases in established manner at 4 remaining markers. 8 decreases worked/welt. 136 (142, 152) stitches.

Welts 22 (23, 24) - 26 (27, 28) Continue to increase 1 stitch at beginning and end of each row and to decrease in established manner at markers in last row of each welt. 8 decreases worked/ welt. 136 (144, 148) stitches.

Welts 27 (28, 29) - 28 (29, 30) No further marker decreases; remove all stitch markers. Continue to increase 1 stitch at beginning and end of each row. 150 (158, 166) stitches.

Welt 29 (30, 31) Cast on 6 stitches at beginning of each row. (Note: To achieve desired sleeve length, add or subtract 4-5 stitches for each inch, distributed across all rows in this and the next four welts; avoid adding stitches in condo row. When casting on at the beginning of a condo row, work cast-on stitches on smaller needle then change to larger needle to work remainder of condo row.) 180 (182, 196) stitches.

Welts 30 (31, 32) – 32 (33, 34) Cast on 6 (7, 6) stitches at beginning of each row. 246 (258, 262) stitches.

Welt 33 (34, 35) Row 1: Cast on 2 stitches at beginning of row. Row 2: Cast on 5 (2, 3) stitches at beginning of row. Row 3: Cast on 3 (11, 1) at beginning of row. Row(s) 4-5 (4, 4-5): Cast on 11 stitches at beginning of (each) row. 278 (284, 290) stitches.

Cuffs

Welts 34 (35, 36) – 40 (42, 44) Place markers 11 stitches in from each end of sleeves to indicate cuff stitches. Use double point needles and add a small bobbin of A at each cuff as necessary. Row 1: With A and smaller needles, purl 11 stitches, slip marker; work stitches between the markers even in established pattern, needle size and yarn to the next marker, slip marker; with A and smaller needles purl 11 stitches. Row 2: With A and smaller needles, k5, k2tog, YO, k4, slip marker; work stitches between the markers even in established pattern, needle size and yarn to the next marker, slip marker; with A and smaller needles, k4, YO, k2tog, k5. Subsequent rows: Work the stitches between the markers even in the established pattern, needle size and yarn, and, at the same time, work the cuff stitches even, repeating the cuff pattern in rows 1 and 2. 278 (284, 290) stitches.

Neck, Front Bodice and Sleeves

In the next welt, stitches in the center of the row are bound off to create the back neck and begin shaping the two front bodice panels. Add a second ball of each yarn as necessary to work both sleeves at the same time. Continue to work cuff stitches in the established stitch pattern and in yarn A only, and the stitches between the markers in the established Welted Stripes with Alternating Condo Row stitch pattern.

Welt 41 (43, 45) Row 1: Work 119 (122, 123) stitches, use basic method to bind off center 40 (40, 44) stitches, work remaining 119 (122, 123) stitches. Row 2: Work in established pattern to the second neck edge, add a second ball of yarn and continue row. Rows 3-5: Work even. 119 (122, 123) stitches/sleeve.

Welts 42 (44, 46) – 47 (50, 53) Work in established pattern, decreasing 1 stitch at each neck edge on row 1 of each welt. 113 (115, 115) stitches/sleeve.

Welt 48 (51, 54) Apply in reverse order any sleeve length changes made in welts 29-33 (30-34, 31-35) in this and the next 5 (4, 4) welts. Continue decreasing at neck edges on row 1. Rows 1-2: Bind off 11 stitches at beginning (sleeve end) of each row. Rows 3-4, Sizes Two and Three only: Bind off 2 (3) stitches at beginning of each row. Row 5, Size Two only: Bind off 6 stitches at beginning of row. 101 (101/95, 100) stitches/sleeve.

Welt 49, Size One Continue to work decreases at neck edges as established. Row 1: Bind off 3 stitches at beginning of row. Row 2: Bind off 5 stitches at beginning of row. Row 3: Bind off 2 stitches at beginning of row. Rows 4-5: Bind off 6 stitches at beginning of each row. 89 stitches/sleeve.

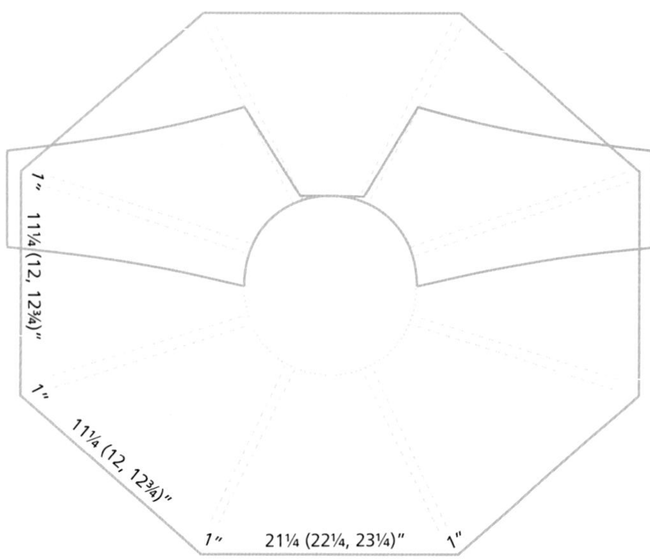

Welt(s) 50-52 (52, 55-58): Continue to work decreases at neck edges as established and, at the same time, bind off 6 (7, 6) stitches at beginning of each row. 50/56 (93/87, 48) stitches/sleeve.

Welt 53, Size Two: Continue to work decreases at neck edges as established. Row 1: Bind off 7 stitches at beginning of row. Rows 2-5: Bind off 6 stitches at the beginning of each row. 73 stitches/sleeve.

Welt 54, Size Two: Continue to work decreases at neck edges as established and, at the same time, bind off 6 stitches at the beginning of each row. 60 stitches/sleeve.

Welt 53 (55), Sizes One and Two: Continue to work decreases at neck edges as established. Rows 1-3 (1-4): Bind off 6 stitches at beginning of each row. Row(s) 5 (4-5): Bind off 1 stitch at the beginning of (each) row. 42 (47) stitches/sleeve.

Welts 54 (56, 59) – 56 (58, 60): Continue to work decreases at neck edges as established and, at the same time, decrease 1 stitch at each sleeve edge each row. 28 (33, 39) stitches/sleeve.

Welts 57(59, 61) – 59 (62, 65): Decrease 1 stitch at each neck edge *every other* row and, at the same time, decrease 1 stitch at the beginning of each row. 7 (9, 7) stitches/sleeve.

Welt 60 (63, 66): Continue to decrease 1 stitch at each neck edge every other row. Rows 1-2: Decrease 1 stitch at each sleeve edge each row. Rows 3-4, Size Two only: Decrease 1 stitch at the beginning of each row. Row(s) 5 (3-4): Sizes Two and Three: Work even at sleeve edges. Bind off remaining 4 (3, 3) stitches/sleeve.

Finishing

Use cast-on yarn tail to sew first rows on Welt 1 together. Weave in ends with the exception of those that will be incorporated into the fringe on the lapel. Block. With tapestry needle and matching yarn, sew neck/front bodice edge to bound-off inner collar edge. Sew underarm seams.

Complete the fringe on the lapel by cutting four 15" (38.1cm) lengths of yarn (2 each A and B) and threading them together through a tapestry needle. On the public side of the lapel, thread the yarn through the fabric so that equal lengths of yarn fall on either side of the start-of-row line immediately adjacent to the existing yarn tails. Divide the yarn strands in the middle and tie in a double overhand knot positioned close against the knitted fabric. Trim ends even. Repeat this process at the top of the welt and at the bottom and top of each subsequent welt in the lapel. Tack cuffs to reinforce rolled shape.

top

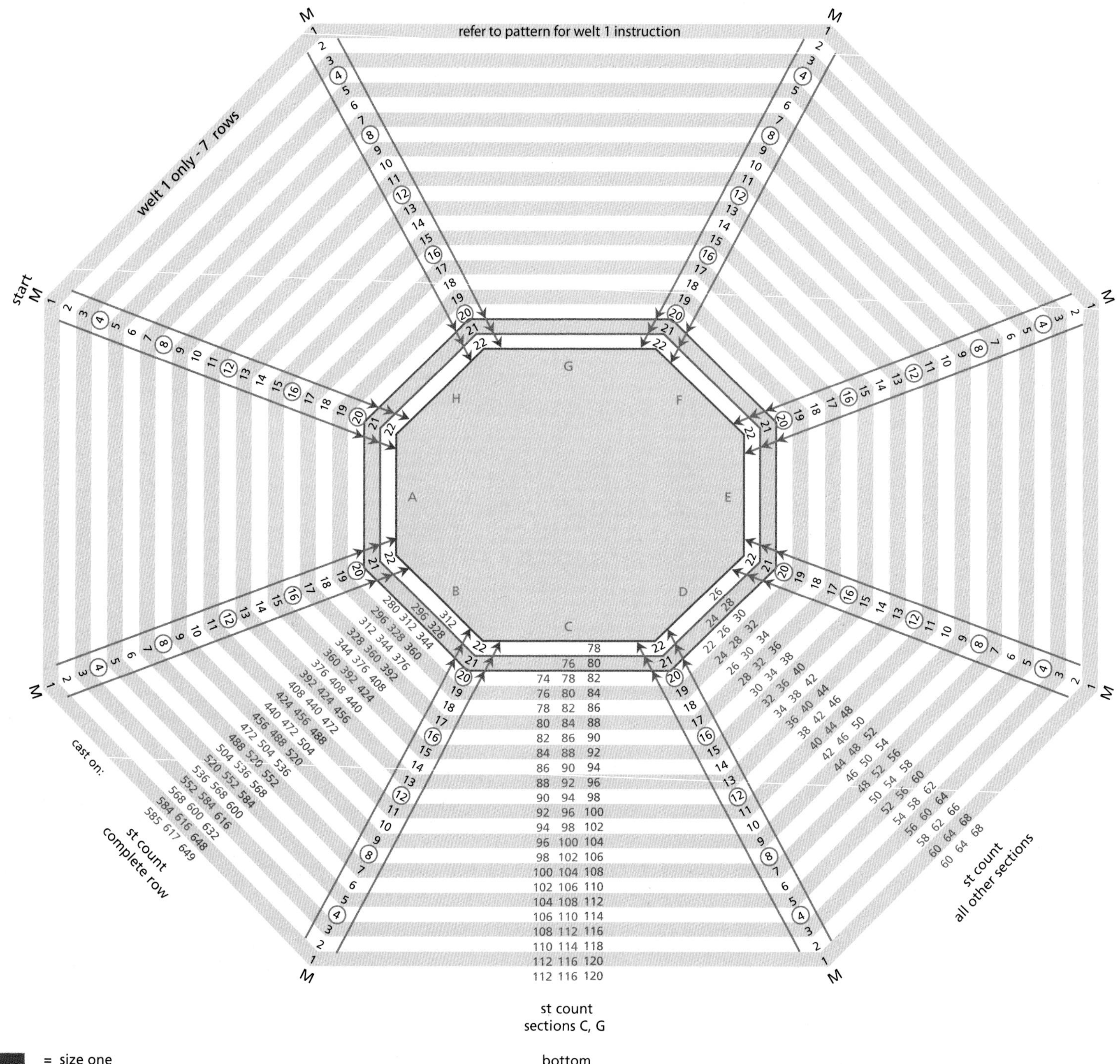

bottom

= size one
= size two
= size three
= all sizes

= Reverse Stockinette stitch welt, 5 rows, yarn A
= Stockinette stitch welt, 4 rows, yarn B
○ = Stockinette stitch with Condo Row, 2 rows, yarn B

M = marker

| = decrease 1 stitch per welt 2 stitches out from marker on last row of welt

AAA = work as directed to this point

Note: All stitch counts refer to the number of stitches at completion of the last row of the welt

WELT #			BO (rw 1) rw 2 rw 3 rw 4 rw 5			st count slv				st count slv			rw 5 rw 4 rw 3 rw 2 (rw 1) BO			st count last row of welt		
								BO		BO						0		
		66			1-1-0-0		BO	3		3	BO		0-0-1-1			6	0	
	63	65		1-1-1-1-0		BO	3	7		7	3	BO		0-1-1-1-1		14	6	0
60	62	64	1-1			4	9	15		15	9	4			1-1	30	18	8
59	61	63				7	15	18		18	15	7				36	30	14
58	60	62				14	22	25		25	22	14				50	44	28
57	59	61				20	25	31	decrease 1 stitch at each neck edge every other row	31	25	20				62	50	40
56	58	60				28	33	39		39	33	28				78	66	56
55	57	59				31	38	42		42	38	31				84	76	62
54	56	58			0-6-0-6	37	44	48		48	44	37	0-6-0-6			96	88	74
53	55	57	0-6-0-1-0	0-6-0-6-0	6-0-6-0-6	42	47	61		61	47	42	0-6-0-6-0	1-0-6-0-6	1-0-6-0-6	122	94	84
52	54	56	0-6	0-6-0-6	6-0	50	60	80		74	60	56	6-0	0-6-0-6	0-6	154	121	106
51	53	55	6-0-6-0-6	7-0-6-0-6	0-6-0-6-0	57	73	87		81	73	63	6-0-6-0-6	0-6-0-6-0	0-6-0-6-0	168	147	120
50	52	54	6-0-6-0	7-0	0-11-0-3	76	93	100		100	87	76	0-3-0-11	7-0	6-0-6-0	200	180	152
49	51	53	0-5-0-6-0	0-11-0-2-0		89	101	115		115	95	89		6-0-2-0-11	6-0-2-0-3	230	196	178
48	50	52	0-11			101	115	116		116	115	101			0-11	232	230	202
47	49	51				113	116	117		117	116	113				234	232	226
46	48	50				114	117	118		118	117	114				236	234	228
45	47	49				115	118	119		119	118	115				238	236	230
44	46	48				116	119	120		120	119	116				240	238	232
43	45	47				117	120	121		121	120	117				242	240	234
42	44	46				118	121	122	dec 1 st at each neck edge on row 1	122	121	118				244	242	236
41	43	45				119	122	123	row 1 BO center 40 (40, 44) sts	123	122	119				246	244	238
40	42	44														290	284	278
39	41	43														290	284	278
38	40	42														290	284	278
37	39	41														290	284	278
36	38	40														290	284	278
35	37	39														290	284	278
34	36	38														290	284	278
33	35	37	0-11-0-5-0												2-0-3-0-11	290	284	278
32	34	36	6-0	11-0-2-0										2-0-11-0	6-0	290	284	246
31	33	35	6-0-6-0-6	7-0-7-0-6	0-11-0-3-0								2-0-1-0-11	0-7-0-7-0	0-6-0-6-0	290	258	234
30	32	34	0-6-0-6	0-6	6-0-6-0								6-0-6-0	0-6	0-6-0-6	262	224	204
29	31	33	0-6-0-6-0	0-6-0-6-0	6-0-6-0-6								0-6-0-6-0	6-0-6-0-6	6-0-6-0-6	238	212	180
28	30	32		6-0-6-0	0-6								0-6	6-0-6-0		208	182	150
27	29	31			0-6-0-6-0								6-0-6-0-6			196	158	146

work cuff on outer 11 sts

WELT #			rw 5 rw 4 rw 3 rw 2 (rw 1) CO			st count cuff - M	M	st count M - M	M	st count M - M	M	st count M - M	M	st count M - cuff	CO (rw 1) rw 2 rw 3 rw 4 rw 5			st count last row of welt		
26	28	30				27		10		62		10		27				166	148	136
25	27	29				24 28		12 12		64 64		12 12		28 24				158	144	136
24	26	28				20 24 27		14 14 14		66 66 66		14 14 14		27 24 20				148	142	134
23	25	27				19 21 26		16 16 16		68 68 68		16 16 16		26 21 19				152	142	138
22	24	26				15 17 22		18 18 18		70 70 70		18 18 18		22 17 15				150	140	136
21	23	25	1-1-0-0-●			12 16 19		20 20 20		72 72 72		20 20 20		19 16 12			●-0-0-1-1	150	144	136
20	22	24		1-0-0-●		12 15		22 22		74 74		22 22		15 12		●-0-0-1		148	142	280
	21	23			1-1-0-0-●	14		24		76		24		14	●-0-0-1-1			152	296	
		22																312		

= size one
= size two
= size three
= all sizes

= Reverse Stockinette stitch welt, 5 rows
= Stockinette stitch welt, 4 rows
= Stockinette stitch with Condo Row welt, 2 rows

M = marker

● ● ● = row 1 use JSSBO to BO 11 (12, 13) sts, work 140 (148, 156) sts*, BO 129 (136, 143) sts; break yarn, rejoin yarn at *; bodice worked on remaining stitches

| | | = decrease 1 stitch per welt 2 stitches out from marker on last row of welt | = decrease at neck edge as directed above

▲ ▲ ▲ = work as directed to this point

⋮ ⋮ ⋮ = increase 1 st at sleeve edge each row (below center line); decrease 1 st at sleeve edge each row (above center line)

Note: All stitch counts refer to the number of stitches at completion of the last row of the welt

CHAPTER FIVE

off-center circles

SILKEN DREAMS

STRATA SPHERE

SHADES OF GREY

PLUM PERFECT

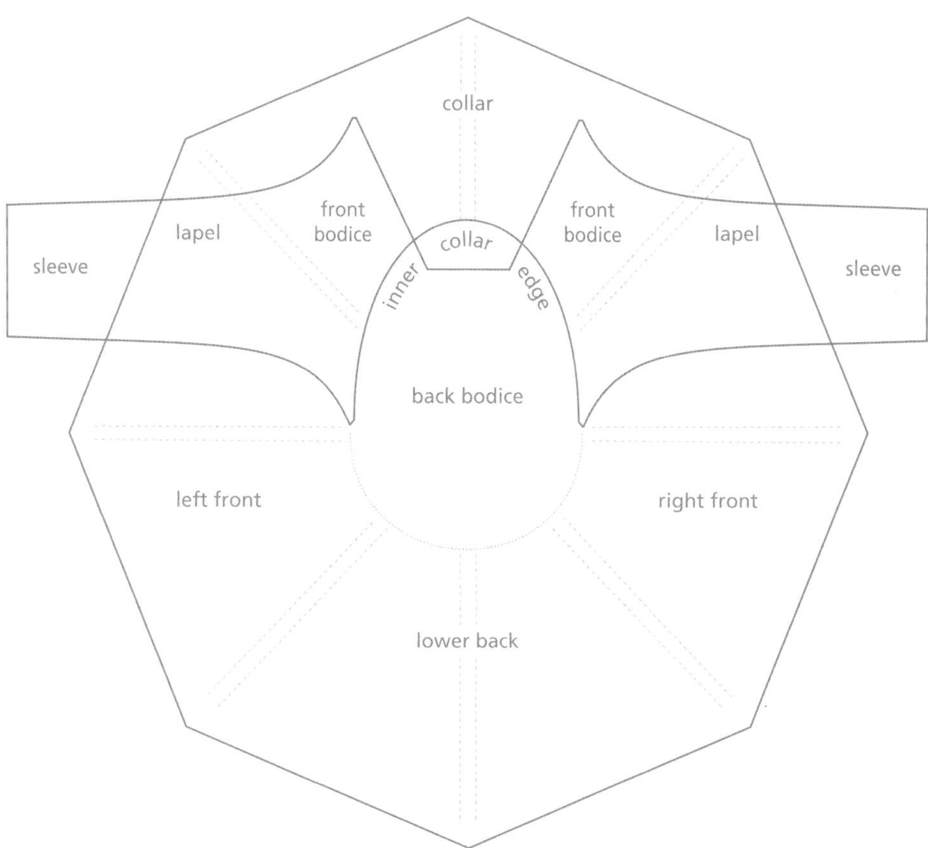

The ***off-center circle silhouette*** compliments a broad range of body types with a gently flared shape that is fitted but still accommodating. The sleeves are tapered with moderate ease around the upper arm. A slimming line is created by the welts that flow diagonally from the narrow collar and lapels down to the softly pointed center back. Just for fun, the mid-length, lighter weight versions of this silhouette can be worn upside down and fastened as waist-length jackets with expansive cape-like collars.

silken dreams

Silken Dreams was born of love, designed to compliment my daughter's pure, simple beauty on her wedding day. Natural spun silk provides a shimmering backdrop for the thousands of tiny glass beads that sparkle on alternating welts and gather in tiny pools at the back of the collar. The structure, length and drape of the coat allow it to glide gracefully over the train of a wedding gown. But you need not wait for a momentous time in life to enjoy this supple, flowing Swirl—a garden party, night on the town or any special day will do.

Sizes
One (Two, Three); shown here in Size Three.

Knitted Measurements
Center Back Collar: 9½ (10½, 11¼)"/24 (27, 29)cm
Center Back: 32¼ (34, 35½)"/82 (86, 90)cm
Center Back Neck to Cuff*: 30¾ (31½, 32½)"/78 (80, 83)cm

Approximate As-Worn Measurements
Center Back Collar: 7¼ (8¼, 9)"/18 (21, 23)cm
Center Back: 34¾ (36½, 38)"/88 (93, 96)cm
Center Back Neck to Cuff*: 36¼ (37¼, 38½)"/92 (95, 98)cm

*Center Back Neck to Cuff measurements include an additional 10% in length to allow for stacking folds at the wrist.

Materials
Single-ply, worsted weight silk yarn, 634 (719, 810) yd/580 (657, 741)m (A); and single-ply worsted weight silk yarn with glass beads, 591 (651, 765) yd/540 (595, 700)m in coordinating color (B). As shown, 3 (3, 4) skeins Tilli Tomas Pure & Simple (100% spun silk, 3½ oz/100g, 260 yd/238m)in color Natural (A); and 4 (5, 6) skeins Tilli Tomas Rock Star (100% spun silk with glass beads, 3½ oz/100g, 150 yd/137m) in same color (B).

One 32 (40, 40)" size 7 (4.5mm) circular needle or size required to obtain gauge; sewing needle and matching thread.

Gauge
18 stitches and 23 rows = 4"/10cm

Before beginning, please review Chapter One, ***Silhouettes and Sizing*** and Chapter Two, ***Tips and Techniques.***

Stitch Pattern: Welted Stripes
Continuous, alternating welts of Reverse Stockinette stitch in yarn A, and Stockinette stitch in yarn B.

Welt 1—Reverse Stockinette Stitch, 5 rows, yarn A
When working in the round: (RS) Purl all rows.
When working flat: Purl on RS rows, knit on WS rows.
Welt 2—Stockinette Stitch, 5 rows, yarn B
When working in the round: (RS) Knit all rows.
When working flat: Knit on RS rows, purl on WS rows.
Repeat welts 1 and 2.

Outer Circle
With A, use a long-tail or double method to cast on 489 (513, 537) stitches, placing a marker in between the following 8 sections of 61 (64, 67) stitches each, with 1 stitch after the last marker. Use a different color marker for the last marker to denote the beginning and end of each row.

Welt 1, Reverse Stockinette Stitch (Note: This outer welt has 7 rows instead of the normal 5 rows. The first 3 rows are worked flat before joining the work into a circle. It is important to the directional integrity of the pattern that the circle be joined at the completion of the third row as instructed.) Row 1: (RS) With A, purl. Row 2: Knit. Row 3: Purl to last stitch, slip 1. Adjust work to ensure that cast-on edge is not twisted around needle. (See *No Twist Join*, Chapter Two.) Join work into a circle by placing the last, slipped stitch from row 3 back onto the left needle. Two stitches are now on the left needle before the marker. Purl these two stitches together.

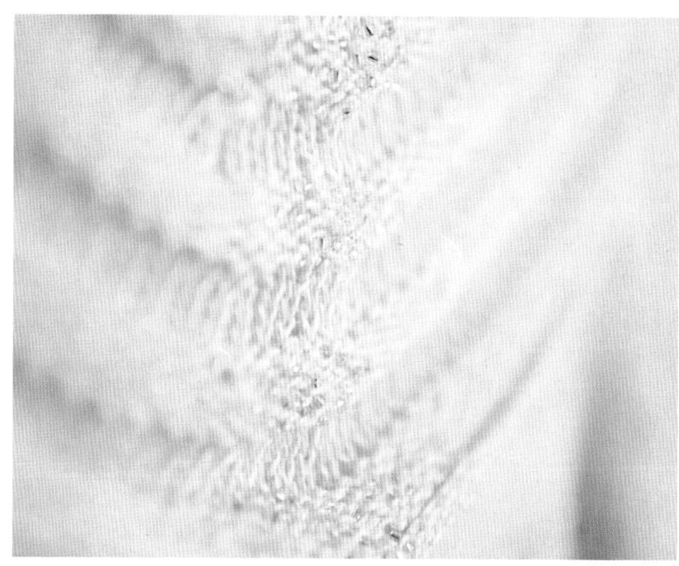

Continue next rows in the round. Rows 4-7: Purl. 488 (512, 536) stitches.

Welt 2, Stockinette Stitch Rows 1- 4: With B, knit. Row 5: *K2, k2tog, knit to within 4 stitches of next marker, k2tog, k2, slip marker; repeat from * across entire row. 472 (496, 520) stitches.

Welt 3, Reverse Stockinette Stitch Rows 1- 4: With A, purl. Row 5: *P2, p2tog, purl to within 4 stitches of next marker, p2tog, p2, slip marker; repeat from * across entire row. 456 (480, 504) stitches.

Welts 4-11 (12, 13) (Note: Continue in Welted Stripes stitch pattern throughout remainder of garment.) Continue decreases at markers in last row of each welt as established. 328 (336, 344) stitches.

Inner Collar Edge

Welt 12 (13, 14) Row 1: Decrease 1 stitch, continue in pattern to last 2 stitches, decrease 1 stitch. Rows 2-5: Turn and change to working-flat version of Welted Stripes stitch pattern. Decrease 1 stitch at beginning and end of each row (collar edge) and, at the same time, continue decreasing at remaining 7 markers on last row of welt as established. 312 (320, 328) stitches.

Welts 13 (14, 15) - 22 (23, 24) Continue to decrease 1 stitch at beginning and end of each row and to decrease in established manner at markers in last row of each welt. (Note: If, following the first neck edge decrease, fewer than 4 stitches remain before the first marker, stop marker-related decreases before the first marker and after the last marker. When decreases from one side of a marker consume its position, remove the marker and stop decreases related to that marker.) 82 (90, 98) stitches.

Back Bodice and Sleeves

After the collar and lapels are completed, the bodice is worked on the remaining live stitches in the center of the garment.

Welt 23 (24, 25) Remove the first and last marker. Rows 1-3: Work even. Row 4: Increase 1 stitch at beginning and end of row. Row 5: Increase 1 stitch at beginning and end of row and continue to decrease in established manner at remaining 3 markers. 6 decreases worked/welt. 80 (88, 96) stitches.

Welts 24 (25, 26) – 26 (27, 28) Continue to increase 1 stitch at beginning and end of each row and to decrease in established manner at markers in last row of each welt. 6 decreases worked/welt. 92 (100, 108) stitches.

Welts 27 (28, 29) – 30 (31, 32) No further decreases at markers; remove all stitch markers. Continue to increase 1 stitch at beginning and end of each row. 132 (140, 148) stitches.

Welt 31 (32, 33) Rows 1-2: Cast on 12 stitches at beginning of each row. Rows 3-5: Cast on 15 stitches at beginning of each row. (Note: To achieve desired sleeve length, add or subtract 3-4 stitches for each inch, distributed across all rows in this and the next welt.) 201 (209, 217) stitches.

Welt 32 (33, 34) Cast on 15 stitches at beginning of each row. 276 (284, 292) stitches.

Cuffs

Welts 33 (34, 35) – 37 (39, 41) Place markers 7 stitches in from each sleeve end to indicate cuff stitches. Work the stitches between the markers even, in the established pattern. At the same time, work the cuff stitches in Stockinette stitch and yarn

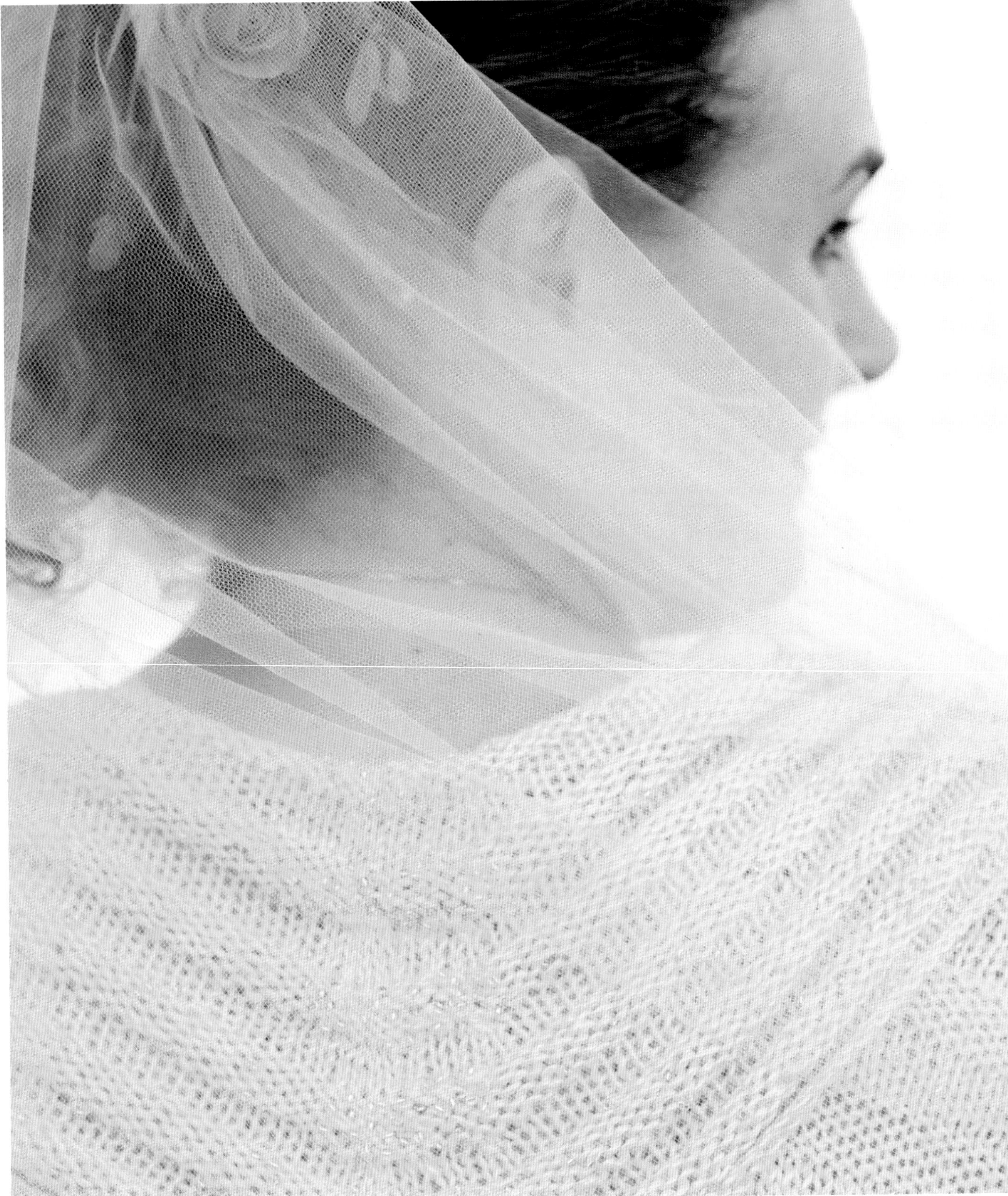

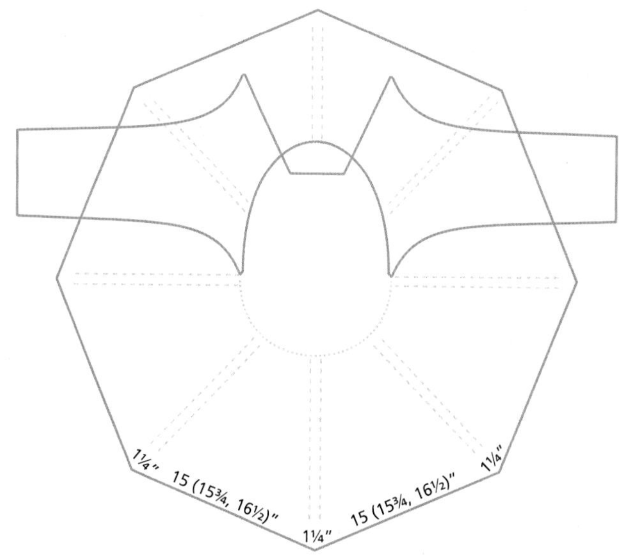

B only, adding a small bobbin of B at each cuff as necessary. 276 (284, 292) stitches.

Neck, Front Bodice and Sleeves

In the next welt, stitches in the center of the row are bound off to create the back neck and begin shaping the two front bodice panels. Add a second ball of each yarn as necessary to work both sleeves at the same time. Continue to work cuff stitches in Stockinette stitch only and the stitches between markers in the established Welted Stripes pattern.

Welt 38 (40, 42) Row 1: Work 126 (129, 131) stitches, use basic method to bind off center 24 (26, 30) stitches, work remaining 126 (129, 131) stitches. Row 2: Work in established pattern to the second neck edge, add a second ball of yarn and continue row. Rows 3-5: Work even. 126 (129, 131) stitches/sleeve.

Welts 39 (41, 43) – 42 (45, 48) Work in established pattern, decreasing 1 stitch at each neck edge on row 1 of each welt. 122 (124, 125) stitches/sleeve.

Welt 43 (46, 49) Apply in reverse order any sleeve length changes made in welts 31-32 (32-33, 33-34) in this and the following welt. Continue decreasing at neck edges on row 1, and, at the same time, bind off 15 stitches at beginning (sleeve end) of each row. 76/91 (78/93, 79/94) stitches/sleeve.

Welt 44 (47, 50) Continue to work decreases at neck edges as established. Rows 1-3: Bind off 15 stitches at beginning of each row. Rows 4-5: Bind off 12 stitches at beginning of each row. 48 (50, 51) stitches/sleeve.

Welts 45 (48, 51) – 51 (54, 56) Continue to work decreases at neck edges as established and, at the same time, decrease 1 stitch at each sleeve edge each row. 6 (8, 15) stitches/sleeve.

Welt 52, Size One Continue to work decreases at neck edges as established. Rows 1-2: Decrease 1 stitch at each sleeve edge each row. Rows 3-5: Work even at sleeve edges. Bind off remaining 3 stitches/sleeve.

Welt 57, Size Three Decrease 1 stitch at each neck edge *every other* row and, at the same time, decrease 1 stitch at each sleeve edge each row. 7 stitches/sleeve.

Welt 55 (58), Sizes Two and Three: Decrease 1 stitch at each neck edge *every other* row. Rows 1-2: Decrease 1 stitch at each sleeve edge each row. Rows 3-5: Work even at sleeve edges. Bind off remaining 3 stitches/sleeve.

Finishing

Carefully pull glass beads from all yarn tails and set aside. Use cast-on yarn tail to sew first rows on Welt 1 together. Weave in ends. Block. With tapestry needle and yarn A, sew neck/front bodice edge to inner collar edge. Sew underarm seams. Tack cuffs to reinforce rolled shape. Use a sewing needle and matching thread to stitch collected glass beads, one at a time, to the public side of the collar so that they are loosely clustered around the start-of-row point and between the decreases on every other welt beginning with Welt 2.

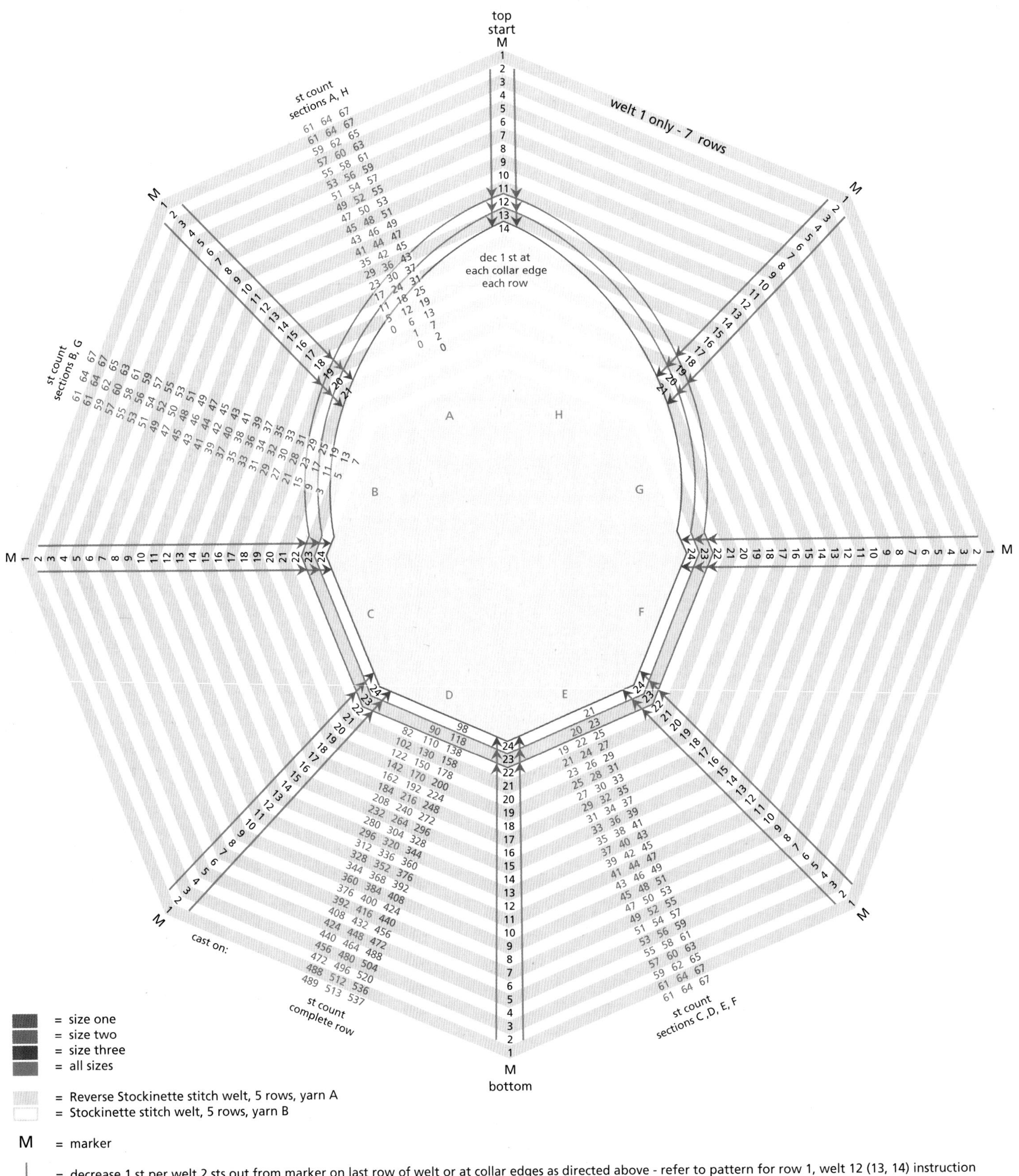

= work as directed to this point

Note: All stitch counts refer to the number of stitches at completion of the last row of the welt

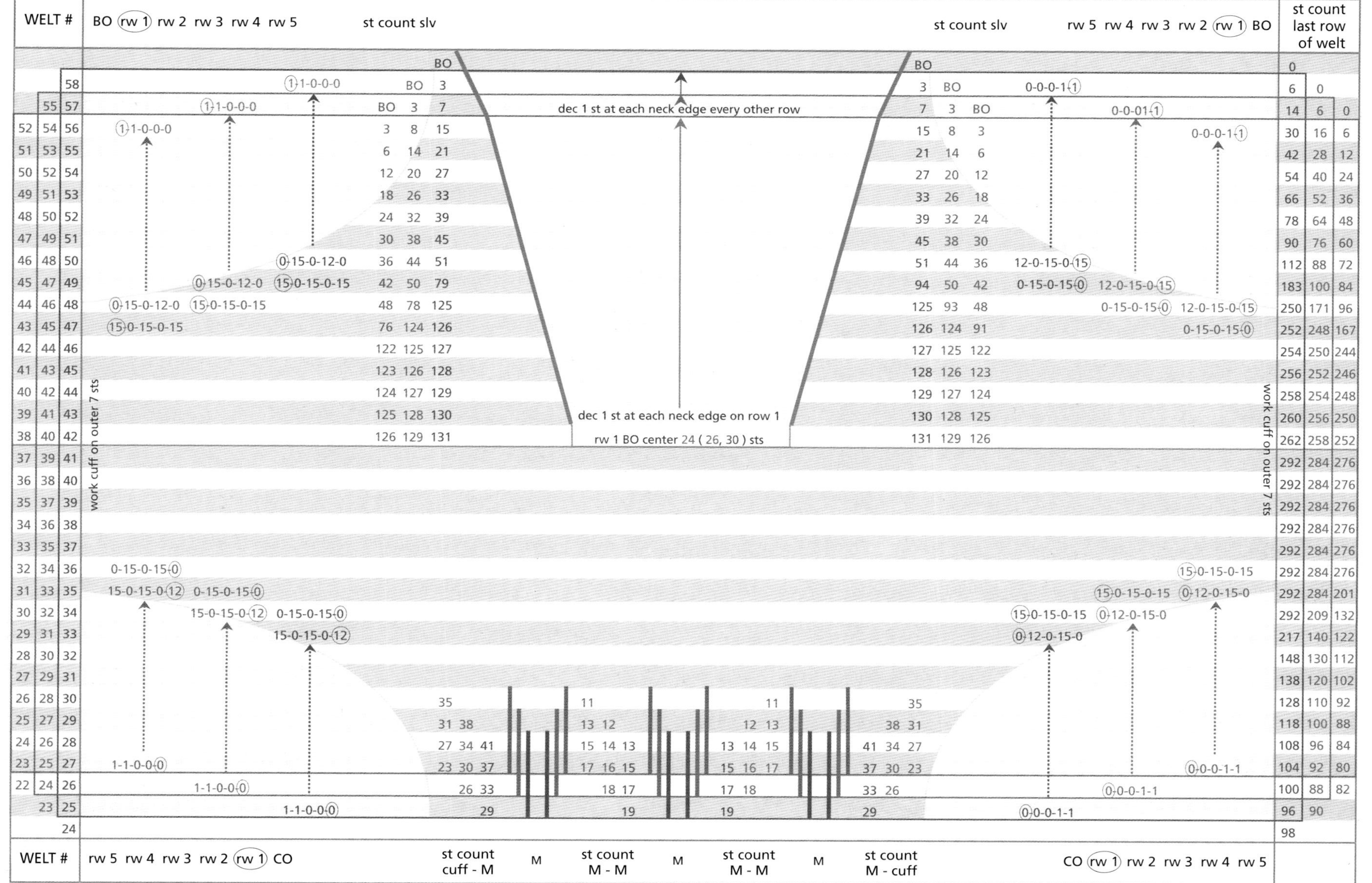

= size one
= size two
= size three
= all sizes

= Reverse Stockinette stitch welt, 5 rows
= Stockinette stitch welt, 5 rows

M = marker

= decrease 1 stitch per welt 2 stitches out from marker on last row of welt

= decrease at neck edge as directed above

= work as directed to this point

= increase 1 st at sleeve edge each row (below center line); decrease 1 st at sleeve edge each row (above center line)

Note: All stitch counts refer to the number of stitches at completion of the last row of the welt

Strata sphere

While the color work in Strata Sphere appears intricate at first glance, one yarn does it all. Swirl jackets are perfect for those deliciously tempting skeins of variegated hand painted yarns that we knitters just can't resist. Swirl construction, with its long revolving rows, scatters the color repeats of hand painted yarns and creates a subtle stratified look in which tiers of color gracefully ebb and flow. Just for fun, wear this design upside down, pinned at the waist and enjoy the ever-changing colors as they whirl across the expansive cape-like collar. Breathtaking!

Sizes
One (Two, Three); shown here in Size Two.

Knitted Measurements
Center Back Collar: 9¾ (10½, 11¼)"/25 (27, 29)cm
Center Back: 32¼ (33½, 35¼)"/82 (85, 89)cm
Center Back Neck to Cuff*: 27¼ (27¾, 28½)"/69 (70, 72)cm

Approximate As-Worn Measurements
Center Back Collar: 6½ (7¼, 8)"/16 (18, 20)cm
Center Back: 33 (34¼, 36)"/84 (87, 91)cm
Center Back Neck to Cuff*: 33¼ (33¾, 34¾)"/84 (86, 88)cm

*Center Back Neck to Cuff measurements do not include the 13 stitches at each sleeve end that become the folded cuff.

Materials
Single-ply, worsted weight silk/mohair/wool yarn, 1593 (1744, 1900) yd/1457 (1595, 1737)m. As shown, 15 (16, 17) balls Noro Silk Garden (45% silk/45% kid mohair/10% lamb's wool, 1¾ oz/50g, 109 yd/100m) in color #84.

One 40 (40, 47)" size 7 (4.5mm) circular needle or size required to obtain gauge.

Gauge
17 stitches and 24 rows = 4"/10cm

Strata Sphere may be worn upside down as shown on opposite page.

Before beginning, please review Chapter One, ***Silhouettes and Sizing*** and Chapter Two, ***Tips and Techniques***.

Stitch Pattern: Welted Stripes
Continuous, alternating welts of Reverse Stockinette stitch and Stockinette stitch.

Welt 1—Reverse Stockinette Stitch, 5 rows
When working in the round: (RS) Purl all rows.
When working flat: Purl on RS rows, knit on WS rows.
Welt 2—Stockinette Stitch, 4 rows
When working in the round: (RS) Knit all rows.
When working flat: Knit on RS rows, purl on WS rows.
Repeat welts 1 and 2.

Outer Circle
Use a long-tail or double method to cast on 537 (561, 585) stitches, placing a marker in between the following 8 sections of 67 (70, 73) stitches each, with 1 stitch after the last marker. Use a different color marker for the last marker to denote the beginning and end of each row.

Welt 1, Reverse Stockinette Stitch (Note: This outer welt has 7 rows instead of the normal 5 rows. The first 3 rows are worked flat before joining the work into a circle. It is important to the directional integrity of the pattern that the circle be joined at the completion of the third row as instructed.) Row 1: (RS) Purl. Row 2: Knit. Row 3: Purl to last stitch, slip 1. Adjust work to ensure that cast-on edge is not twisted around needle. (See *No Twist Join*, Chapter Two.) Join work into a circle by placing the last, slipped stitch from row 3 back onto the left needle. Two stitches are now on the left needle before the marker. Purl these two stitches together. Continue next rows in the round. Rows 4-7: Purl. 536 (560, 584) stitches.

Welt 2, Stockinette Stitch Rows 1-3: Knit. Row 4: *K2, k2tog, knit to within 4 stitches of next marker, k2tog, k2, slip marker; repeat from * across entire row. 520 (544, 568) stitches.

Welt 3, Reverse Stockinette Stitch Rows 1-4: Purl. Row 5: *P2, p2tog, purl to within 4 stitches of next marker, p2tog, p2, slip marker; repeat from * across entire row. 504 (528, 552) stitches.

Welts 4 - 13 (14, 15) (Note: Continue in Welted Stripes stitch pattern throughout remainder of garment.) Continue decreases at markers in last row of each welt as established. 344 (352, 360) stitches.

Inner Collar Edge
Welt 14 (15, 16) Row 1: Decrease 1 stitch, continue in pattern to last 2 stitches, decrease 1 stitch. Rows 2-4 (2-5, 2-4): Turn and change to working-flat version of Welted Stripes stitch pattern. Decrease 1 stitch at beginning and end of each row (collar edge) and, at the same time, continue decreasing at remaining 7 markers on last row of welt as established. 322 (328, 338) stitches.

Welts 15 (16, 17) - 25 (26, 27) Continue to decrease 1 stitch at beginning and end of each row and to decrease in established manner at markers in last row of each welt. (Note: If, following the first neck edge decrease, fewer than 4 stitches remain before the first marker, stop marker-related decreases before the first marker and after the last marker. When decreases from one side of a marker consume its position, remove the marker and stop decreases related to that marker.) 86 (94, 102) stitches.

Back Bodice and Sleeves

After the collar and lapels are completed, the bodice is worked on the remaining live stitches in the center of the garment.

Welt 26 (27, 28) No further decreases at markers; remove all stitch markers. Rows 1-3: Work even. Row(s) 4 (4-5, 4): Increase 1 stitch at beginning and end of each row. 88 (98, 104) stitches.

Welts 27 (28, 29) – 33 (34, 35) Continue to increase 1 stitch at beginning and end of each row. 152 (160, 168) stitches.

Welt 34 (35, 36) Cast on 6 stitches at beginning of each row. (Note: To achieve desired sleeve length, add or subtract 3-4 stitches for each inch, distributed across all rows in this and the next welt.) 176 (190, 192) stitches.

Welt 35 (36, 37) Row(s) 1-2 (1, 1-2): Cast on 6 stitches at beginning of each row. Row 3 (2, 3): Cast on 21 (20, 20) stitches at beginning of row. Row 4 (3, 4): Cast on 42 (40, 40) stitches at beginning of row. Row 5 (4, 5): Cast on 21 (20, 20) stitches at beginning of row. 272 (276, 284) stitches.

Cuffs

Welts 36 (37, 38) – 43 (45, 47) (Note: At finishing, the 13 stitches at each sleeve end will be folded back to form the cuffs.) Work stitches even in the established pattern, slipping the first sleeve edge stitch in each row. 272 (276, 284) stitches.

Neck, Front Bodice and Sleeves

In the next welt, stitches in the center of the row are bound off to create the back neck and begin shaping the two front bodice panels. Continue to work in the established Welted Stripes pattern.

Welt 44 (46, 48) Continue to slip the first sleeve edge stitch in each row. Row 1: Work 113 (114, 117) stitches, use basic method to bind off center 46 (48, 50) stitches, work remaining 113 (114, 117) stitches. Row 2: Work in established pattern to the second neck edge, add a second ball of yarn and continue row. Rows 3-4: Work even. 113 (114, 117) stitches/sleeve.

Welts 45 (47, 49) – 51 (54, 57) Continue slipping stitches at sleeve edges as established and, at the same time, decrease 1 stitch at each neck edge on last row of each welt. 106 (106, 108) stitches/sleeve.

Welt 52 (55, 58) Apply in reverse order any sleeve length changes made in welts 34-35 (35-36, 36-37) in this and the next welt. Continue slipping stitches at sleeve edges as established and decreasing at neck edges on row 4 (5, 4). Row 1: Bind off 21 (20, 20) stitches at beginning (sleeve end) of row. Row 2: Bind off 42 (40, 40) stitches at beginning (sleeve end) of row. Row 3: Bind off 21 (20, 20) stitches at beginning of row. Row 4: Bind off 6 stitches at beginning of row. Row 5, Size 2 only: Bind off 6 stitches at beginning of row. 63/57 (59, 67/61) stitches/sleeve.

Welt 53 (56, 59) Continue to work decreases at neck edges as established and, at the same time, bind off 6 stitches at beginning of each row. 44 (46, 48) stitches/sleeve.

Welts 54 (57, 60) – 60 (62, 64) Continue to work decreases at neck edges as established and, at the same time, decrease 1 stitch at each sleeve edge each row. 6 (13, 21) stitches/sleeve.

Welt 61, Size One Decrease 1 stitch at each neck edge *every other* row beginning with row 2. Row 1: Decrease 1 stitch

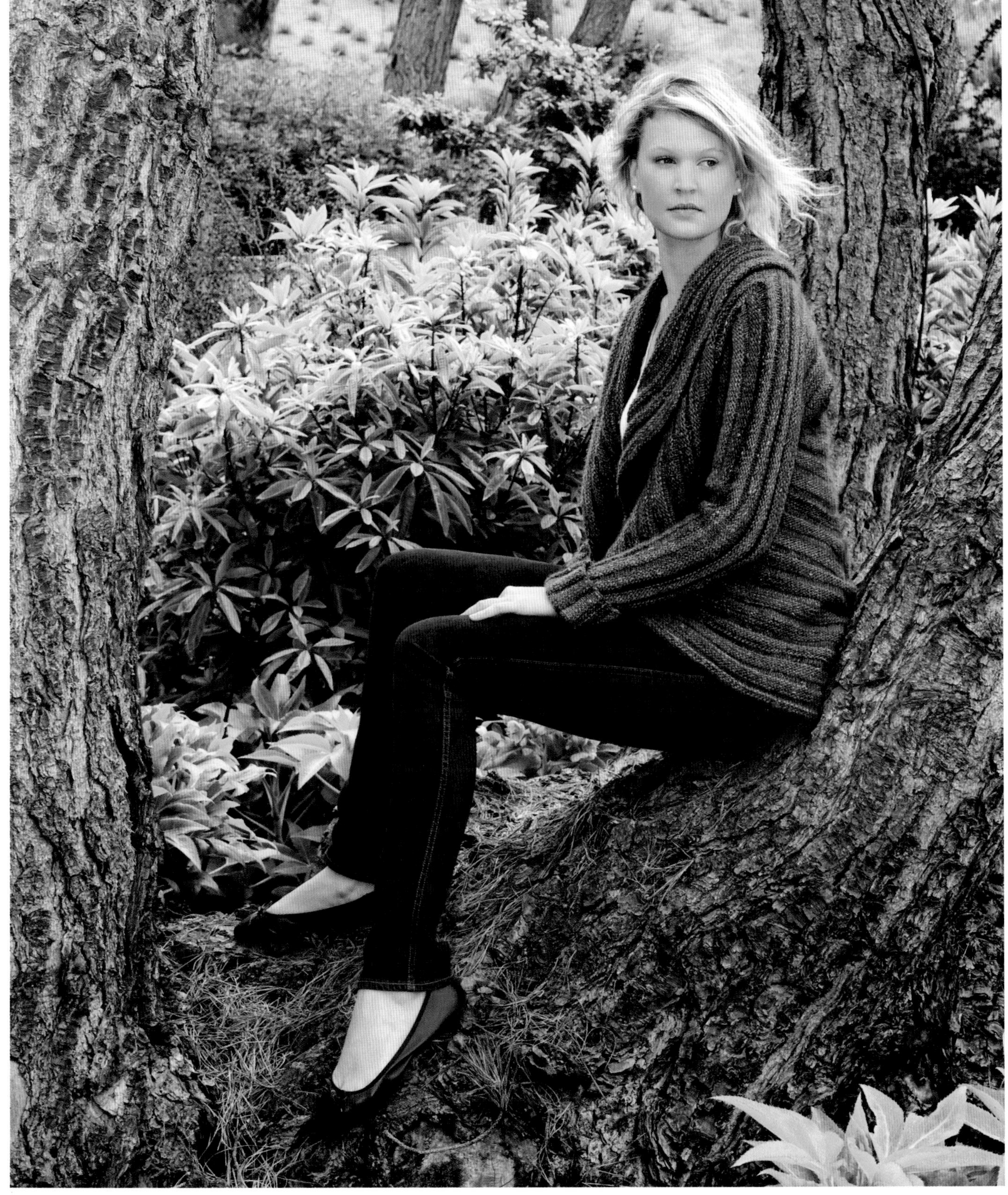

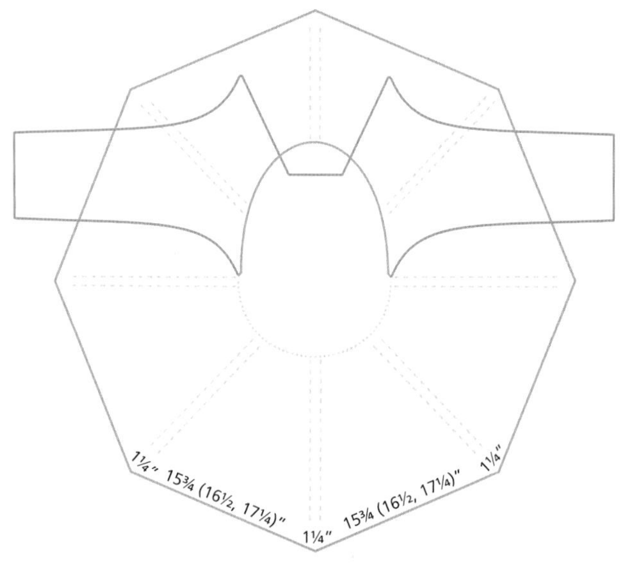

at each sleeve edge each row. Rows 2-5: Work even at sleeve edges. Bind off remaining 3 stitches/sleeve.

Welt(s) 63 (65-66), Sizes Two and Three Decrease 1 stitch at each neck edge *every other* row beginning with row 2 and, at the same time, decrease 1 stitch at each sleeve edge each row. 6 (8) stitches/sleeve.

Welt 64 (67), Sizes Two and Three Continue to decrease 1 stitch at each neck edge every other row. Row(s) 1 (1-2): Decrease 1 stitch at each sleeve edge each row. Rows 2-4 (3-5): Work even at sleeve edges. Bind off remaining 3 stitches/sleeve.

Finishing

Use cast-on yarn tail to sew first rows on Welt 1 together. Weave in ends. Block. With tapestry needle and matching yarn, sew neck/front bodice edge to inner collar edge. Sew underarm seams so that the finished seam is outside on the sleeves and inside on the 13 stitches that make up the cuff. Fold cuffs back and tack to hold in place at the seam.

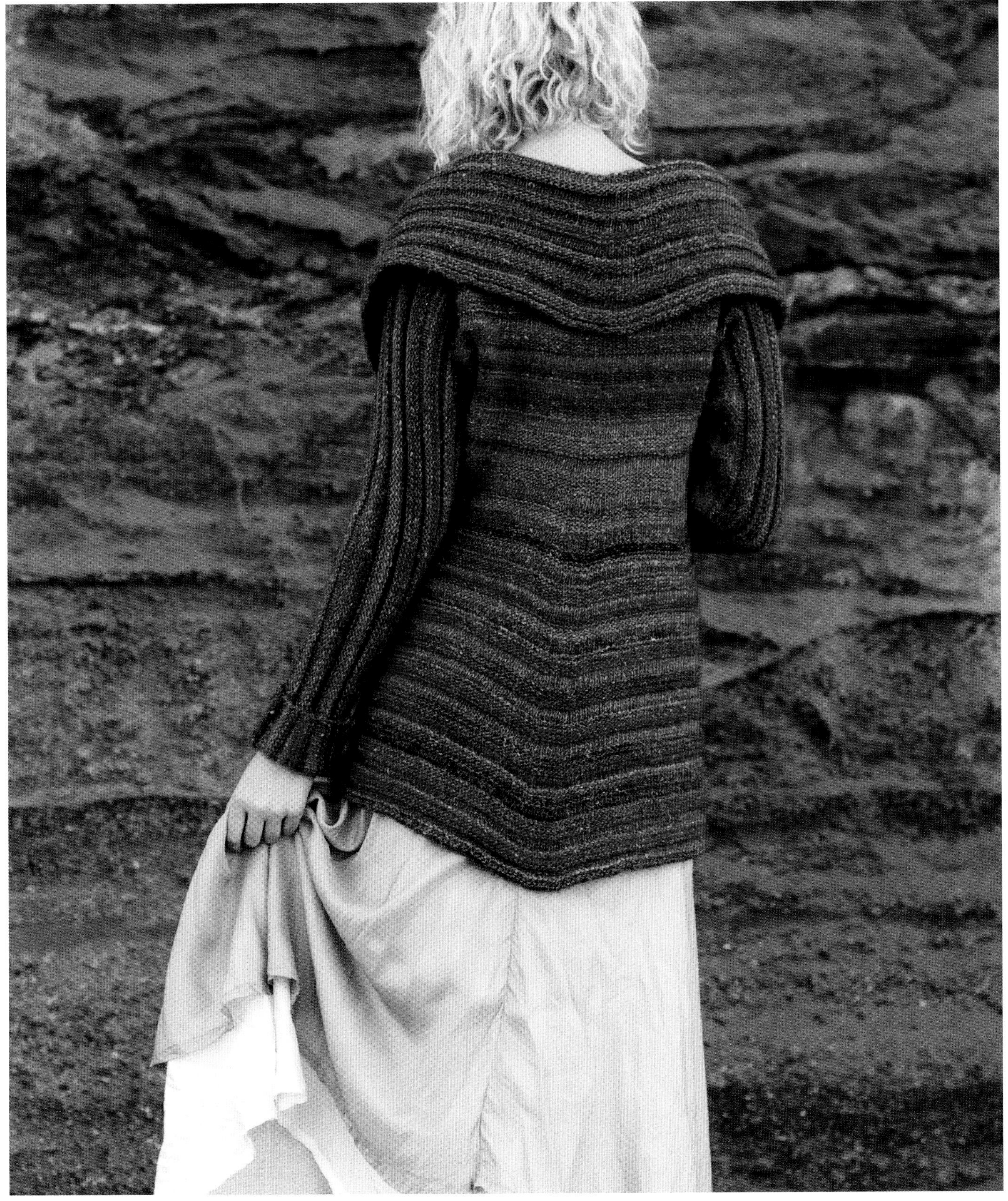

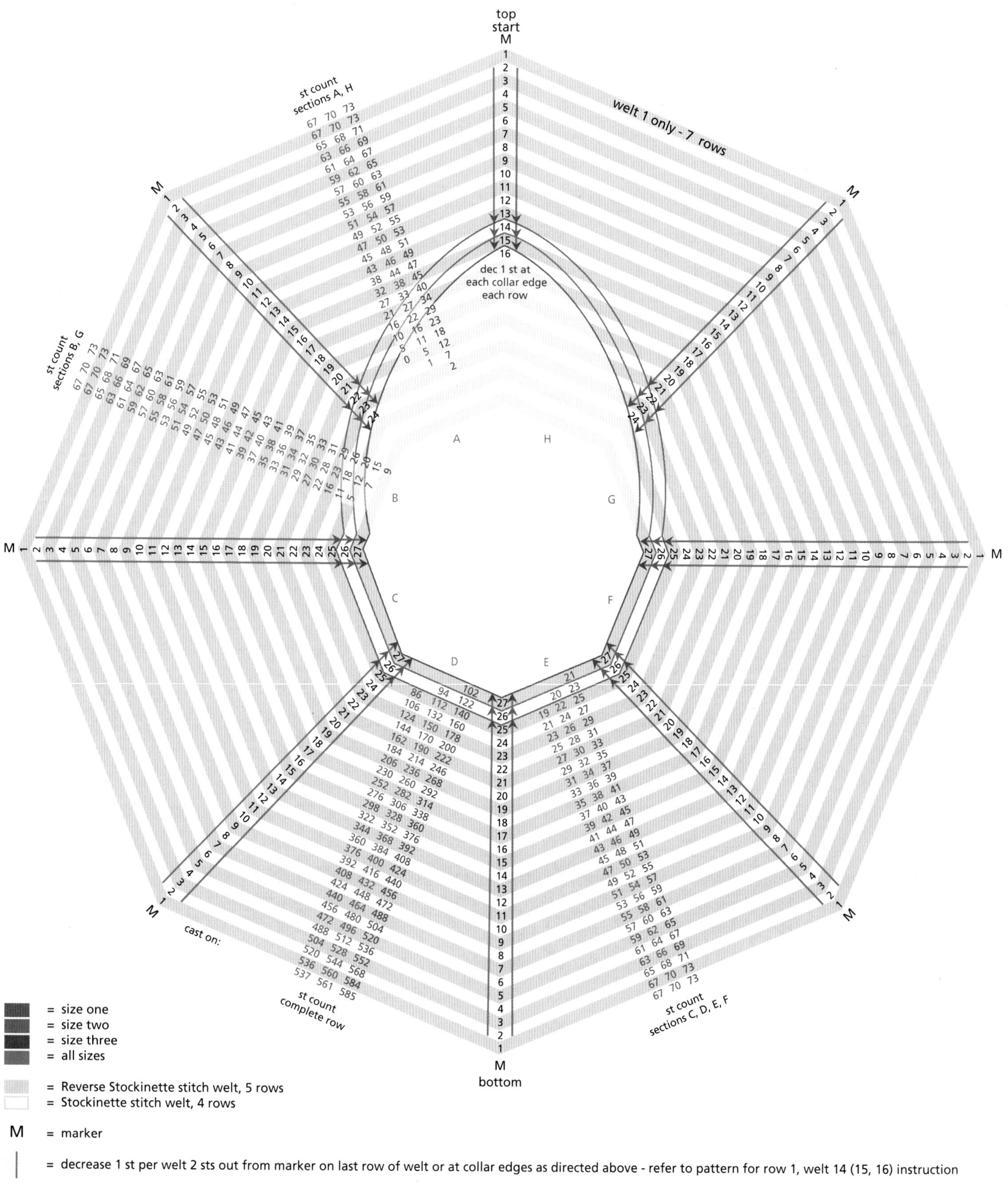

= size one
= size two
= size three
= all sizes

= Reverse Stockinette stitch welt, 5 rows
= Stockinette stitch welt, 4 rows

M = marker

= decrease 1 st per welt 2 sts out from marker on last row of welt or at collar edges as directed above - refer to pattern for row 1, welt 14 (15, 16) instruction

▲▲▲ = work as directed to this point

Note: All stitch counts refer to the number of stitches at completion of the last row of the welt

WELT #			BO (rw 1) rw 2 rw 3 rw 4 rw 5			st count slv				st count slv			rw 5 rw 4 rw 3 rw 2 (rw 1) BO			st count last row of welt		
								BO		BO						0		
		67			(1)-1-0-0-0		BO	3		3	BO		0-0-0-1-(1)			6	0	
	64	66		(1)-0-0-0		BO	3	8		8	3	BO		0-0-0-(1)		16	6	0
61	63	65	(1)-0-0-0-0			3	6	14	beginning row 2, dec 1 st at each neck edge every other row	14	6	3			0-0-0-0-(1)	28	12	6
60	62	64				6	13	21		21	13	6				42	26	12
59	61	63				11	18	26		26	18	11				52	36	22
58	60	62				17	24	32		32	24	17				64	48	34
57	59	61				22	29	37		37	29	22				74	58	44
56	58	60				28	35	43		43	35	28				86	70	56
55	57	59			(6)-0-6-0-6	33	40	48		48	40	33	0-6-0-6-(0)			96	80	66
54	56	58		(6)-0-6-0	(20)-0-20-0	39	46	67		61	46	39	6-0-40-(0)	6-0-6-(0)		128	92	78
53	55	57	(6)-0-6-0-6	(0)-40-0-6-0		44	59	108		108	59	44		6-0-20-0-(20)	0-6-0-6-(0)	216	118	88
52	54	56	(21)-0-21-0			63	106	109		109	106	57			6-0-42-(0)	218	212	120
51	53	55				106	107	110		110	107	106				220	214	212
50	52	54				107	108	111		111	108	107				222	216	214
49	51	53				108	109	112		112	109	108				224	218	216
48	50	52				109	110	113		113	110	109				226	220	218
47	49	51				110	111	114		114	111	110				228	222	220
46	48	50				111	112	115		115	112	111				230	224	222
45	47	49				112	113	116	dec 1 st at each neck edge on last row	116	113	112				232	226	224
44	46	48				113	114	117	row 1 BO center 46 (48, 50) sts	117	114	113				234	228	226
43	45	47														284	276	272
42	44	46														284	276	272
41	43	45														284	276	272
40	42	44														284	276	272
39	41	43														284	276	272
38	40	42														284	276	272
37	39	41														284	276	272
36	38	40														284	276	272
35	37	39	0-42-0-6-(0)												(6)-0-21-0-21	284	276	272
34	36	38	6-0-6-(0)	0-40-0-(6)										(0)-20-0-20	(6)-0-6-0	284	276	176
33	35	37		0-6-0-6-(0)	0-40-0-6-(0)								(6)-0-20-0-20	(6)-0-6-0-6		284	190	152
32	34	36			6-0-6-(0)								(6)-0-6-0			192	160	142
31	33	35														168	152	134
30	32	34														158	142	124
29	31	33														150	134	116
28	30	32														140	124	106
27	29	31														132	116	98
26	28	30	1-0-0-(0)												(0)-0-0-1	122	106	88
25	27	29		1-1-0-0-(0)										(0)-0-0-1-1		114	98	86
	26	28			1-0-0-(0)								(0)-0-0-1			104	94	
		27														102		
WELT #			rw 5 rw 4 rw 3 rw 2 (rw 1) CO										CO (rw 1) rw 2 rw 3 rw 4 rw 5					

slip first stitch at sleeve edge each row (left edge, welts 38–49 of size one)

slip first stitch at sleeve edge each row (right edge)

- = size one
- = size two
- = size three
- = all sizes
- = Reverse Stockinette stitch welt, 5 rows
- = Stockinette stitch welt, 4 rows
- M = marker
- | | | = decrease 1 stitch per welt 2 stitches out from marker on last row of welt
- | = decrease at neck edge as directed above
- ▲ ▲ ▲ = work as directed to this point
- ⋮ ⋮ ⋮ = increase 1 st at sleeve edge each row (below center line); decrease 1 st at sleeve edge each row (above center line)

Note: All stitch counts refer to the number of stitches at completion of the last row of the welt

shades of grey

Surprises await the knitter as the shifting spirals of black and white broaden then taper, gather then fade, knitting together in ever-varying shades of grey. A touch of red, bold at the border then scattering outward toward the center, defines the swirling shape before making one last appearance in an elongating run down each sleeve. This yarn is an unusual blend of linen and wool that produces an intriguing fabric that manages to be robust yet supple, rustic yet sleek. A quick knit without a bulky look—what could be better?

Sizes
One (Two, Three); shown here in Size Two.

Knitted Measurements
Center Back Collar: 9¼ (10, 10¾)"/23 (25, 27)cm
Center Back: 33¼ (35, 36½)"/84 (89, 93)cm
Center Back Neck to Cuff: 24½ (25¼, 26)"/62 (64, 66)cm

Approximate As-Worn Measurements
Center Back Collar: 6¼ (7, 7¾)"/16 (18, 20)cm
Center Back: 34 (35¾, 37¼)"/86 (91, 95)cm
Center Back Neck to Cuff: 32¾ (33¾, 34¾)"/83 (86, 88)cm

Materials
Single-ply, aran weight wool/linen yarn, 142 (149, 156) yd/130 (136, 143)m (A); and same yarn in contrasting color, 1295 (1439, 1568) yd/1184 (1316, 1433)m (B). As shown, 1 (1, 1) skein Cascade Yarns Rustic (79% wool/21% linen, 3½ oz/100g, 196 yd/179m) in color 01 (A); and 7 (8, 8) skeins of the same yarn in color 12 (B).

One 40 (40, 47)" size 8 (5.0mm) circular needle or size required to obtain gauge.

Gauge
19 stitches and 24 rows = 4"/10cm

Before beginning, please review Chapter One, ***Silhouettes and Sizing*** and Chapter Two, ***Tips and Techniques***.

STITCH PATTERN: WELTED STRIPES
Continuous, alternating welts of Reverse Stockinette stitch and Stockinette stitch in yarn B. Welt 1, welt 41 (43, 45) and the first row only of welts 4, 10, 16 and 22 in yarn A.

Welt 1— Reverse Stockinette Stitch, 5 rows
When working in the round: (RS) Purl all rows.
When working flat: Purl on RS rows, knit on WS rows.
Welt 2—Stockinette Stitch, 5 rows
When working in the round: (RS) Knit all rows.
When working flat: Knit on RS rows, purl on WS rows.
Repeat welts 1 and 2.

OUTER CIRCLE
With A, use a long-tail or double method to cast on 521 (545, 569) stitches, placing a marker in between the following 8 sections of 65 (68, 71) stitches each. Continue next rows in the round. Use a different color marker for the last marker to denote the beginning and end of each row.

Welt 1, Reverse Stockinette Stitch (Note: This outer welt has 7 rows instead of the normal 5 rows. The first 3 rows are worked flat before joining the work into a circle. It is important to the directional integrity of the pattern that the circle be joined at the completion of the third row as instructed.) Row 1: (RS) With A, purl. Row 2: Knit. Row 3: Purl to last stitch, slip 1. Adjust work to ensure that cast-on edge is not twisted around needle. (See *No Twist Join*, Chapter Two.) Join work into a circle by placing the last, slipped stitch from row 3 back onto the left needle. Two stitches are now on the left needle before the marker. Purl these two stitches together. Continue next rows in the round. Rows 4-7: Purl. 520 (544, 568) stitches.

Welt 2, Stockinette Stitch Rows 1-4: With B, knit. Row 5: *K2, k2tog, knit to within 4 stitches of next marker, k2tog, k2, slip marker; repeat from * across entire row. 504 (528, 552) stitches.

Welt 3, Reverse Stockinette Stitch Row 1: Purl. Rows 2-4: Purl. Row 5: *P2, p2tog, purl to within 4 stitches of next marker, p2tog, p2, slip marker; repeat from * across entire row. 488 (512, 536) stitches.

Welts 4 - 11 (12, 13) (Note: Continue in Welted Stripes stitch pattern throughout remainder of garment.) Work the first row of welts 4 and 10 in yarn A. Continue decreases at markers in last row of each welt as established. 360 (368, 376) stitches.

INNER COLLAR EDGE
Welt 12 (13, 14) Row 1: Decrease 1 stitch, continue in pattern to last 2 stitches, decrease 1 stitch. Rows 2-5: Turn and change to working-flat version of Welted Stripes stitch pattern. Decrease 1 stitch at beginning and end of each row (collar edge) and, at the same time, continue decreasing at remaining 7 markers on last row of welt as established. 344 (352, 360).

Welts 13 (14, 15) - 23 (24, 25) Work the first row of welts 16 and 22 in yarn A. Continue to decrease 1 stitch at beginning and end of each row and to decrease in established manner at markers in last row of each welt. (Note: If, following the first neck edge decrease, fewer than 4 stitches remain before the first marker, stop marker-related decreases before

the first marker and after the last marker. When decreases from one side of a marker consume its position, remove the marker and stop decreases related to that marker.) 92 (100, 106) stitches.

Back Bodice and Sleeves

After the collar and lapels are completed, the bodice is worked on the remaining live stitches in the center of the garment.

Welt 24 (25, 26) Rows 1-3: Work even. Row 4: Increase 1 stitch at beginning and end of row. Row 5: Increase 1 stitch at beginning and end of row and continue decreases in established manner at the 3 center markers and at the inside only of the 2 outer markers. 8 decreases worked/welt. 88 (96, 102) stitches.

Welt 25 (26, 27) Continue to increase 1 stitch at beginning and end of each row and to decrease in established manner at markers in last row of welt. 8 decreases worked/welt. 90 (98, 104) stitches.

Welts 26 (27, 28) – 31 (32, 33) No further decreases at markers; remove all stitch markers. Continue to increase 1 stitch at beginning and end of each row. 150 (158, 164) stitches.

Welt 32 (33, 34) Rows 1-2: Cast on 3 (3, 4) stitches at beginning of each row. Rows 3-5: Cast on 5 stitches at beginning of each row. (Note: To achieve desired sleeve length, add or subtract 3-4 stitches for each inch, distributed across all rows in these and the next 3 welts.) 171 (179, 187) stitches.

Welts 33 (34, 35) – 35 (36, 37) Cast on 5 stitches at beginning of each row. 246 (254, 262) stitches.

Cuffs

Welts 36 (37, 38) – 40 (42, 44) Place markers 7 stitches in from each sleeve end to indicate cuff stitches. Work the stitches between the markers even, in the established pattern. At the same time, work the cuff stitches in Reverse Stockinette stitch only. 246 (254, 262) stitches.

Welt 41 (43, 45) Rows 1-4: Work the first 7 cuff stitches of row 1, change to yarn A and continue to work the stitches between the markers even, in the established pattern; work the cuffs in Reverse Stockinette stitch only. Row 5: Work the first 7 cuff stitches, change to yarn B and continue to work the stitches between the markers even, in the established pattern; work the cuffs in Reverse Stockinette stitch only. 246 (254, 262) stitches.

Neck, Front Bodice and Sleeves

In the next welt, stitches in the center of the row are bound off to create the back neck and begin shaping the two front bodice panels. Continue to work cuff stitches in Reverse Stockinette stitch only and the stitches between markers in the established Welted Stripes pattern.

Welt 42 (44, 46) Row 1: Work 107 (110, 113) stitches, use basic method to bind off center 32 (34, 36) stitches, work remaining 107 (110, 113) stitches. Row 2: Work in established pattern to second neck edge, add a second ball of yarn and continue row. Rows 3-5: Work even. 107 (110, 113) stitches/sleeve.

Welts 43 (45, 47) – 47 (50, 53) Work in established pattern, decreasing 1 stitch at each neck edge on row 1 of each welt. 102 (104, 106) stitches/sleeve.

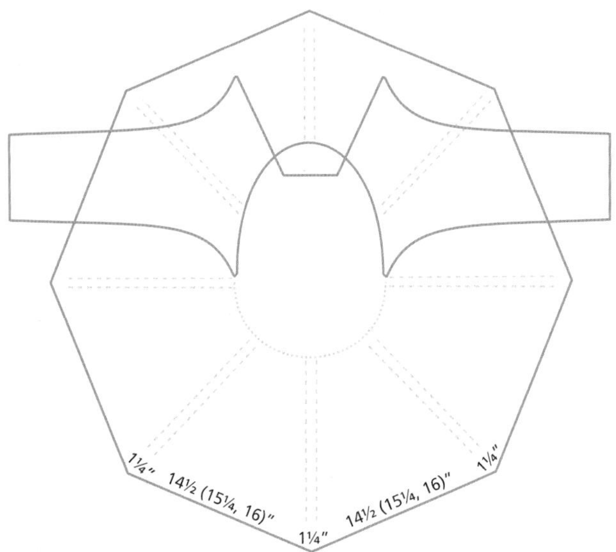

Welts 48 (51, 54) – 50 (53, 56) Apply in reverse order any sleeve length changes made in welts 32-35 (33-36, 34-37) in this and the next 3 welts. Continue to work decreases at neck edges on row 1 of each welt and, at the same time, bind off 5 stitches at beginning of each row. 64/59 (66/61, 68/63) stitches/sleeve.

Welt 51 (54, 57) Continue decreasing at neck edges as established. Rows 1-3: Bind off 5 stitches at beginning (sleeve end) of each row. Rows 4-5: Bind of 3 (3, 4) stitches at beginning of each row. 50 (52, 53) stitches/sleeve.

Welts 52 (55, 58) – 57 (59, 61) Continue to work decreases at neck edges as established and, at the same time, decrease 1 stitch at each sleeve edge each row. 14 (22, 29) stitches/sleeve.

Welt(s) 58 (60-61, 62-64) Decrease 1 stitch at each neck edge *every other* row and, at the same time, decrease 1 stitch at each sleeve edge each row. 6 (7, 6) stitches/sleeve.

Welt 59 (62, 65) Continue to decrease 1 stitch at neck edges every other row. Rows 1-2: Decrease 1 stitch at each sleeve edge. Rows 3-5: Work even at sleeve edges. Bind off remaining 2 stitches/sleeve.

Finishing

Use cast-on tail to sew first rows on Welt 1 together. Weave in ends. Block. With tapestry needle and matching yarn, sew neck/front bodice edge to inner collar edge. Sew underarm seams so that the finished seam is outside on the sleeves and inside on the cuffs. Tack cuffs to reinforce rolled shape.

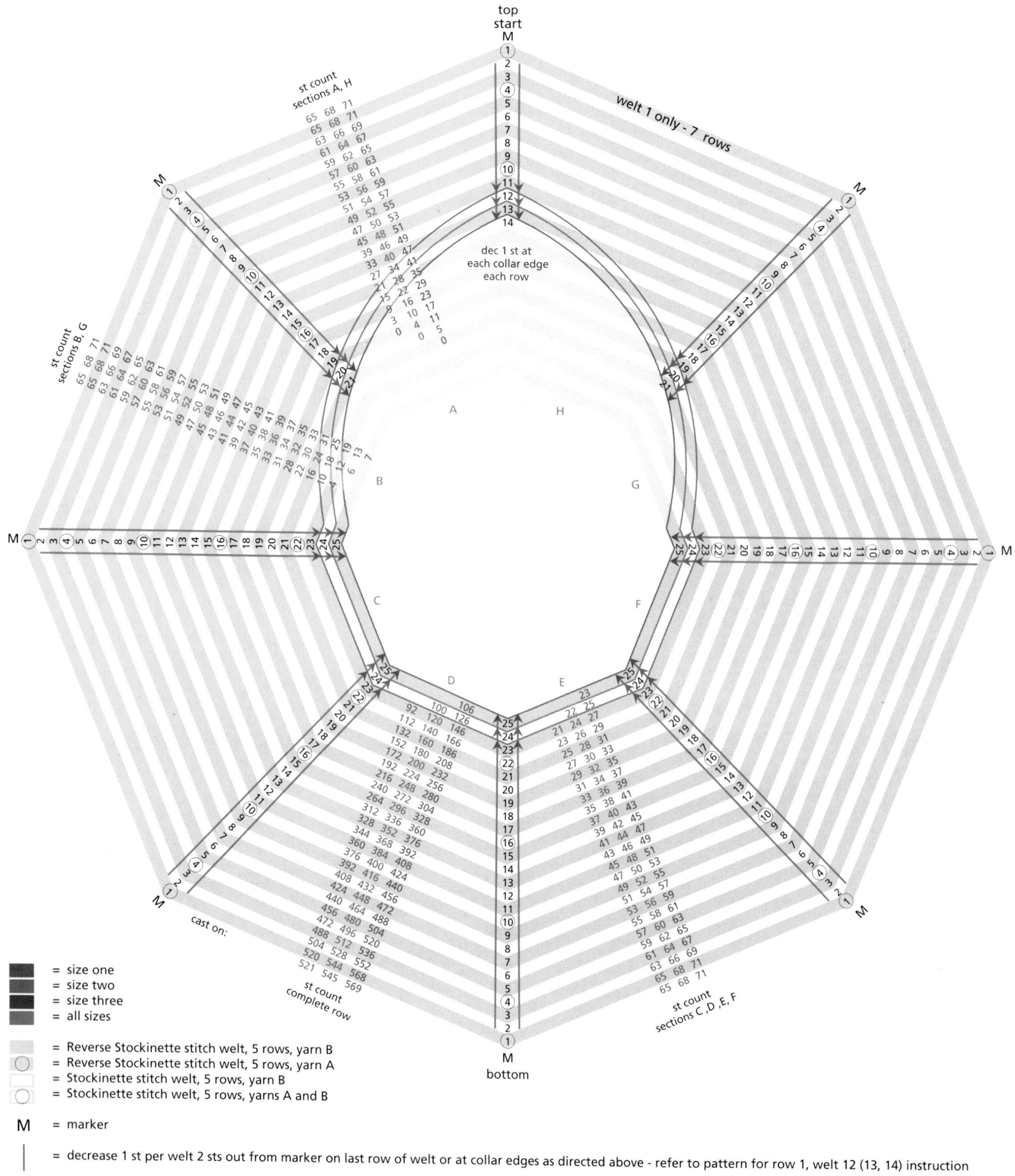

Note: All stitch counts refer to the number of stitches at completion of the last row of the welt

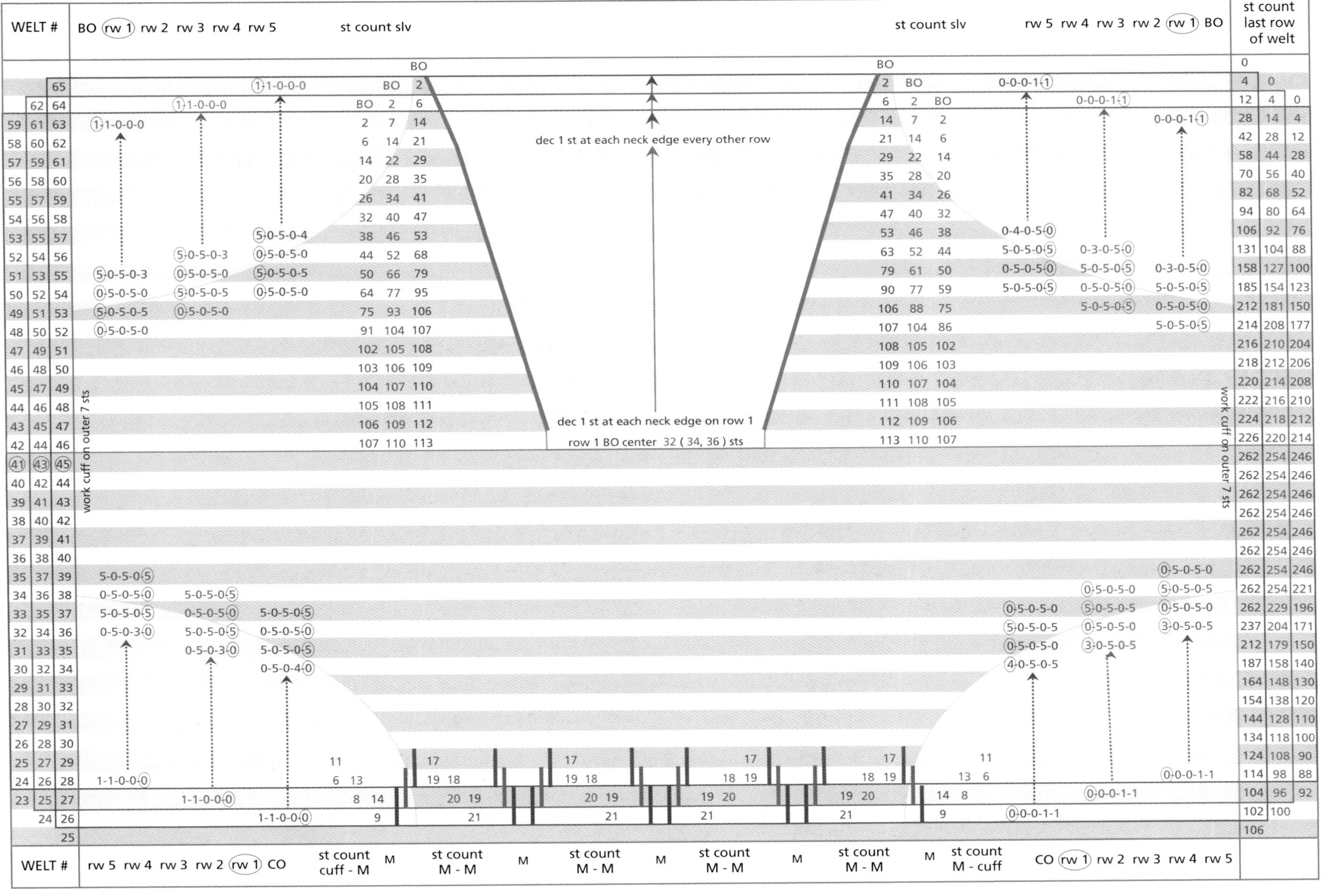

= size one
= size two
= size three
= all sizes

= Reverse Stockinette stitch welt, 5 rows
= Reverse Stockinette stitch welt, 5 rows
= Stockinette stitch welt, 5 rows

M = marker

= decrease 1 stitch per welt 2 stitches out from marker on last row of welt

= decrease at neck edge as directed above

= work as directed to this point

= increase 1 st at sleeve edge each row (below center line); decrease 1 st at sleeve edge each row (above center line)

Note: All stitch counts refer to the number of stitches at completion of the last row of the welt

plum perfect

Tucked within the folds of this velvety soft jacket lie narrow bands of jewel toned, hand painted cashmere. Their opulence is rivaled by the deep, resonant plum color that takes center stage. Not to be outdone, the jewel tones make a concluding statement in the tufts that adorn the back of the slender collar. Semi-fitted, sleekly tapered and mid-length when worn in the usual manner, this design can also be worn upside down and fastened to create a waist length jacket with a gently gathered shawl collar of dramatic proportion. Plum Perfect is perfectly luscious either way.

Sizes
One (Two, Three); shown here in Size One.

Knitted Measurements
Center Back Collar: 9¾ (10½, 11¼)"/25 (27, 29)cm
Center Back: 29 (30½, 32)"/74 (77, 81)cm
Center Back Neck to Cuff: 30¼ (31, 31¾)"/77 (79, 81)cm

Approximate As-Worn Measurements
Center Back Collar: 7½ (8¼, 8¾)"/19 (21, 22)cm
Center Back: 30¾ (32¼, 33½)"/78 (82, 85)cm
Center Back Neck to Cuff: 33 (34, 35)"/84 (86, 89)cm

Materials
Multiple-ply, worsted weight solid cashmere/mohair blend yarn 1216 (1320, 1461) yd/1112 (1207, 1336)m (A); and multiple-ply, worsted weight variegated cashmere yarn 297 (332, 351) yd/272 (304, 321)m (B). As shown, 10 (11, 12) balls Classic Elite Charmed (85% cashmere/15% mohair, 1¾ oz/50g, 130 yd/100m) in color #709, Heathered Plum (A); and 4 (4, 4) skeins Mountain Colors Cashmere (100% superfine cashmere, 1 oz/25g, 95 yd/87m) in colorway Wild Raspberry (B).

One 40 (40, 47)" size 8 (5.0mm) circular needle or size required to obtain gauge.

Gauge
18 stitches and 26 rows = 4"/10cm

Plum Perfect may be worn upside down as shown to the left and on page 161.

Before beginning, please review Chapter One, ***Silhouettes and Sizing*** and Chapter Two, ***Tips and Techniques***.

STITCH PATTERN: WELTED STRIPES
Continuous, alternating welts of Reverse Stockinette stitch in yarn A, and Stockinette stitch in yarns A and B.

Welt 1— Reverse Stockinette Stitch, 5 rows, yarn A
When working in the round: (RS) Purl all rows.
When working flat: Purl on RS rows, knit on WS rows.
Welt 2—Stockinette Stitch, 4 rows, yarns A and B
Work rows 1, 4 in yarn A and rows 2, 3 in yarn B.
When working in the round: (RS) Knit all rows.
When working flat: Knit on RS rows, purl on WS rows.
Repeat welts 1 and 2.

OUTER CIRCLE
With A, use a long-tail or double method to cast on 513 (537, 561) stitches, placing a marker in between the following 8 sections of 64 (67, 70) stitches each, with 1 stitch after the last marker. Use a different color marker for the last marker to denote the beginning and end of each row.

Welt 1, Reverse Stockinette Stitch (Note: This outer welt has 7 rows instead of the normal 5 rows. The first 3 rows are worked flat before joining the work into a circle. It is important to the directional integrity of the pattern that the circle be joined at the completion of the third row as instructed.) Row 1: (RS) With A, purl. Row 2: Knit. Row 3: Purl to last stitch, slip 1. Adjust work to ensure that cast-on edge is not twisted around needle. (See *No Twist Join*, Chapter Two.) Join work into a circle by placing the last, slipped stitch from row 3 back onto the left needle. Two stitches are now on the left needle before the marker. Purl these two stitches together. Continue next rows in the round. Rows 4-7: Purl. 512 (536, 560) stitches.

Welt 2, Stockinette Stitch Row 1: With A, knit. Rows 2-3: With B, knit. Row 4: With A, *K2, k2tog, knit to within 4 stitches of next marker, k2tog, k2, slip marker; repeat from * across entire row. 496 (520, 544) stitches.

Welt 3, Reverse Stockinette Stitch Rows 1-4: With A, purl. Row 5: *P2, p2tog, purl to within 4 stitches of next marker, p2tog, p2, slip marker; repeat from * across entire row. 480 (504, 528) stitches.

Welts 4 - 14 (15, 16) (Note: Continue in Welted Stripes stitch pattern throughout remainder of garment.) Continue decreases at markers in last row of each welt as established. 304 (312, 320) stitches.

INNER COLLAR EDGE
Welt 15 (16, 17) Row 1: Decrease 1 stitch, continue in pattern to last 2 stitches, decrease 1 stitch. Rows 2-5 (2-4, 2-5): Turn and change to working-flat version of Welted Stripes stitch pattern. Decrease 1 stitch at beginning and end of each row (collar edge) and, at the same time, continue decreasing at remaining 7 markers on last row of welt as established. 280 (290, 296) stitches.

Welts 16 (17, 18) - 24 (25, 26) Continue to decrease 1 stitch at beginning and end of each row and to decrease in established manner at markers in last row of each welt. (Note: If, following the first neck edge decrease, fewer than 4 stitches remain before the first marker, stop marker-related decreases before the first marker and after the last marker. When decreases from

one side of a marker consume its position, remove the marker and stop decreases related to that marker.) 88 (96, 104) stitches.

Back Bodice and Sleeves

After the collar and lapels are completed, the bodice is worked on the remaining live stitches in the center of the garment.

Welt 25 (26, 27) No further decreases at markers; remove all stitch markers. Rows 1-3: Work even. Row(s) 4-5 (4, 4-5): Increase 1 stitch at beginning and end of each row. 92 (98, 108) stitches.

Welts 26 (27, 28) – 31 (32, 33) Continue to increase 1 stitch at beginning and end of each row. 146 (152, 162) stitches.

Welt 32 (33, 34) Cast on 10 stitches at beginning of each row. (Note: To achieve desired sleeve length, add or subtract 4 stitches for each inch, distributed across all rows in this and the next welt.) 186 (202, 202) stitches.

Welt 33 (34, 35) Row(s) 1-2 (1, 1-2): Cast on 10 stitches at beginning of each row. Row 3 (2, 3): Cast on 16 (16, 15) stitches at beginning of row. Row 4 (3, 4): Cast on 33 (33, 31) stitches at beginning of row. Row 5 (4, 5): Cast on 17 (17, 16) stitches at beginning of row. 272 (278, 284) stitches.

Cuffs

Welts 34 (35, 36) – 42 (44, 46) Work stitches even in the established pattern, slipping the first sleeve edge stitch in each row. 272 (278, 284) stitches.

Neck, Front Bodice and Sleeves

In the next welt, stitches in the center of the row are bound off to create the back neck and begin shaping the two front bodice panels. Add a second ball of each yarn as necessary to work both sleeves at the same time. Continue to work in the established Welted Stripes pattern.

Welt 43 (45, 47) Continue to slip the first sleeve edge stitch in each row. Row 1: Work 114 (115, 116) stitches, use basic method to bind off center 44 (48, 52) stitches, work remaining 114 (115, 116) stitches. Row 2: Work in established pattern to the second neck edge, add a second ball of yarn and continue row. Rows 3-5: Work even. 114 (115, 116) stitches/sleeve.

Welts 44 (46, 48) – 51 (54, 57) Continue slipping stitches at sleeve edges as established. Work even, decreasing 1 stitch at each neck edge on first row of each welt. 106 (106, 106) stitches/sleeve.

Welt 52 (55, 58) Apply in reverse order any sleeve length changes made in welts 32-33 (33-34, 34-45) in this and next welt. Continue slipping stitches at sleeve edges as established and decreasing at neck edges on row 1. Row 1: Bind off 17 (17, 16) stitches at beginning (sleeve end) of row. Row 2: Bind off 33 (33, 31) stitches at beginning (sleeve end) of row. Row 3: Bind off 16 (16, 15) stitches at beginning of row. Row 4 (4-5, 4): Bind off 10 stitches at beginning of each row. 72/62 (62, 74/64) stitches/sleeve.

Welt 53 (56, 59) Continue to work decreases at neck edges as established and, at the same time, bind off 10 stitches at beginning of each row. 41 (41, 43) stitches/sleeve.

Welts 54 (57, 60) – 59 (61, 63) Continue to work decreases at neck edges as established and, at the same time, decrease 1 stitch at each sleeve edge each row. 8 (13, 21) stitches/sleeve.

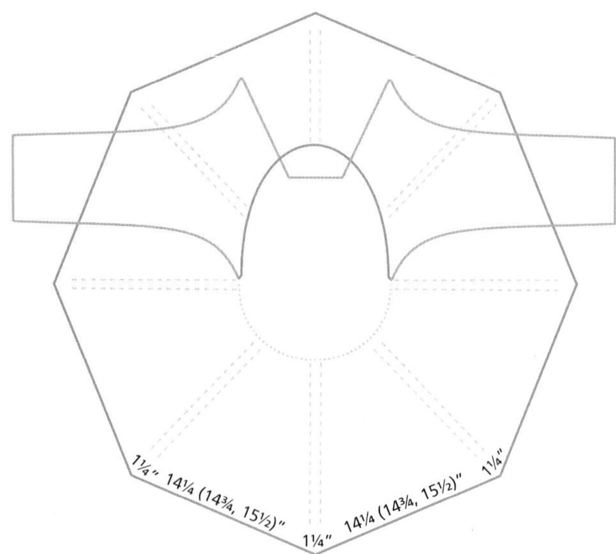

Welt 60, Size One Decrease 1 stitch at each neck edge *every other* row. Rows 1-3: Decrease 1 stitch at each sleeve edge. Row 4: Work even. Bind off remaining 3 stitches/sleeve.

Welt(s) 62 (64 - 65), Sizes Two and Three Decrease 1 stitch at each neck edge *every other* row and, at the same time, decrease 1 stitch at each sleeve edge each row. 7 (7) stitches/sleeve.

Welt 63 (66), Sizes Two and Three Continue to decrease 1 stitch at each neck edge every other row. Row(s) 1 (1-2): Decrease 1 stitch at each sleeve edge each row. Rows 2-5 (3-4): Work even at sleeve edges. Bind off remaining 3 stitches/sleeve.

Finishing

Use cast-on yarn tail to sew first rows on Welt 1 together. Weave in ends. Block. With tapestry needle and matching yarn, sew neck/front bodice edge to inner collar edge. Sew underarm seams.

Complete the tufts of fringe at the back of the collar by cutting 98 (98, 112) 3" (7.6 cm) lengths of yarn. Using a crochet hook and one length of yarn, fold yarn in half and, with the public side of the collar facing up, insert the hook and draw the folded end through a stitch at the start-of-row point on a 4 row welt. Use the hook to pull the ends of the strands through the loop. Tighten. Repeat the process placing remaining strands close to one another to create a tightly clustered tuft of fringe made up of 14 strands (28 ends) centered on the start-of-row line in each 4 row welt. Trim tuft ends even to approximately ½" (1.3 cm) in depth.

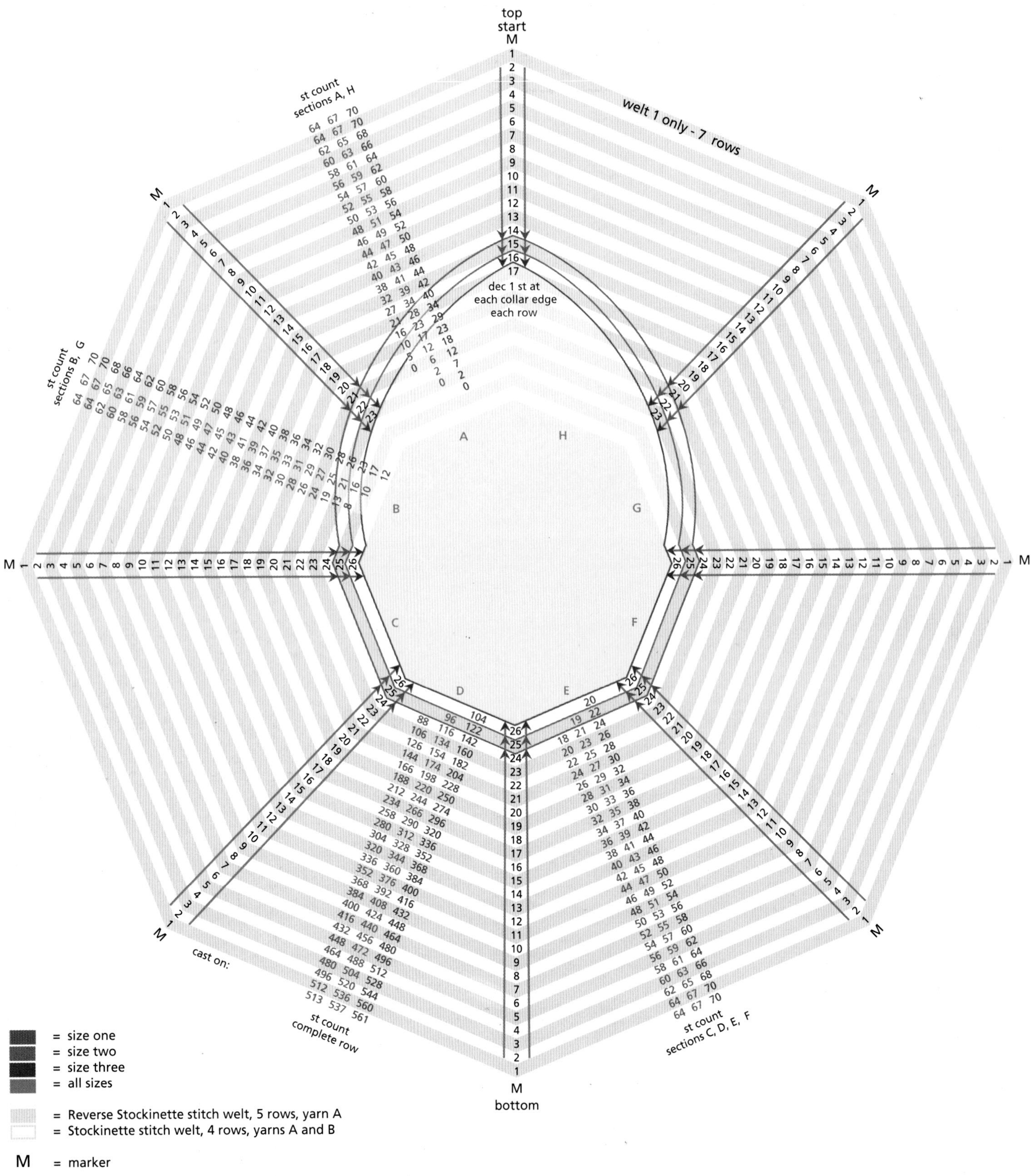

= decrease 1 st per welt 2 sts out from marker on last row of welt or at collar edges as directed above - refer to pattern for row 1, welt 15 (16, 17) instruction

= work as directed to this point

Note: All stitch counts refer to the number of stitches at completion of the last row of the welt

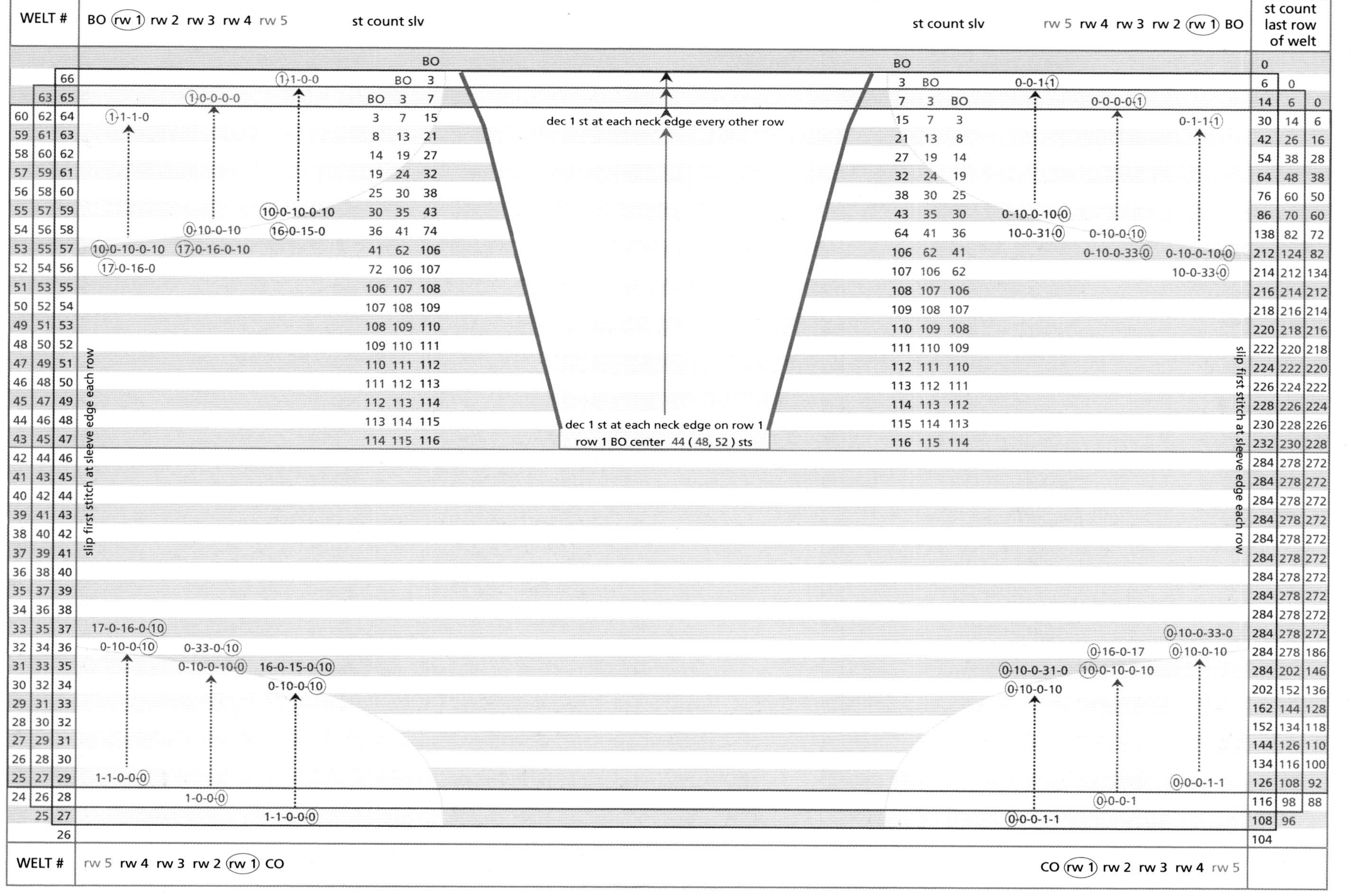

= size one
= size two
= size three
= all sizes

= Reverse Stockinette stitch welt, 5 rows
= Stockinette stitch welt, 4 rows

M = marker

= decrease 1 stitch per welt 2 stitches out from marker on last row of welt

= decrease at neck edge as directed above

= work as directed to this point

= increase 1 st at sleeve edge each row (below center line); decrease 1 st at sleeve edge each row (above center line)

Note: All stitch counts refer to the number of stitches at completion of the last row of the welt

CHAPTER SIX *off-center ovals*

SHEER BEAUTY

WILD THYME

COAT OF MANY COLORS

SILHOUETTE IN THE SUN

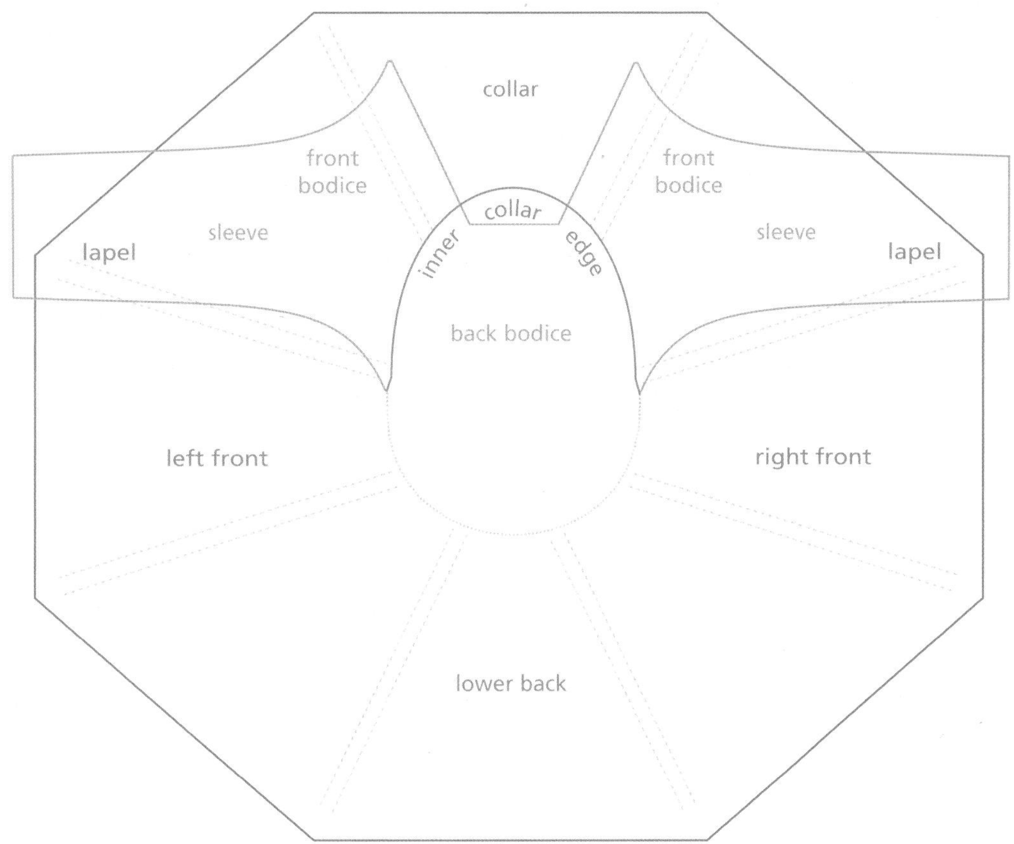

The ***off-center oval silhouette*** presents an elegant, elongated profile that gains emphasis from the repeating horizontal lines that travel across the length of the beautifully sculptured back panel. The narrow collar flows into long, draping lapels that can be worn in a variety of ways. The sleeves are slender throughout. Unique among this group of patterns is *Silhouette in the Sun* which was designed with minimal shaping through the torso and falls expansively from the shoulders with its slim rolled collar worn dipped down low at the back.

sheer beauty

Lacy gossamer streams, so delicate that they almost disappear from sight, flow between dense, richly hand painted golden bands that at times appear to float in space. This long, lean, gently flared and fitted Swirl was designed to be worn over bare arms, hence its sleeves are cut narrow with just a bit of extra length to allow soft gathers to form at the wrist. Whether pinned closed or worn open and flowing, admiring glances will always follow this sheer beauty.

Sizes

One (Two, Three); shown here in Size One.

Knitted Measurements

Center Back Collar: 9½ (10, 10¾)"/24 (25, 27)cm
Center Back: 25½ (26½, 27¾)"/65 (67, 70)cm
Center Back Neck to Cuff: 25½ (26, 26½)"/65 (66, 67)cm

Approximate As-Worn Measurements

Center Back Collar: 6½ (7, 7¾)"/16 (18, 20)cm
Center Back: 30 (31, 32¼)"/76 (79, 82)cm
Center Back Neck to Cuff: 35¾ (36½, 37¼)"/91 (93, 95cm

Materials

Multiple-ply, DK weight wool/silk yarn, 806 (879, 959) yd/737 (799, 877)m (A); and lace weight brushed mohair/silk yarn in coordinating color, 689 (757, 816) yd/630 (692, 746)m (B). As shown, 7 (7, 8) skeins Alchemy Yarns Sanctuary (70% wool/30% silk, 1¾ oz/50g, 125 yd/114m) in color #11C-Full Metal Alchemist (A); and 3 (3, 3) skeins Alchemy Yarn Haiku (60% mohair/40% silk, ¾ oz/25g, 325 yd/ 297m) in same color (B).

One 32 (32, 40)" size 7 (4.5mm) circular needle or size required to obtain gauge.

Gauge

23 stitches and 30 rows = 4"/10cm

Before beginning, please review Chapter One, ***Silhouettes and Sizing*** and Chapter Two, ***Tips and Techniques***.

Stitch Pattern: Welted Stripes
Continuous, alternating welts of Reverse Stockinette stitch in yarn A, and Stockinette stitch in yarn B.

Welt 1—Reverse Stockinette Stitch, 4 rows, yarn A
When working in the round: (RS) Purl all rows.
When working flat: Purl on RS rows, knit on WS rows.
Welt 2—Stockinette Stitch, 4 rows, yarn B
When working in the round: (RS) Knit all rows.
When working flat: Knit on RS rows, purl on WS rows.
Repeat welts 1 and 2.

Outer Oval
With A, use a long-tail or double method to cast on 633 (665, 697) stitches, placing a marker after the first stitch and then in between the following 8 sections: Three sections of 70 (74, 78) stitches, 106 (110, 114) stitches, three sections of 70 (74, 78) stitches,106 (110, 114) stitches, with 1 stitch after the last marker. Use a different color marker for the last marker to denote the beginning and end of each row.

Welt 1, Reverse Stockinette Stitch (Note: This outer welt has 6 rows instead of the normal 4 rows. The first 3 rows are worked flat before joining the work into an oval. It is important to the directional integrity of the pattern that the oval be joined at the completion of the third row as instructed.) Row 1: (RS) With A, purl. Row 2: Knit. Row 3: Purl to last stitch, slip 1. Adjust work to ensure that cast-on edge is not twisted around needle. (See *No Twist Join*, Chapter Two.) Join work into an oval by placing the last, slipped stitch from row 3 back onto the left needle. Two stitches are now on the left needle before the marker. Purl these two stitches together. Continue next rows in the round. Rows 4-6: Purl. 632 (664, 696) stitches.

Welt 2, Stockinette Stitch Rows 1-3: With B, knit. Row 4: *K2, k2tog, knit to within 4 stitches of next marker, k2tog, k2, slip marker; repeat from * across entire row. 616 (648, 680) stitches.

Welt 3, Reverse Stockinette Stitch Rows 1-3: With A, purl. Row 4: *P2, p2tog, purl to within 4 stitches of next marker, p2tog, p2, slip marker; repeat from * across entire row. 600 (632, 664) stitches.

Welts 4 - 18 (19, 20) (Note: Continue in Welted Stripes stitch pattern throughout remainder of garment.) Continue decreases at markers in last row of each welt as established. 360 (376, 392) stitches.

Inner Collar Edge
Welt 19 (20, 21) Row 1: Break yarn and slip first 26 (23, 20) stitches to reposition beginning of row. Using Jeny's Surprisingly Stretchy Bind Off method, rejoin yarn and bind off 20 (28, 36) stitches. Continue in pattern working remaining stitches followed by stitches originally slipped at beginning of row. Rows 2-4: Change to working-flat version of Welted Stripes stitch pattern. Decrease 1 stitch at beginning and end of each row (collar edge) and, at the same time, continue decreasing at markers in last row as established. 318 (326, 334) stitches.

Welts 20 (21, 22) - 29 (30, 31) Continue to decrease 1 stitch at beginning and end of each row and to decrease in established

manner at markers in last row of each welt. (Note: If, following the first neck edge decrease, fewer than 4 stitches remain before the first marker, stop marker-related decreases before the first marker and after the last marker. When decreases from one side of a marker consume its position, remove the marker and stop decreases related to that marker.) 106 (116, 126) stitches.

Back Bodice and Sleeves

After the collar and lapels are completed, the bodice is worked on the remaining live stitches in the center of the garment.

Welt 30 (31, 32) Rows 1-2: Bind off 7 (8, 9) stitches at the beginning of each row. Row 3: Work even. Row 4: Increase 1 stitch at beginning and end of row and continue decreases in established manner at the 4 remaining markers. 8 decreases worked/welt. 86 (94, 102) stitches.

Welt 31 (32, 33) Continue to increase 1 stitch at beginning and end of each row and to decrease in established manner at markers in last row of welt. 8 decreases worked/welt. 86 (94, 102) stitches.

Welts 32 (33, 34) – 33 (34, 35) No further decreases at markers; remove all stitch markers. Continue to increase 1 stitch at beginning and end of each row. 102 (110, 118) stitches.

Welts 34 (35, 36) - 41 (41, 42) Cast on 6 stitches at beginning of each row. (Note: To achieve desired sleeve length, add or subtract 4 stitches for each inch, distributed across all rows in these welts and the next welt in sizes 2 and 3.) 294 (278, 286) stitches.

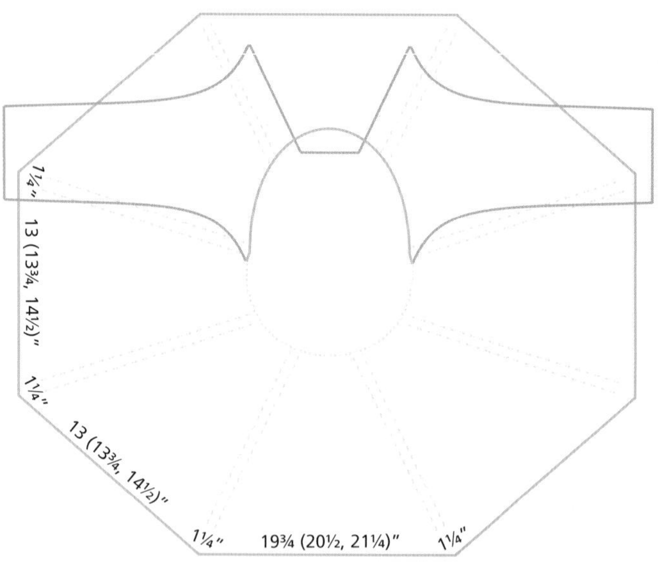

Welt 42 (43), Sizes 2 and 3 Rows 1-2: Cast on 5 (4) stitches at beginning of each row. Rows 3-4: Cast on 6 stitches at the beginning of each row. 300 (306) stitches.

Cuffs

Welts 42 (43, 44) – 48 (50, 52) Place markers 6 stitches in from each sleeve end to indicate cuff stitches. Work the stitches between the markers even, in the established pattern. At the same time, work the cuff stitches in Stockinette stitch only and in yarn A only, adding small bobbin of A at each cuff. 294 (300, 306) stitches.

Neck, Front Bodice and Sleeves

In the next welt, stitches in the center of the row are bound off to create the back neck and begin shaping the two front bodice panels. Add a second ball of each yarn as needed to work both sleeves at the same time. Continue to work cuff stitches in Stockinette stitch only and yarn A only and the stitches between markers in the established Welted Stripes pattern.

Welt 49 (51, 53) Row 1: Work 133 (135, 137) stitches, use basic method to bind off center 28 (30, 32) stitches, work remaining 133 (135, 137) stitches. Row 2: Work in established pattern to second neck edge, add a second ball of yarn and continue row. Rows 3-4: Work even. 133 (135, 137) stitches/sleeve.

Welts 50 (52, 54) – 55 (58, 61) Work in established pattern, decreasing 1 stitch at each neck edge on row 1 of each welt. 127 (128, 129) stitches/sleeve.

Welt 56 (59, 62) Apply in reverse order any sleeve length changes made in welts 34-41 (35-42, 36-43) in this and the following seven welts. Continue decreasing at neck edges on row 1. Rows 1-2: Bind off 6 stitches at beginning of each row. Rows 3-4: Bind off 6 (5, 4) stitches at beginning of each row. 114 (116, 118) stitches/sleeve.

Welts 57 (60, 63) - 63 (66, 68) Continue to work decreases at neck edges as established and, at the same time, bind off 6 stitches at beginning (sleeve end) of each row. 23 (25, 40) stitches/sleeve.

Welt 64, Size One Continue to work decreases at neck edges as established and, at the same time, decrease 1 stitch at each sleeve edge each row. 18 stitches/sleeve.

Welt 69, Size Three Decrease 1 stitch at each neck edge *every other* row and, at same time, bind off 6 stitches at beginning of each row. 26 stitches/sleeve.

Welts 65 (67, 70) – 66 (69, 72) Decrease 1 stitch at each neck edge *every other* row and, at the same time, decrease 1 stitch at each sleeve edge each row. 6 (7, 8) stitches/sleeve.

Welt 67 (70, 73) Continue to decrease 1 stitch at neck edges every other row. Row 1: Decrease 1 stitch at each sleeve edge. Row 2: Decrease 0 (1, 1) stitch at each sleeve edge. Row 3: Decrease 0 (0, 1) stitch at each sleeve edge. Row 4: Work even at sleeve edges. Bind off remaining 3 stitches/sleeve.

Finishing

Use cast-on yarn tail to sew first rows on Welt 1 together. Weave in ends. Block. With tapestry needle and matching yarn, sew neck/front bodice edge to inner collar edge. Sew underarm seams. Tack cuffs to reinforce rolled shape.

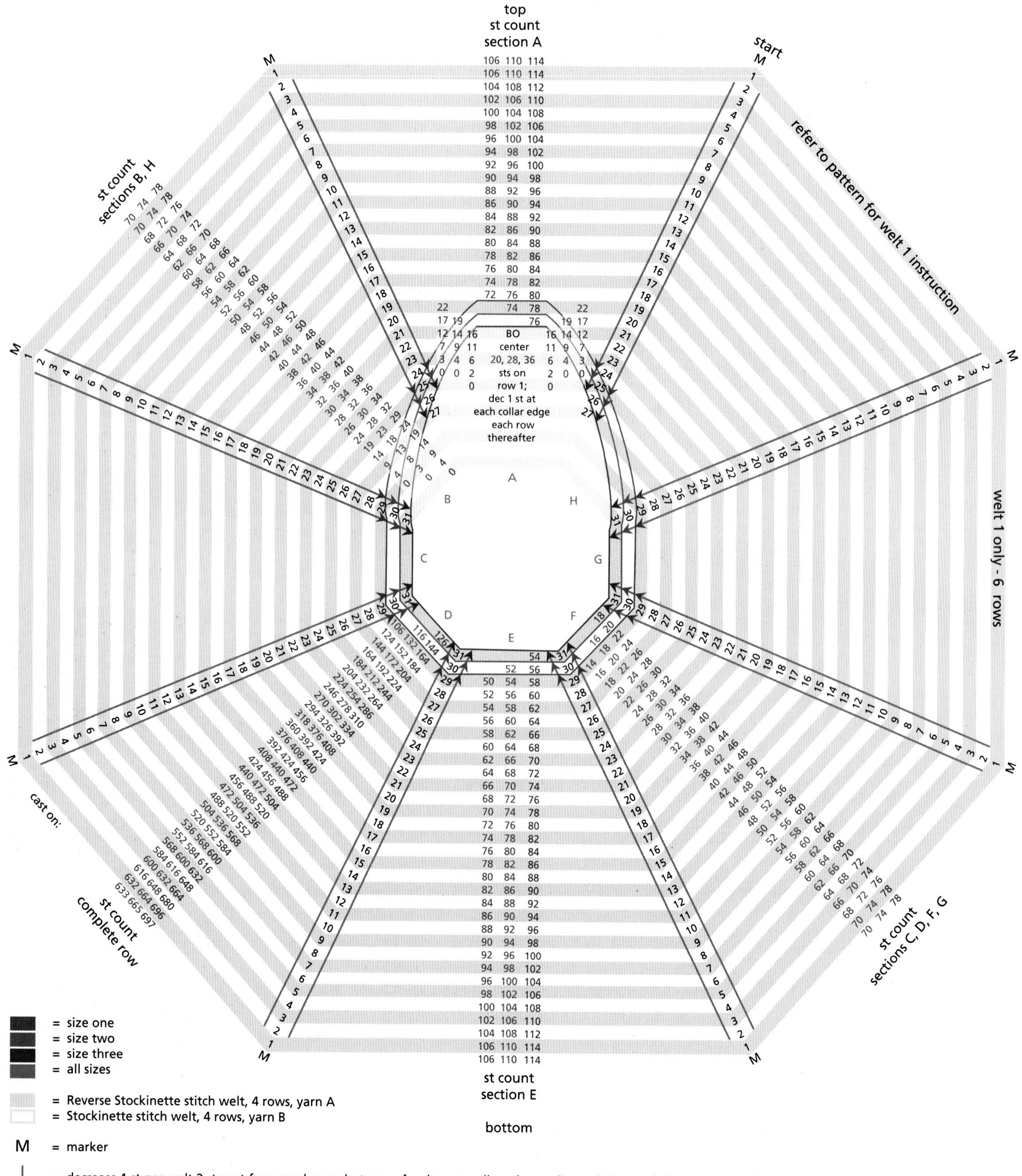

= size one
= size two
= size three
= all sizes

= Reverse Stockinette stitch welt, 4 rows, yarn A
= Stockinette stitch welt, 4 rows, yarn B

M = marker

| = decrease 1 st per welt 2 sts out from marker on last row of welt or at collar edge as directed above - refer to pattern for row 1, welt 19 (20, 21) instruction

▲▲▲ = work as directed to this point

Note: All stitch counts refer to the number of stitches at completion of the last row of the welt.

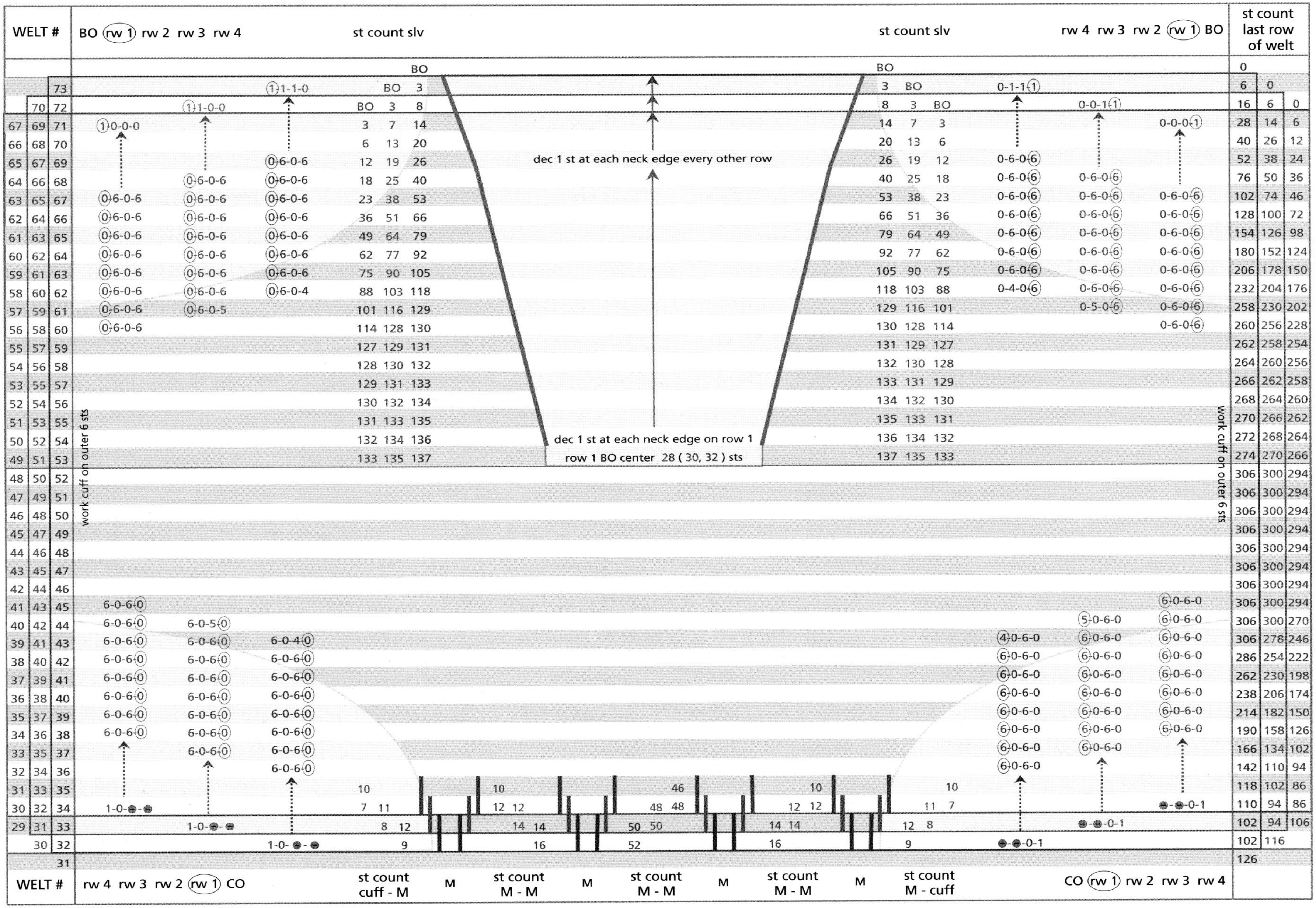

WELT #			BO (rw 1) rw 2 rw 3 rw 4			st count slv				st count slv			rw 4 rw 3 rw 2 (rw 1) BO			st count last row of welt		
								BO		BO						0		
		73			(1)1-1-0		BO	3		3	BO		0-1-1(1)			6	0	
	70	72		(1)1-0-0		BO	3	8		8	3	BO		0-0-1(1)		16	6	0
67	69	71	(1)0-0-0			3	7	14		14	7	3			0-0-0(1)	28	14	6
66	68	70				6	13	20		20	13	6				40	26	12
65	67	69			(0)6-0-6	12	19	26	dec 1 st at each neck edge every other row	26	19	12	0-6-0(6)			52	38	24
64	66	68		(0)6-0-6	(0)6-0-6	18	25	40		40	25	18	0-6-0(6)	0-6-0(6)		76	50	36
63	65	67	(0)6-0-6	(0)6-0-6	(0)6-0-6	23	38	53		53	38	23	0-6-0(6)	0-6-0(6)	0-6-0(6)	102	74	46
62	64	66	(0)6-0-6	(0)6-0-6	(0)6-0-6	36	51	66		66	51	36	0-6-0(6)	0-6-0(6)	0-6-0(6)	128	100	72
61	63	65	(0)6-0-6	(0)6-0-6	(0)6-0-6	49	64	79		79	64	49	0-6-0(6)	0-6-0(6)	0-6-0(6)	154	126	98
60	62	64	(0)6-0-6	(0)6-0-6	(0)6-0-6	62	77	92		92	77	62	0-6-0(6)	0-6-0(6)	0-6-0(6)	180	152	124
59	61	63	(0)6-0-6	(0)6-0-6	(0)6-0-6	75	90	105		105	90	75	0-6-0(6)	0-6-0(6)	0-6-0(6)	206	178	150
58	60	62	(0)6-0-6	(0)6-0-6	(0)6-0-4	88	103	118		118	103	88	0-4-0(6)	0-6-0(6)	0-6-0(6)	232	204	176
57	59	61	(0)6-0-6	(0)6-0-5		101	116	129		129	116	101		0-5-0(6)	0-6-0(6)	258	230	202
56	58	60	(0)6-0-6			114	128	130		130	128	114			0-6-0(6)	260	256	228
55	57	59				127	129	131		131	129	127				262	258	254
54	56	58				128	130	132		132	130	128				264	260	256
53	55	57				129	131	133		133	131	129				266	262	258
52	54	56				130	132	134		134	132	130				268	264	260
51	53	55	work cuff on outer 6 sts			131	133	135		135	133	131			work cuff on outer 6 sts	270	266	262
50	52	54				132	134	136	dec 1 st at each neck edge on row 1	136	134	132				272	268	264
49	51	53				133	135	137	row 1 BO center 28 (30, 32) sts	137	135	133				274	270	266
48	50	52														306	300	294
47	49	51														306	300	294
46	48	50														306	300	294
45	47	49														306	300	294
44	46	48														306	300	294
43	45	47														306	300	294
42	44	46														306	300	294
41	43	45	6-0-6(0)												(6)0-6-0	306	300	294
40	42	44	6-0-6(0)	6-0-5(0)										(5)0-6-0	(6)0-6-0	306	300	270
39	41	43	6-0-6(0)	6-0-6(0)	6-0-4(0)								(4)0-6-0	(6)0-6-0	(6)0-6-0	306	278	246
38	40	42	6-0-6(0)	6-0-6(0)	6-0-6(0)								(6)0-6-0	(6)0-6-0	(6)0-6-0	286	254	222
37	39	41	6-0-6(0)	6-0-6(0)	6-0-6(0)								(6)0-6-0	(6)0-6-0	(6)0-6-0	262	230	198
36	38	40	6-0-6(0)	6-0-6(0)	6-0-6(0)								(6)0-6-0	(6)0-6-0	(6)0-6-0	238	206	174
35	37	39	6-0-6(0)	6-0-6(0)	6-0-6(0)								(6)0-6-0	(6)0-6-0	(6)0-6-0	214	182	150
34	36	38	6-0-6(0)	6-0-6(0)	6-0-6(0)								(6)0-6-0	(6)0-6-0	(6)0-6-0	190	158	126
33	35	37		6-0-6(0)	6-0-6(0)								(6)0-6-0	(6)0-6-0		166	134	102
32	34	36			6-0-6(0)								(6)0-6-0			142	110	94

WELT #			rw 4 rw 3 rw 2 (rw 1) CO			st count cuff - M	M	st count M - M	M	st count M - M	M	st count M - M	M	st count M - cuff	CO (rw 1) rw 2 rw 3 rw 4			st count last row of welt		
31	33	35				10		10		46		10		10				118	102	86
30	32	34	1-0-●-●			7 11		12 12		48 48		12 12		11 7			●-●-0-1	110	94	86
29	31	33		1-0-●-●		8 12		14 14		50 50		14 14		12 8		●-●-0-1		102	94	106
	30	32			1-0-●-●	9		16		52		16		9	●-●-0-1			102	116	
		31																126		

= size one
= size two
= size three
= all sizes

= Reverse Stockinette stitch welt, 4 rows
= Stockinette stitch welt, 4 rows

M = marker

● ● ● = on rows 1-2, bind off 7 (8, 9) stitches at beginning of row; bodice worked on remaining stitches

| | | = decrease 1 st per welt 2 sts out from marker on last row of welt | = decrease at neck edge as directed above

▲ ▲ ▲ = work as directed to this point

⋮ ⋮ ⋮ = increase 1 st at sleeve edge each row (below center line); decrease 1 st at sleeve edge each row (above center line)

Note: All stitch counts refer to the number of stitches at completion of the last row of the welt

wild thyme

The dappled hues of wild thyme flow rhythmically through the soft tufts of tightly looped bouclé and the crisply defined stitches of its worsted-spun counterpart. The yarns are light, luxuriant blends of alpaca and merino with a bit of silk in one, bamboo in the other. Both are hand painted in the same rich blend of colors. Worn with the broad, square-back collar wrapped just over the edge of the shoulders, the result is a jacket that is closely fitted through the torso and at the waist. Gather the collar in close at the neckline allowing the outer edges to flare outward from the bodice and, voilà, it becomes a swing coat.

Sizes

One (Two, Three); shown here in Size One.

Knitted Measurements

Center Back Collar: 8½ (9¼, 10)"/22 (23, 25)cm
Center Back: 27¼ (28½, 30)"/69 (72, 76)cm
Center Back Neck to Cuff: 27½ (28½, 29½)"/70 (72, 75)cm

Approximate As-Worn Measurements

Center Back Collar: 8 (8¾, 9½)"/20 (22, 24)cm
Center Back: 32 (33¼, 34¾)"/81 (84, 88)cm
Center Back Neck to Cuff: 32¾ (33¾, 34¾)"/83 (86, 88)cm

Materials

Small loop bouclé, heavy worsted weight merino/alpaca yarn, 665 (723, 801) yd/608 (661, 732)m (A); and multiple-ply, heavy worsted weight alpaca/merino/silk yarn in coordinating colorway, 711 (791, 880) yd/650 (723, 805)m (B). As shown, 2 (2, 2) skeins Blue Moon Fiber Arts "Baby Bouclé" (35% merino/30% alpaca/30% bamboo/5% nylon, 8 oz/226g, 500 yd/457m) in colorway Covelite (A); and 2 (2, 2) skeins Blue Moon Fiber Arts "Peru" (50% alpaca/30% merino/20% silk, 8 oz/226g, 500 yd/457m) in same colorway (B).

One 40 (40, 47)" size 8 (5.0mm) circular needle or size required to obtain gauge.

Gauge

18 stitches and 27 rows = 4"/10cm

Before beginning, please review Chapter One, ***Silhouettes and Sizing*** and Chapter Two, ***Tips and Techniques***.

Stitch Pattern: Welted Stripes

Continuous, alternating welts of Reverse Stockinette stitch in yarn A, and Stockinette stitch in yarn B.

Welt 1—Reverse Stockinette Stitch, 4 rows, yarn A
When working in the round: (RS) Purl all rows.
When working flat: Purl on RS rows, knit on WS rows.
Welt 2—Stockinette Stitch, 5 rows, yarn B
When working in the round: (RS) Knit all rows.
When working flat: Knit on RS rows, purl on WS rows.

Outer Oval

With A, use a long-tail or double method to cast on 497 (521, 545) stitches, placing a marker in between the following 8 sections: 55 (58, 61) stitches, 64 (66, 68) stitches, 55 (58, 61) stitches, 74 (78, 82) stitches, 55 (58, 61) stitches, 64 (66, 68) stitches, 55 (58, 61) stitches, 74 (78, 82) stitches, with 1 stitch after the last marker. Use a different color marker for the last marker to denote the beginning and end of each row.

Welt 1, Reverse Stockinette Stitch (Note: This outer welt has 6 rows instead of the normal 4 rows. The first 3 rows are worked flat before joining the work into an oval. It is important to the directional integrity of the pattern that the oval be joined at the completion of the third row as instructed.) Row 1: (RS) With A, purl. Row 2: Knit. Row 3: Purl to last stitch, slip 1. Adjust work to ensure that cast-on edge is not twisted around needle. (See *No Twist Join*, Chapter Two.) Join work into an oval by placing the last, slipped stitch from row 3 back onto the left needle. Two stitches are now on the left needle before the marker. Purl these two stitches together. Continue next rows in the round. Rows 4-6: Purl. 496 (520, 544) stitches.

Welt 2, Stockinette Stitch When changing yarns at the beginning and end of a row in welts 2-13 (14, 15), leave approximately 7" (17.8cm) of yarn tail at back of work at each end. These strands will be incorporated into the looped trim on the collar. Rows 1-4: With B, knit. Row 5: *K2, k2tog, knit to within 4 stitches of next marker, k2tog, k2, slip marker; repeat from * across entire row. 480 (504, 528) stitches.

Welt 3, Reverse Stockinette Stitch Rows 1-3: With A, purl. Row 4: *P2, p2tog, purl to within 4 stitches of next marker, p2tog, p2, slip marker; repeat from * across entire row. 464 (488, 512) stitches.

Welts 4 – 13 (14, 15) (Note: Continue in Welted Stripes stitch pattern throughout remainder of garment.) Continue decreases at markers in last row of each welt as established. 304 (312, 320) stitches.

Inner Collar Edge

Welt 14 (15, 16) Row 1: Break yarn and slip first 25 (26, 27) stitches to reposition beginning of row. Rejoin yarn and decrease 1 stitch. Continue in pattern working remaining stitches, followed by stitches originally slipped at beginning of row, to last two stitches and decrease 1 stitch. Rows 2-5 (2-4, 2-5): Turn and change to working-flat version of Welted Stripes stitch pattern. Decrease 1 stitch at beginning and end of each row (collar edge) and, at the same time, continue decreasing at markers in last row as established. 278 (288, 294) stitches.

Welts 15 (16, 17) - 23 (24, 25) Continue to decrease 1 stitch at beginning and end of each row and to decrease in established manner at markers in last row of each welt. (Note: If, following the first neck edge decrease, fewer than 4 stitches remain before the first marker, stop marker-related decreases before the first marker and after the last marker. When decreases from one side of a marker consume its position, remove the marker and stop decreases related to that marker.) 86 (90, 98) stitches.

Back Bodice and Sleeves

After the collar and lapels are completed, the bodice is worked on the remaining live stitches in the center of the garment.

Welt 24 (25, 26) Rows 1-3: Work even. Row 4, Sizes One and Three: Increase 1 stitch at beginning and end of row. Row 5 (4, 5): Increase 1 stitch at beginning and end of row and continue decreases in established manner at the 4 remaining markers. 8 decreases worked/welt. 82 (84, 94) stitches.

Welts 25 (26, 27) - 27 (28, 29) Continue to increase 1 stitch at beginning and end of each row and to decrease in established manner at markers in last row of welt. 8 decreases worked/ welt. 84 (88, 96) stitches.

Welts 28 (29, 30) - 29 (30, 31) No further decreases at markers; remove all stitch markers. Continue to increase 1 stitch at beginning and end of each row. 102 (106, 114) stitches.

Welt 30 (31, 32) Row 1: Cast on 0 (1, 1) stitches at beginning (sleeve end) of row. Row 2: Cast on 1 (3, 3) stitches at beginning (sleeve end) of row. Row 3: Cast on 1 (2, 2) stitches at beginning of row. Row(s) 4-5 (4, 4-5) Cast on 6 stitches at beginning of (each) row. (Note: To achieve desired sleeve length, add or subtract 3-4 stitches for each inch, distributed across all rows in this and the next 5 welts.) 116 (118, 132) stitches.

Welts 31 (32, 33) - 35 (36, 37) Cast on 6 stitches at the beginning of each row. 248 (256, 264) stitches.

Cuffs

Welts 36 (37, 38) - 41 (43, 45) Place markers 7 stitches in from each sleeve end to indicate cuff stitches. Work the stitches between the markers even, in the established pattern. At the same time, work the cuff stitches in Stockinette stitch only and in yarn A only, adding small bobbin of A at each cuff. 248 (256, 264) stitches.

Neck, Front Bodice and Sleeves

In the next welt, stitches in the center of the row are bound off to create the back neck and begin shaping the two front bodice panels. Add a second ball of each yarn as needed to work both sleeves at one time. Continue to work cuff stitches in Stockinette stitch only and yarn A only and the stitches between markers in the established Welted Stripes pattern.

Welt 42 (44, 46) Row 1: Work 113 (116, 119) stitches, use basic method to bind off center 22 (24, 26) stitches, work remaining 113 (116, 119) stitches. Row 2: Work in established pattern to second neck edge, add a second ball of yarn and continue row. Rows 3-5: Work even. 113 (116, 119) stitches/sleeve.

Welts 43 (45, 47) – 47 (50, 53) Work in established pattern, decreasing 1 stitch at each neck edge on last row of each welt. 108 (110, 112) stitches/sleeve.

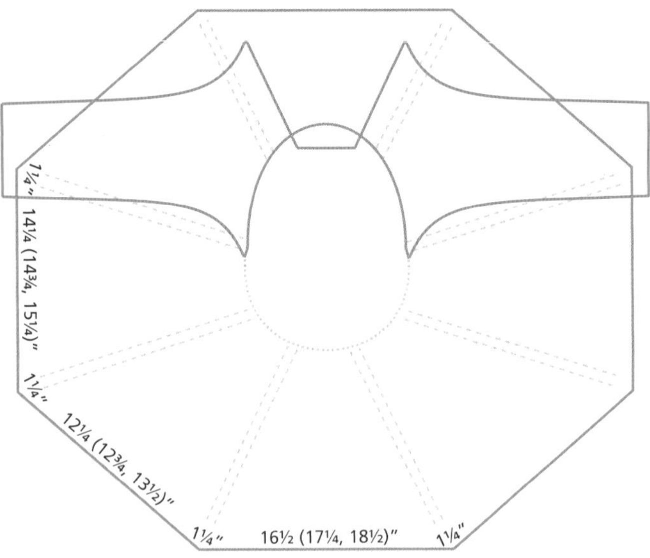

Welts 48 (51, 54) – 51 (53, 55) Apply in reverse order any sleeve length changes made in welts 30-35 (31-36, 32-37) in this and the next 5 welts. Continue to work decreases at neck edges as established and, at the same time, bind off 6 stitches at beginning (sleeve end) of each row. 50 (65, 86/80) stitches/sleeve.

Welt 52 (54, 56) No decrease at neck edges in this welt. Bind off 6 stitches at beginning of each row. 38 (53, 74/68) stitches/sleeve.

Welt(s) 55 (57-58) Sizes Two and Three Work decreases at neck edges on last row of *every other welt.* Bind off 6 stitches at beginning of each row. 40/34 (43) stitches/sleeve.

Welt 53 (56, 59) Work decreases at neck edges on last row of *every other welt.* Row(s) 1-2 (1, 1-2): Bind off 6 stitches at beginning of (each) row. Row 3 (2, 3): Bind off 1 (2, 2) stitches at beginning of row. Row 4 (3, 4): Bind off 1 (3, 3) stitches at beginning of row. Row 5 (4, 5): Bind off 0 (1, 1) stitches at beginning of row. 30 (31, 33) stitches/sleeve.

Welts 54 (57, 60) - 58 (61, 63) Continue to work decrease at neck edges as established and, at the same time, decrease 1 stitch at each sleeve edge each row. 5 (6, 13) stitches/sleeve.

Welt 59 Size One Continue to work decreases at neck edges as established. Row 1: Decrease 1 stitch at each sleeve edge. Rows 2-4: Work even at sleeve edges. Bind off remaining 3 stitches/sleeve.

Welt 64 Size Three Work decreases at neck edges on last row of welt and, at the same time, decrease 1 stitch at each sleeve edge each row. 7 stitches/sleeve.

Welt 62 (65) Sizes Two and Three Work decreases at neck edges on last row of welt. Rows 1-2 (1-3): Decrease 1 stitch at each sleeve edge. Row(s) 3-5 (4): Work even at sleeve edges. Bind off remaining 3 stitches/sleeve.

Finishing

Use cast-on yarn tail to sew first rows on Welt 1 together. Weave in ends with the exception of those that will be incorporated into the looped fringe across the collar. Block. With tapestry needle and matching yarn, sew neck/front bodice edge to inner collar edge. Sew underarm seams.

Complete the looped fringe on the collar by tying the 2 yarn tails found at the top and bottom of each side collar welt into a simple bow. Hold the loop and end together on each side of bow. Tie the two sides together in a simple overhand knot.

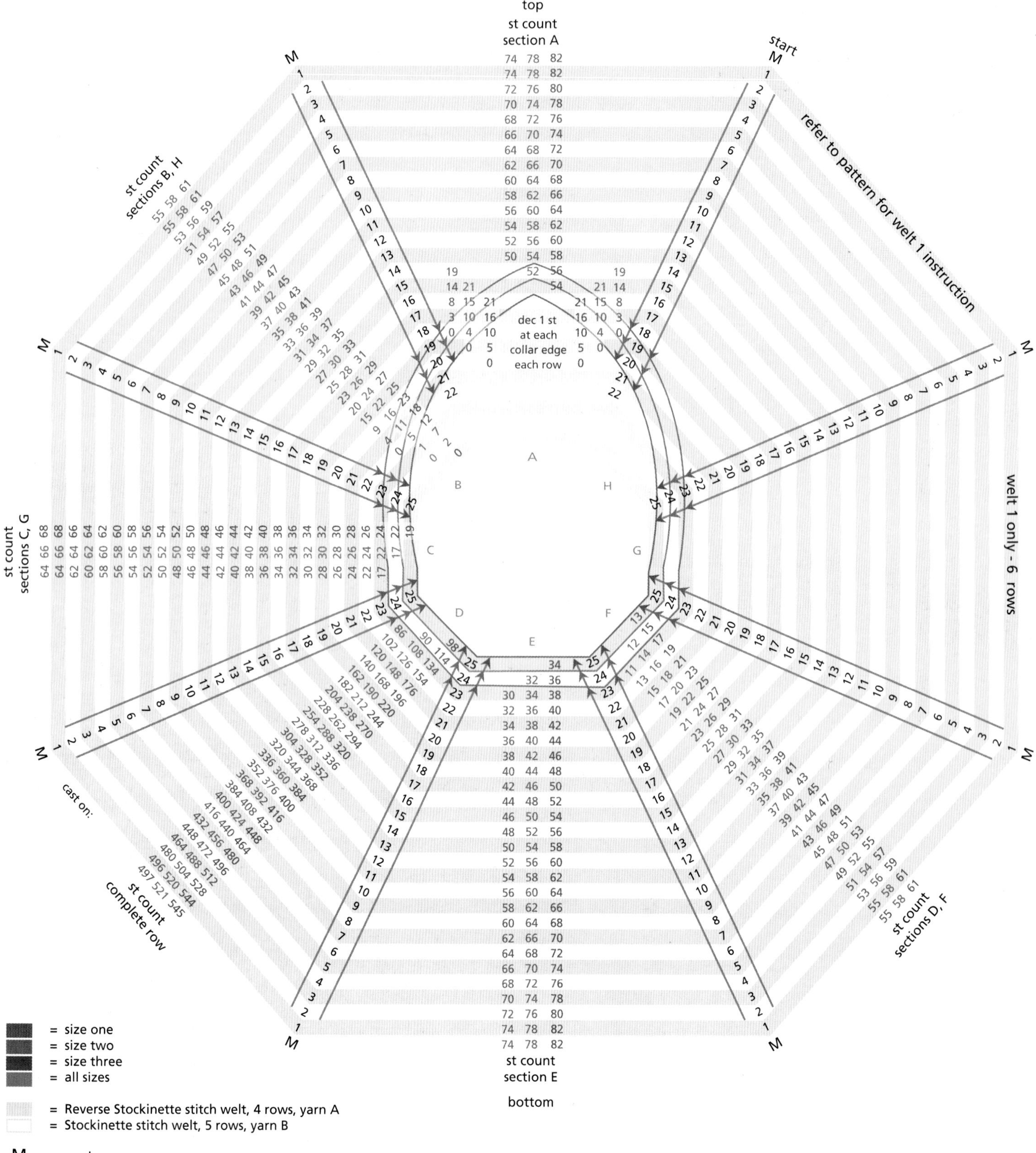

M = marker

| = decrease 1 st per welt 2 sts out from marker on last row of welt or at collar edge as directed above - refer to pattern for row 1, welt 14 (15, 16) instruction

AAA = work as directed to this point

Note: All stitch counts refer to the number of stitches at completion of the last row of the welt

WELT #			BO (rw 1) rw 2 rw 3 rw 4 rw 5			st count slv				st count slv			rw 5 rw 4 rw 3 rw 2 (rw 1) BO			st count last row of welt		
								BO		BO						0		
		65			(1)-1-1-0		BO	3		3	BO		0-1-1-(1)			6	0	
	62	64		(1)-1-0-0-0		BO	3	7	dec 1 st at each neck edge on last row	7	3	BO		0-0-0-1-(1)		14	6	0
59	61	63	(1)-0-0-0			3	6	13		13	6	3			0-0-0-(1)	26	12	6
58	60	62				5	11	18		18	11	5				36	22	10
57	59	61				10	16	23		23	16	10				46	32	20
56	58	60				15	21	28		28	21	15				56	42	30
55	57	59			(0)-6-0-3-0	20	26	33		33	26	20	1-0-2-0-(6)			66	52	40
54	56	58		(6)-0-3-0	(0)-6-0-6	25	31	43		43	31	25	0-6-0-(6)	1-0-2-(0)		86	62	50
53	55	57	(6)-0-1-0-0	(0)-6-0-6-0	(6)-0-6-0-6	30	40	55	dec 1 st at each neck edge on last row every other welt	55	34	30	0-6-0-6-(0)	6-0-6-0-(6)	0-1-0-6-(0)	110	74	60
52	54	56	(6)-0-6-0	(0)-6-0-6	(6)-0-6-0	38	53	74	work even	68	53	38	6-0-6-(0)	0-6-0-(6)	6-0-6-(0)	142	106	76
51	53	55	(0)-6-0-6-0	(6)-0-6-0-6	(0)-6-0-6-0	50	65	86		80	65	50	6-0-6-0-(6)	0-6-0-6-(0)	6-0-6-0-(6)	166	130	100
50	52	54	(0)-6-0-6	(6)-0-6-0	(0)-6-0-6	63	84	99		99	78	69	0-6-0-(6)	6-0-6-(0)	0-6-0-(6)	198	162	132
49	51	53	(6)-0-6-0-6	(0)-6-0-6-0		76	97	112		112	91	82		6-0-6-0-(6)	0-6-0-6-(0)	224	188	158
48	50	52	(6)-0-6-0			95	110	113		113	110	95			6-0-6-(0)	226	220	190
47	49	51				108	111	114		114	111	108				228	222	216
46	48	50				109	112	115		115	112	109				230	224	218
45	47	49	work cuff on outer 7 sts			110	113	116		116	113	110	work cuff on outer 7 sts			232	226	220
44	46	48				111	114	117		117	114	111				234	228	222
43	45	47				112	115	118	dec 1 st at each neck edge on last row	118	115	112				236	230	224
42	44	46				113	116	119	row 1 BO center 22 (24, 26) sts	119	116	113				238	232	226
41	43	45														264	256	248
40	42	44														264	256	248
39	41	43														264	256	248
38	40	42														264	256	248
37	39	41														264	256	248
36	38	40														264	256	248
35	37	39	0-6-0-(6)												(0)-6-0-6	264	256	248
34	36	38	0-6-0-6-(0)	0-6-0-6-(0)										(6)-0-6-0-6	(6)-0-6-0-6	264	256	224
33	35	37	6-0-6-(0)	6-0-6-(0)	0-6-0-(6)								(0)-6-0-6	(6)-0-6-0	(6)-0-6-0	264	226	194
32	34	36	6-0-6-0-(6)	6-0-6-0-(6)	0-6-0-6-(0)								(6)-0-6-0-6	(0)-6-0-6-0	(0)-6-0-6-0	240	202	170
31	33	35	0-6-0-(6)	0-6-0-(6)	6-0-6-(0)								(6)-0-6-0	(0)-6-0-6	(0)-6-0-6	210	172	140
30	32	34	0-6-0-1-(0)	0-6-0-6-(0)	6-0-6-0-(6)								(0)-6-0-6-0	(6)-0-6-0-6	(0)-0-1-0-6	186	148	116
29	31	33		6-0-3-(0)	0-6-0-(6)								(0)-6-0-6	(1)-0-2-0		156	118	102
28	30	32			0-6-0-3-(0)								(1)-0-2-0-6			132	106	94

WELT #			rw 5 rw 4 rw 3 rw 2 (rw 1) CO			st count cuff - M			M	st count M - M			M	st count M - M			M	st count M - M			M	st count M - cuff			CO (rw 1) rw 2 rw 3 rw 4 rw 5			st count last row of welt		
27	29	31				28				3						22				3				28				114	96	84
26	28	30				25	28			5	4				24	24			4	5			28	25				106	88	84
25	27	29				21	24	30		7	6	5		26	26	26		5	6	7		30	24	21				96	86	82
24	26	28	1-1-0-0-(0)			18	21	27		9	8	7		28	28	28		7	8	9		27	21	18			(0)-0-0-1-1	96	86	82
23	25	27		1-0-0-(0)			17	23			10	9		30	30			9	10			23	17			(0)-0-0-1		94	84	86
	24	26			1-1-0-0-(0)		20				11				32				11				20		(0)-0-0-1-1			94	90	
		25																										98		

■ = size one
■ = size two
■ = size three
■ = all sizes

= Reverse Stockinette stitch welt, 4 rows
= Stockinette stitch welt, 5 rows

M = marker

| | | = decrease 1 stitch per welt 2 stitches out from marker on last row of welt

| = decrease at neck edge as directed above

▲ ▲ ▲ = work as directed to this point

⋮ ⋮ ⋮ = increase 1 st at sleeve edge each row (below center line); decrease 1 st at sleeve edge each row (above center line)

Note: All stitch counts refer to the number of stitches at completion of the last row of the welt

coat of many colors

Every knitter knows the dilemma. There before you in your favorite local yarn shop are shelves of glorious hand painted yarns, stunningly beautiful, each and every one. You covet them all. You will never be able to choose just one! Fear not, Coat of Many Colors invites you to indulge, choose a range of your favorites and then enjoy working them together in ever-changing waves of color and intensity. Or perhaps you've already treated yourself to a skein here, a skein there and are now wondering what to do with all those odd lots. The blending approach in a Coat of Many Colors offers a solution. Experiment with some swatches and see what wonders unfold.

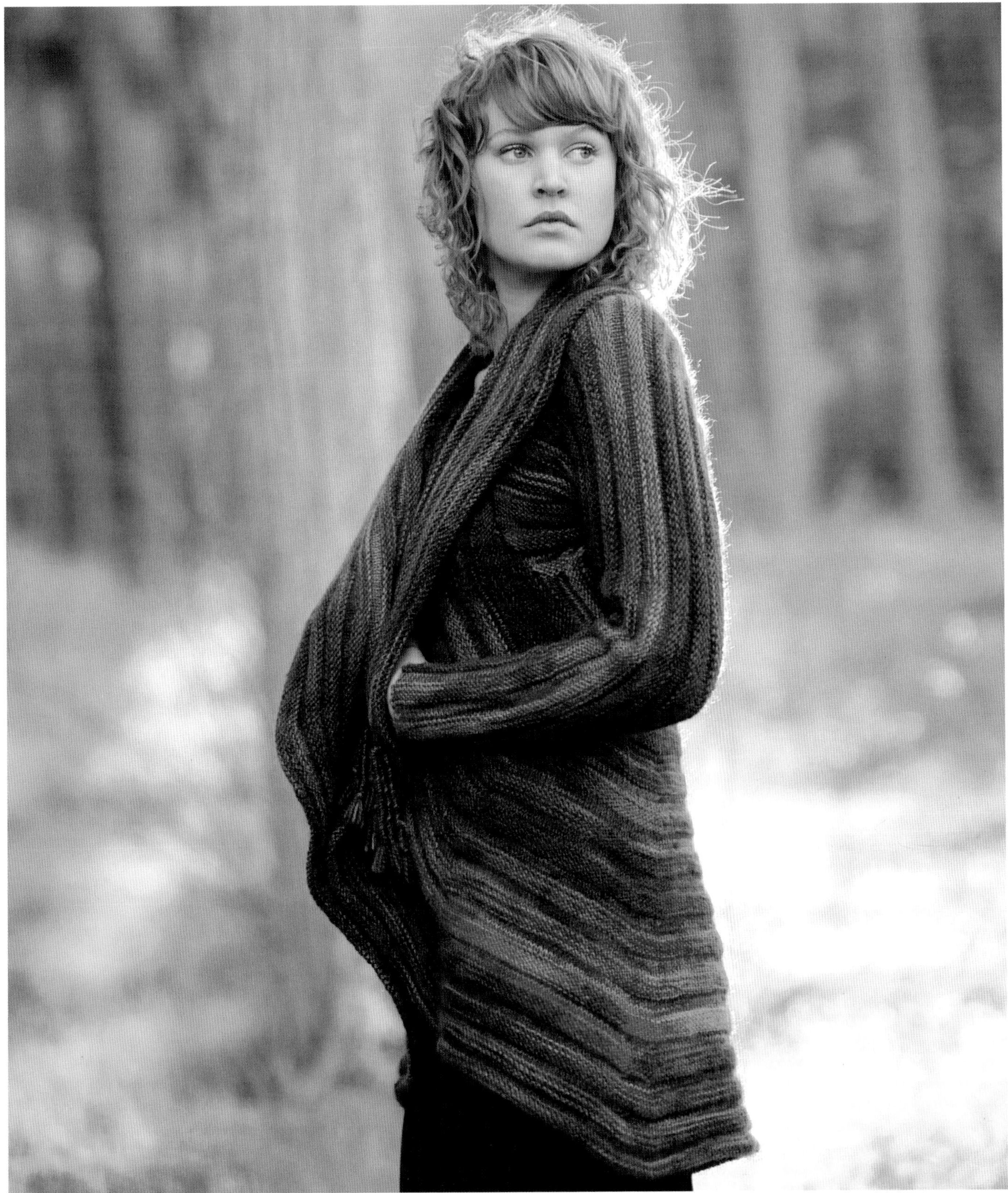

Sizes
One (Two, Three); shown here in Size Two.

Knitted Measurements
Center Back Collar: 9¾ (10½, 11¼)"/25 (27, 28)cm
Center Back: 32 (34, 36)"/81 (86, 91)cm
Center Back Neck to Cuff: 27¾(28½, 29¼)"/70 (72, 74)cm

Approximate As-Worn Measurements
Center Back Collar: 6¾ (7½, 8¼)"/17 (19, 21)cm
Center Back: 33 (35, 37)"/84 (89, 94)cm
Center Back Neck to Cuff: 33 (33¾, 34¾)"/84 (86, 88)cm

Materials
Multiple-ply, worsted weight mohair/wool yarn in 9 colorways, 1579 (1631, 1785) yd/1444 (1491, 1632)m (A-I). As shown, 10 (10, 11) skeins Mountain Colors "Mountain Goat" (55% mohair/45% wool, 3½ oz/100g, 230 yd/210m) in colors Indian Corn (A), 2 skeins; Firestorm (B), 1 (1, 2) skeins; and 1 skein each Raspberry (C), Crazy Woman (D), Wildflower (E), Sun River (F), Ruby River (G), Rosehip (H), Pheasant (I).

One 40 (40, 47)" size 7 (4.5mm) circular needle or size required to obtain gauge.

Gauge
20 stitches and 25 rows = 4"/10cm

Before beginning, please review Chapter One, ***Silhouettes and Sizing*** and Chapter Two, ***Tips and Techniques***.

STITCH PATTERN: WELTED STRIPES

Continuous, alternating welts of Reverse Stockinette stitch and Stockinette stitch in 9 colorways.

Welt 1—Reverse Stockinette Stitch, 5 rows, single yarn (yarns A, B, C, D, E, F, G, H, I rotating throughout Reverse Stockinette stitch welts per instructions on oval schematic.)
When working in the round: (RS) Purl all rows.
When working flat: Purl on RS rows, knit on WS rows.
Welt 2—Stockinette Stitch, 5 rows, 2 yarns alternating each row; (yarns A and B, yarns B and C, yarns C and D, yarns D and E, yarns E and F, yarns F and G, yarns G and H, yarns H and I, yarns I and A. Yarn pairs rotate throughout Stockinette stitch welts per instructions on oval schematic. Use yarn listed first within a pair for rows 2 and 4, and yarn listed second for rows 1, 3, 5.
When working in the round: (RS) Knit all rows.
When working flat: Knit on RS rows, purl on WS rows.

OUTER OVAL

With A, use a long-tail or double method to cast on 537 (569, 601) stitches, placing a marker in between the following 8 sections: cast on two sections of 58 (62, 66) stitches, 94 (98, 102) stitches, three sections of 58 (62, 66) stitches, 94 (98, 102) stitches, 58 (62, 66) stitches, with 1 stitch after the last marker. Use a different color marker for the last marker to denote the beginning and end of each row.

Welt 1, Reverse Stockinette Stitch (Note: This outer welt has 7 rows instead of the normal 5 rows. The first 3 rows are worked flat before joining the work into an oval. It is important to the directional integrity of the pattern that the oval be joined at the completion of the third row as instructed.) Row 1: (RS) With A, purl. Row 2: Knit. Row 3: Purl to last stitch, slip 1. Adjust work to ensure that cast-on edge is not twisted around needle. (See *No Twist Join*, Chapter Two.) Join work into an oval by placing the last, slipped stitch from row 3 back onto the left needle. Two stitches are now on the left needle before the marker. Purl these two stitches together. Continue next rows in the round. Rows 4-7: Purl. 536 (568, 600) stitches.

Welt 2, Stockinette Stitch (Note: When changing yarns at the beginning and end of a row in this and all subsequent outer oval welts, leave approximately 4"/10.2 cm of yarn tail at back of work at each end. These strands will be incorporated into the braided fringe across the collar.) Row 1: With B, knit. Row 2: With A, knit. Row 3: With B, knit. Row 4: With A, knit. Row 5: With B, *K2, k2tog, knit to within 4 stitches of next marker, k2tog, k2, slip marker; repeat from * across entire row. 520 (552, 584) stitches.

Welt 3, Reverse Stockinette Stitch Rows 1-4: With B, purl. Row 5: *P2, p2tog, purl to within 4 stitches of next marker, p2tog, p2, slip marker; repeat from * across entire row. 504 (536, 568) stitches.

Welt 4, Stockinette Stitch Row 1: With C, knit. Row 2: With B, knit. Row 3: With C, knit. Row 4: With B, knit. Row 5: With C, *K2, k2tog, knit to within 4 stitches of next marker, k2tog, k2, slip marker; repeat from * across entire row. 488 (520, 552) stitches.

Welts 5 - 12 (13, 14) (Note: Continue in Welted Stripes stitch pattern rotating yarns A - I in alphabetical order as described

in stitch pattern and oval schematic throughout remainder of garment.) Continue decreases at markers in last row of each welt as established. 360 (376, 392) stitches.

Inner Collar Edge

Welt 13 (14, 15) Row 1: Break yarn and slip last 25 (26, 27) stitches to reposition beginning of row. Rejoin yarn, decrease 1 stitch, continue in pattern to last 2 stitches, decrease 1 stitch. Rows 2-5: Turn and change to working-flat version of Welted Stripes stitch pattern. Decrease 1 stitch at beginning and end of each row (collar edge) and, at the same time, continue decreasing at markers on the last row of welt as established. 334 (350, 366) stitches.

Welts 14 (15, 16) - 24 (25, 26) Continue to decrease 1 stitch at beginning and end of each row and to decrease in established manner at remaining markers in last row of each welt. (Note: If, following the first neck edge decrease, fewer than 4 stitches remain before the first marker, stop marker-related decreases before the first marker and after the last marker. When decreases from one side of a marker consume its position, remove the marker and stop decreases related to that marker.) 84 (98, 110) stitches.

Back Bodice and Sleeves

After the collar and lapels are completed, the bodice is worked on the remaining live stitches in the center of the garment.

Welt 25 (26, 27) Rows 1-2: Bind off 0 (2, 3) stitches at the beginning of each row. Row 3: Work even. Row 4: Increase 1 stitch at beginning and end of row. Row 5: Increase 1 stitch at beginning and end of row and continue decreases in established manner at the 4 remaining markers. 8 decreases worked/welt. 80 (90, 100) stitches.

Welt 26 (27, 28) Continue to increase 1 stitch at beginning and end of each row and to decrease in established manner at markers in last row of welt. 8 decreases worked/welt. 82 (92, 102) stitches.

Welts 27 (28, 29) – 29 (30, 31) No further decreases at markers; remove all stitch markers. Continue to increase 1 stitch at beginning and end of each row. 112 (122, 132) stitches.

Welts 30 (31, 32) – 31 (32, 33) Cast on 6 stitches at beginning of each row. (Note: To achieve desired sleeve length, add or subtract 4-5 stitches for each inch, distributed across all rows in these and the next 4 welts.) 172 (182, 192) stitches.

Welts 32 (33, 34) – 34 (35, 36) Cast on 5 stitches at beginning of each row. 247 (257, 267) stitches.

Welt 35 (36, 37) Rows 1-3: Cast on 5 stitches at beginning of each row. Rows 4-5: Cast on 8 (6, 5) stitches at beginning of each row. 278 (284, 292) stitches.

Cuffs

Welts 36 (37, 38) – 41 (43, 45) Work stitches even in the established pattern, slipping the first sleeve edge stitch in each row. 278 (284, 292) stitches.

Neck, Front Bodice and Sleeves

In the next welt, stitches in the center of the row are bound off to create the back neck and begin shaping the two front bodice panels. Add a second ball of each yarn as needed to work both sleeves at the same time. Continue to work in the established Welted Stripes pattern and yarn rotation.

Welt 42 (44, 46) Continue to slip the first sleeve edge stitch in each row. Row 1: Work 124 (125, 127) stitches, use basic method to bind off center 30 (34, 38) stitches, work remaining 124 (125, 127) stitches. Row 2: Work in established pattern to the second neck edge, add a second ball of yarn and continue row. Rows 3-5: Work even. 124 (125, 127) stitches/sleeve.

Welts 43 (45, 47) – 47 (50, 53) Work in established pattern, decreasing 1 stitch at each neck edge on row 1 of each welt. 119 (119, 120) stitches/sleeve.

Welt 48 (51, 54) Apply in reverse order any sleeve length changes made in welts 30-35 (31-36, 32-37) in this and the next 5 welts. Continue decreasing at neck edges on row 1. Rows 1-2: Bind off 8 (6, 5) stitches at beginning (sleeve end) of each row. Rows 3-5: Bind off 5 stitches at beginning of each row. 100/105 (102/107, 104/109) stitches/sleeve.

Welts 49 (52, 55) – 51 (54, 57) Continue to work decreases at neck edges as established, and, at the same time bind off 5 stitches at beginning of each row. 62 (64, 66) stitches/sleeve.

Welts 52 (55, 58) – 53 (56, 59) Continue to work decreases at neck edges as established and, at the same time, decrease 6 stitches at each sleeve edge each row. 30 (32, 34) stitches/sleeve.

Welts 54 (57, 60) - 57 (60, 62) Continue to work decrease at neck edges as established and, at the same time, decrease 1 stitch at each sleeve edge each row. 6 (8, 16) stitches/sleeve.

Welt 58, Size One Continue to decrease 1 stitch at neck edges as established. Rows 1-2: Decrease 1 stitch at each sleeve edge.

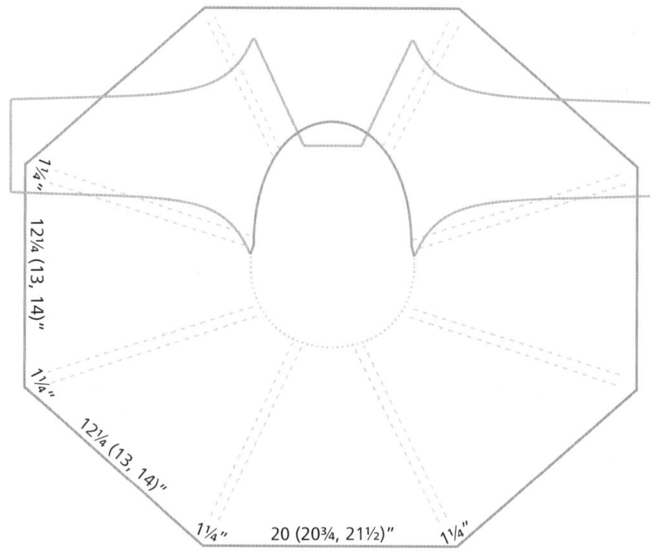

Rows 3-5: Work even at sleeve edges. Bind off remaining 3 stitches/sleeve.

Welt 63, Size Three Decrease 1 stitch at each neck edge *every other* row and, at the same time, decrease 1 stitch at each sleeve edge each row. 8 stitches/sleeve.

Welt 61 (64), Sizes Two and Three Decrease 1 stitch at each neck edge *every other* row. Rows 1-2 (1-3): Decrease 1 stitch at each sleeve edge. Rows 3-5 (4-5): Work even at sleeve edges. Bind off remaining 3 stitches/sleeve.

Finishing

Use cast-on yarn tail to sew first rows on Welt 1 together. Weave in ends. Block. With tapestry needle and matching yarn, sew neck/front bodice edge to inner collar edge. Sew underarm seams.

To create the braid fringe, cut five 12"/61cm lengths of yarn, 3 of yarn A and 2 of yarn B. Thread strands together through a tapestry needle. With the public side of the collar facing you, begin at the outer edge of welt 2 at the start-of-row line immediately adjacent to the existing yarn B tail. Thread the yarn through the fabric so that the needle enters 1 stitch to the right and exits 1 stitch to the left of the start-of-row line. Remove the needle and adjust the strands of yarn so that all are of equal length and divided into 2 groups of 2 strands on each side and 1 center group of 2 strands plus the existing yarn tail. Hold 2 groups in one hand and 3 in the other. *Braid, moving the outermost of the 3 groups held in one hand to the center and adding it to the groups held with the other hand. Repeat from * until braid measures approximately 4"/10.2cm. Tie a simple overhand knot at the end. Trim yarn strands even approximately 1"/2.5cm beneath knot. Create a second braid at the inner edge of welt 2, using 2 strands of yarn B and 3 strands of yarn A. Repeat, creating a braid at the outer and inner edges of all even numbered welts in the outer oval using the yarns worked in that welt.

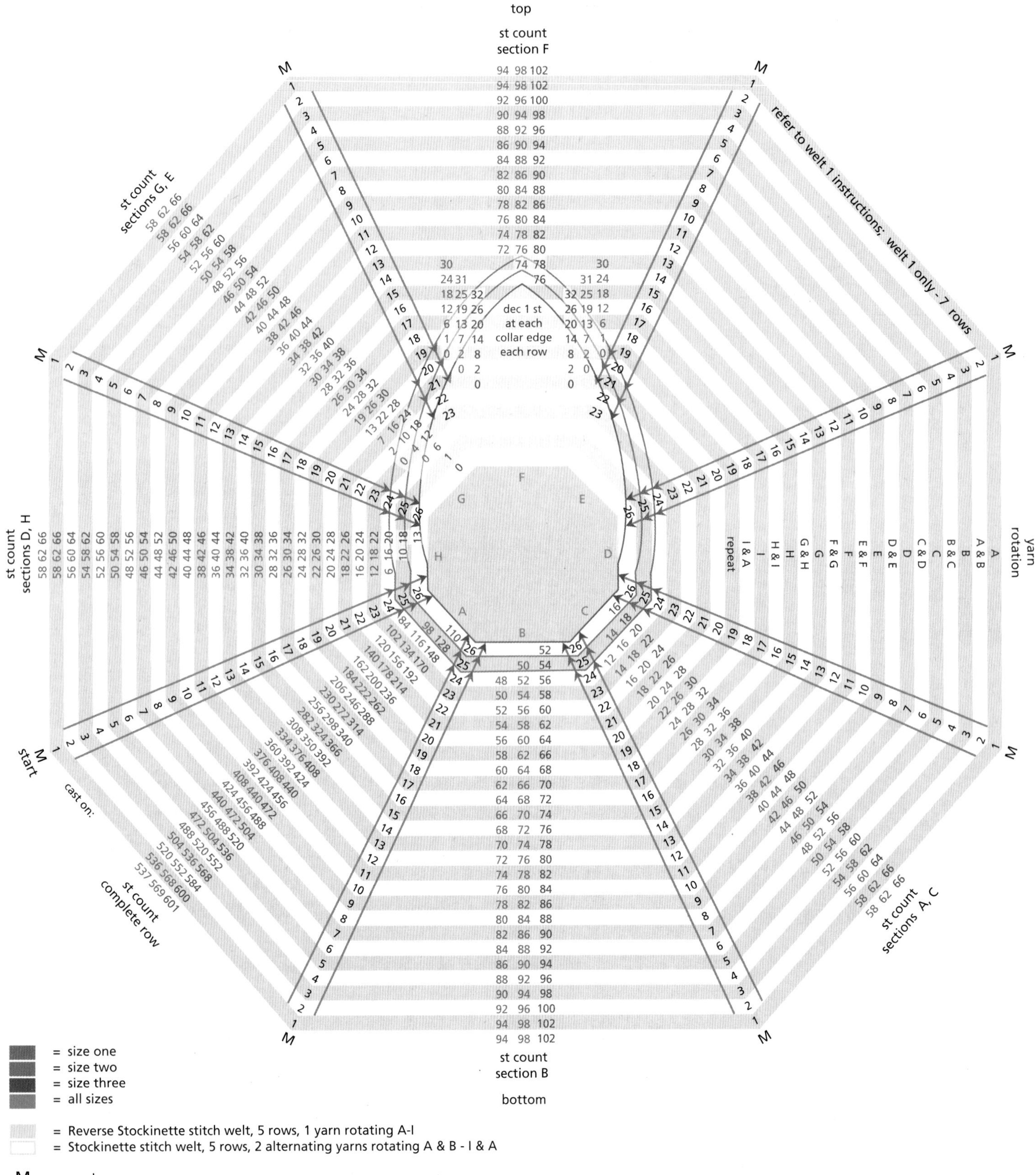

= Reverse Stockinette stitch welt, 5 rows, 1 yarn rotating A-I

= Stockinette stitch welt, 5 rows, 2 alternating yarns rotating A & B - I & A

M = marker

| = decrease 1 st per welt 2 sts out from marker on last row of welt or at collar edge as directed above - refer to pattern for row 1, welt 13 (14, 15) instruction

▲▲▲ = work as directed to this point

Note: All stitch counts refer to the number of stitches at completion of the last row of the welt

WELT #			BO (rw 1) rw 2 rw 3 rw 4 rw 5			st count slv				st count slv			rw 5 rw 4 rw 3 rw 2 (rw 1) BO			st count last row of welt		
								BO		BO						0		
		64			(1)-1-1-0-0		BO	3		3	BO		0-0-1-1-(1)			6	0	
	61	63		(1)-1-0-0-0		BO	3	8	dec 1 st at each neck edge every other row	8	3	BO		0-0-0-1-(1)		16	6	0
58	60	62	(1)-1-0-0-0			3	8	16		16	8	3			0-0-0-1-(1)	32	16	6
57	59	61				6	14	22		22	14	6				44	28	12
56	58	60				12	20	28		28	20	12				56	40	24
55	57	59			(0)-6-0-6-0	18	26	34		34	26	18	6-0-6-0-(6)			68	52	36
54	56	58		(0)-6-0-6-0	(6)-0-6-0-6	24	32	47		53	32	24	0-6-0-6-(0)	6-0-6-0-(6)		100	64	48
53	55	57	(0)-6-0-6-0	(6)-0-6-0-6	(0)-5-0-5-0	30	45	66		66	51	30	5-0-5-0-(5)	0-6-0-6-(0)	6-0-6-0-(6)	132	96	60
52	54	56	(6)-0-6-0-6	(0)-5-0-5-0	(5)-0-5-0-5	43	64	77		82	64	49	0-5-0-5-(0)	5-0-5-0-(5)	0-6-0-6-(0)	159	128	92
51	53	55	(0)-5-0-5-0	(5)-0-5-0-5	(0)-5-0-5-0	62	75	93		93	80	62	5-0-5-0-(5)	0-5-0-5-(0)	5-0-5-0-(5)	186	155	124
50	52	54	(5)-0-5-0-5	(0)-5-0-5-0	(5)-0-5-0-5	73	91	104		109	91	78	0-5-0-5-(0)	5-0-5-0-(5)	0-5-0-5-(0)	213	182	151
49	51	53	(0)-5-0-5-0	(6)-0-5-0-5		89	102	120		120	107	89		0-5-0-6-(0)	5-0-5-0-(5)	240	209	178
48	50	52	(8)-0-5-0-5			100	119	121		121	119	105			0-5-0-8-(0)	242	238	205
47	49	51				119	120	122		122	120	119				244	240	238
46	48	50				120	121	123		123	121	120				246	242	240
45	47	49				121	122	124		124	122	121				248	244	242
44	46	48				122	123	125		125	123	122				250	246	244
43	45	47				123	124	126	dec 1 st at each neck edge on row 1	126	124	123				252	248	246
42	44	46				124	125	127	row 1 BO center 30 (34, 38) sts	127	125	124				254	250	248
41	43	45														292	284	278
40	42	44														292	284	278
39	41	43														292	284	278
38	40	42														292	284	278
37	39	41														292	284	278
36	38	40														292	284	278
35	37	39	0-8-0-5-(0)												(5)-0-5-0-8	292	284	278
34	36	38	5-0-5-0-(5)	0-6-0-5-(0)										(5)-0-5-0-6	(0)-5-0-5-0	292	284	247
33	35	37	0-5-0-5-(0)	5-0-5-0-(5)	0-5-0-5-(0)								(5)-0-5-0-5	(0)-5-0-5-0	(5)-0-5-0-5	292	257	222
32	34	36	5-0-5-0-(5)	0-5-0-5-(0)	5-0-5-0-(5)								(0)-5-0-5-0	(5)-0-5-0-5	(0)-5-0-5-0	267	232	197
31	33	35	0-6-0-6-(0)	5-0-5-0-(5)	0-5-0-5-(0)								(5)-0-5-0-5	(0)-5-0-5-0	(6)-0-6-0-6	242	207	172
30	32	34	6-0-6-0-(6)	0-6-0-6-(0)	5-0-5-0-(5)								(0)-5-0-5-0	(6)-0-6-0-6	(0)-6-0-6-0	217	182	142
29	31	33		6-0-6-0-(6)	0-6-0-6-(0)								(6)-0-6-0-6	(0)-6-0-6-0		192	152	112
28	30	32			6-0-6-0-(6)								(0)-6-0-6-0			162	122	102
27	29	31														132	112	92

WELT #			rw 5 rw 4 rw 3 rw 2 (rw 1) CO			st count cuff - M	M	st count M - M	M	st count M - M	M	st count M - M	M	st count M - cuff	CO (rw 1) rw 2 rw 3 rw 4 rw 5			st count last row of welt		
26	28	30				11		8		44		8		11				122	102	82
25	27	29	1-1-0-●-●			7 13		10 10		46 46		10 10		13 7			●-●-0-1-1	112	92	80
24	26	28		1-1-0-●-●		9 15		12 12		48 48		12 12		15 9		●-●-0-1-1		102	90	84
	25	27			1-1-0-●-●	11		14		50		14		11	●-●-0-1-1			100	98	
		26																110		

slip first stitch at sleeve edge each row

slip first stitch at sleeve edge each row

= size one
= size two
= size three
= all sizes

= Reverse Stockinette stitch welt, 5 rows
= Stockinette stitch welt, 5 rows

M = marker

● ● ● = on rows 1-2, bind off 0 (2, 3) stitches at beginning of row; bodice worked on remaining stitches

| | | = decrease 1 st per welt 2 sts out from marker on last row of welt | = decrease at neck edge as directed above

⋀ ⋀ ⋀ = work as directed to this point

⋮ ⋮ ⋮ = increase 1 st at sleeve edge each row (below center line); decrease 1 st at sleeve edge each row (above center line)

Note: All stitch counts refer to the number of stitches at completion of the last row of the welt

silhouette in the sun

It is the negative spaces swirling within that define the form and describe the movement of this elegant coat of sweeping proportions. Glimpses of light and surrounding colors come and go, framed at all times by concentric circles of black. A narrow collar and trim lapels flow into the gently shaped torso and softly billowing back. The sumptuous aran weight blend of royal alpaca and merino provides the crisp stitch definition that makes this study in contrasts sing. Go ahead, strike a pose and create your own memorable silhouette in the sun.

Sizes
One (Two, Three); shown here in Size Three.

Knitted Measurements
Center Back Collar: 6½ (7¼, 8)"/16 (18, 20)cm
Center Back: 31½ (33½, 35½)"/80 (85, 90)cm
Center Back Neck to Cuff: 25 (25½, 26¼)"/63 (65, 67)cm

Approximate As-Worn Measurements
Center Back Collar: 5 (5½, 6)"/13 (14, 15)cm
Center Back: 34 (36, 38)"/86 (91, 96)cm
Center Back Neck to Cuff: 33 (34, 35)"/84 (86, 89)cm

Materials
Multiple-ply, aran weight alpaca/merino yarn, 1320 (1488, 1659) yd/1207 (1361, 1417)m. As shown, 17 (19, 21) skeins Blue Sky Alpacas Worsted Hand Dyes (50% royal alpaca, 50% merino, 3½ oz/100g, 100 yd/91m) in color #2006.

One 40 (40, 47)" size 9 (5.5mm) circular needle or size required to obtain gauge.

Gauge
17 stitches and 23 rows = 4"/10cm

Before beginning, please review Chapter One, ***Silhouettes and Sizing*** and Chapter Two, ***Tips and Techniques***.

Stitch Pattern: Welted Stripes with Eyelets
Continuous, alternating welts of Reverse Stockinette stitch and Stockinette stitch with eyelets.

Welt 1—Reverse Stockinette Stitch, *5* rows
When working in the round: (RS) Purl all rows.
When working flat: Purl on RS rows, knit on WS rows.
Welt 2—Stockinette Stitch with Eyelets, *5* rows
When working in the round: (RS) Knit all rows, working eyelet row on row 3.
When working flat: Knit on RS rows, purl on WS rows, working eyelet row on row 3.
Eyelet Row: *Work 2 stitches together, YO; repeat from * across entire row.
Repeat welts 1 and 2.

Outer Oval
Use a long-tail or double method to cast on 473 (505, 537) stitches, placing a marker in between the following 8 sections: 80 (84, 88) stitches, three sections of 52 (56, 60) stitches, 80 (84, 88) stitches, three sections of 52 (56, 60) stitches, with 1 stitch after marker. Use a different color marker for the last marker to denote the beginning and end of each row.

Welt 1, Reverse Stockinette Stitch (Note: This outer welt has 7 rows instead of the normal 5 rows. The first 3 rows are worked flat before joining the work into an oval. It is important to the directional integrity of the pattern that the oval be joined at the completion of the third row as instructed.) Row 1: (RS) Purl. Row 2: Knit. Row 3: Purl to last stitch, slip 1. Adjust work to ensure that cast-on edge is not twisted around needle. (See *No Twist Join*, Chapter Two.) Join work into an oval by placing the last, slipped stitch from row 3 back onto the left needle. Two stitches are now on the left needle before the marker. Purl these two stitches together. Continue next rows in the round. Rows 4-7: Purl. 472 (504, 536) stitches.

Welt 2, Stockinette Stitch with Eyelets Rows 1-4: Work first 4 rows of Stockinette stitch with eyelets. Row 5: *K2, k2tog, knit to within 4 stitches of next marker, k2tog, k2, slip marker; repeat from * across entire row. 456 (488, 520) stitches.

Welt 3, Reverse Stockinette Stitch Rows 1-4: Purl. Row 5: *P2, p2tog, purl to within 4 stitches of next marker, p2tog, p2, slip marker; repeat from * across entire row. 440 (472, 504) stitches.

Welts 4 - 7 (8, 9) (Note: Continue in Welted Stripes with Eyelets stitch pattern throughout remainder of garment.) Continue decreases at markers in last row of each welt as established. 376 (392, 408) stitches.

Inner Collar Edge
Welt 8 (9, 10) Row 1: Work in pattern to last marker, slip marker, work 31 (31, 29) stitches, use Jeny's Surprisingly Stretchy Bind Off method to bind off 6 (8, 14) stitches, work remaining 31 (31, 29) stitches. Break yarn. Slip 31 (31, 29) stitches just worked back on to left needle. (Note: this action repositions the beginning of row going forward.) Change to working-flat version of Welted Stripes with Eyelets stitch pattern. Rejoin yarn. Row 2: Decrease 1 stitch at beginning and end of each row (collar edge). Row 3: Decrease 1

stitch at beginning of row, then begin eyelet row (work 2 stitches together, YO) and continue until two stitches remain on needle, decrease 1. Rows 4-5: Decrease 1 stitch at beginning and end of each row (collar edge) and, at the same time, continue decreasing at markers on last row as established. 346 (360, 370) stitches.

Welts 9 (10, 11) - 18 (19, 20) Continue to decrease 1 stitch at beginning and end of each row as established above and to decrease in established manner at markers in last row of each welt. (Note: If, following the first neck edge decrease, fewer than 4 stitches remain before the first marker, stop marker-related decreases before the first marker and after the last marker. When decreases from one side of a marker consume its position, remove the marker and stop decreases related to that marker.) 116 (128, 138) stitches.

Back Bodice and Sleeves

After the collar and lapels are completed, the bodice is worked on the remaining live stitches in the center of the garment.

Welt 19 (20, 21) No further decreases at outer marker each side; remove outer stitch marker each side. Rows 1-3: Work even. Row 4: Increase 1 stitch at beginning and end of row. Row 5: Increase 1 stitch at beginning and end of row and continue decreases in established manner at the 2 remaining markers. 4 decreases worked/welt. 116 (128, 138) stitches.

Welts 20 (21, 22) - 28 (29, 30) Continue to increase 1 stitch at beginning and end of each row and to decrease in established manner at markers in last row of welt. 4 decreases worked/welt. 170 (182, 192) stitches.

Welt 29 (30, 31) No further decreases at markers; remove both stitch markers. Continue to increase 1 stitch at beginning and end of each row. 180 (192, 202) stitches.

Welt 30 (31, 32) Row 1: Work even. Rows 2-3: Cast on 8 (6, 5) stitches at beginning of each row. Rows 4-5: Cast on 8 (7, 6) stitches at beginning of each row. (Note: To lengthen sleeve length, add or subtract 3 stitches for each inch, distributed across all rows in this welt.) 212 (218, 224) stitches.

Cuffs

Welts 31 (32, 33) – 35 (37, 39) Place markers 5 stitches in from each sleeve end to indicate cuff stitches. Work the stitches between the markers even, in the established pattern. At the same time, work the cuff stitches in Reverse Stockinette stitch only. 212 (218, 224) stitches.

Neck, Front Bodice and Sleeves

In the next welt, stitches in the center of the row are bound off to create the back neck and begin shaping the two front bodice panels. Continue to work cuff stitches in Reverse Stockinette stitch only and the stitches between markers in the established Welted Stripes with Eyelets pattern.

Welt 36 (38, 40) Row 1: Work 96 (97, 98) stitches, use basic method to bind off center 20 (24, 28) stitches, work remaining 96 (97, 98) stitches. Row 2: Work in established pattern to the second neck edge, add a second ball of yarn and continue row. Rows 3-5: Work even. 96 (97, 98) stitches/sleeve.

Welts 37 (39, 41) – 40 (43, 46) Work in established pattern, decreasing 1 stitch at each neck edge on row 1 of each welt. 92 (92, 92) stitches/sleeve.

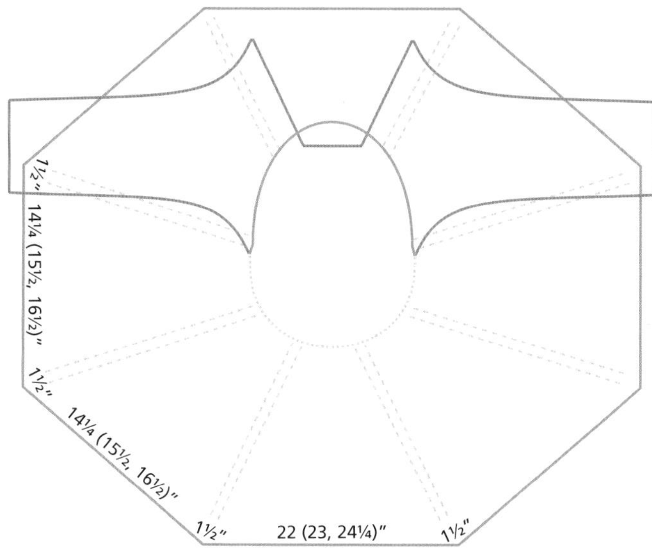

Welt 41 (44, 47) Apply in reverse order any sleeve length changes made in welt 30 (31, 32) in this welt. Continue decreasing at neck edges on row 1. Rows 1-2: Bind off 8 (7, 6) stitches at beginning (sleeve end) of each row. Rows 3-4: Bind off 8 (6, 5) stitches at beginning (sleeve end) of each row. Row 5: Work even at sleeve edges. 75 (78, 80) stitches/sleeve.

Welts 42 (45, 48) – 46 (48, 50) Continue to work decreases at neck edges as established, and, at the same time decrease 1 stitch at each sleeve edge each row. 45 (54, 62) stitches/sleeve.

Welts 47 (49, 51) – 51 (54, 57) Decrease 1 stitch at each neck edge *every other* row and, at the same time, decrease 1 stitch at each sleeve edge each row. 7 (9, 9) stitches/sleeve.

Welt 52 (55, 58) Continue to decrease 1 stitch at neck edges every other row. Rows 1-2: Decrease 1 stitch at each sleeve edge. Row 3: Decrease 0 (1, 1) stitch at each sleeve edge each row. Row 4: Decrease 0 (0, 1) stitch at each sleeve edge. Row 5: Work even at sleeve edges. Bind off remaining 3 stitches/sleeve.

Finishing

Use cast-on yarn tail to sew first rows on Welt 1 together. Weave in ends. Block. With tapestry needle and matching yarn, sew neck/front bodice edge to collar edge of outer oval. Sew underarm seams so that the finished seam is outside on the sleeves and inside on the cuffs. Tack cuffs to reinforce rolled shape.

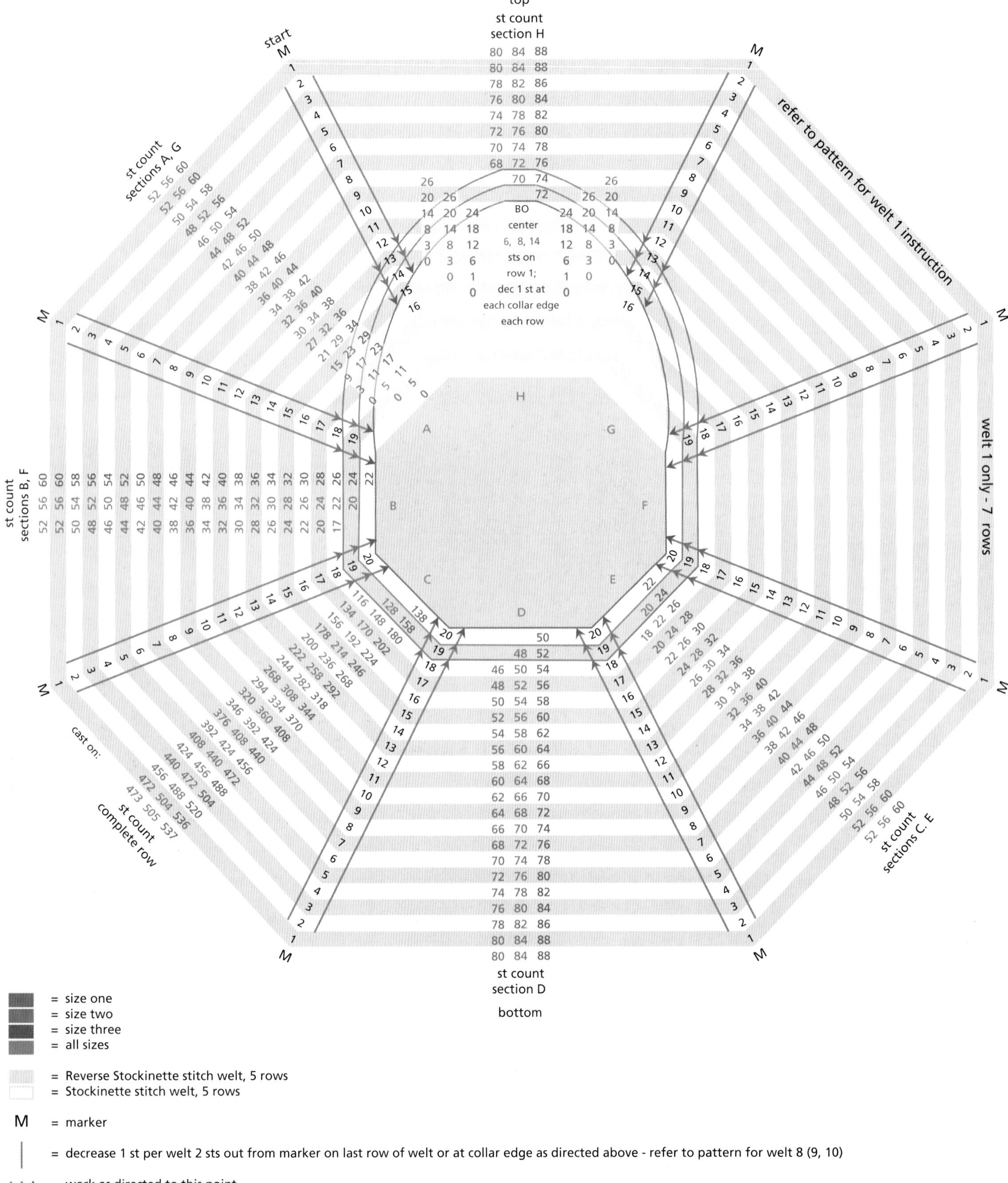

Note: All stitch counts refer to the number of stitches at completion of the last row of the welt

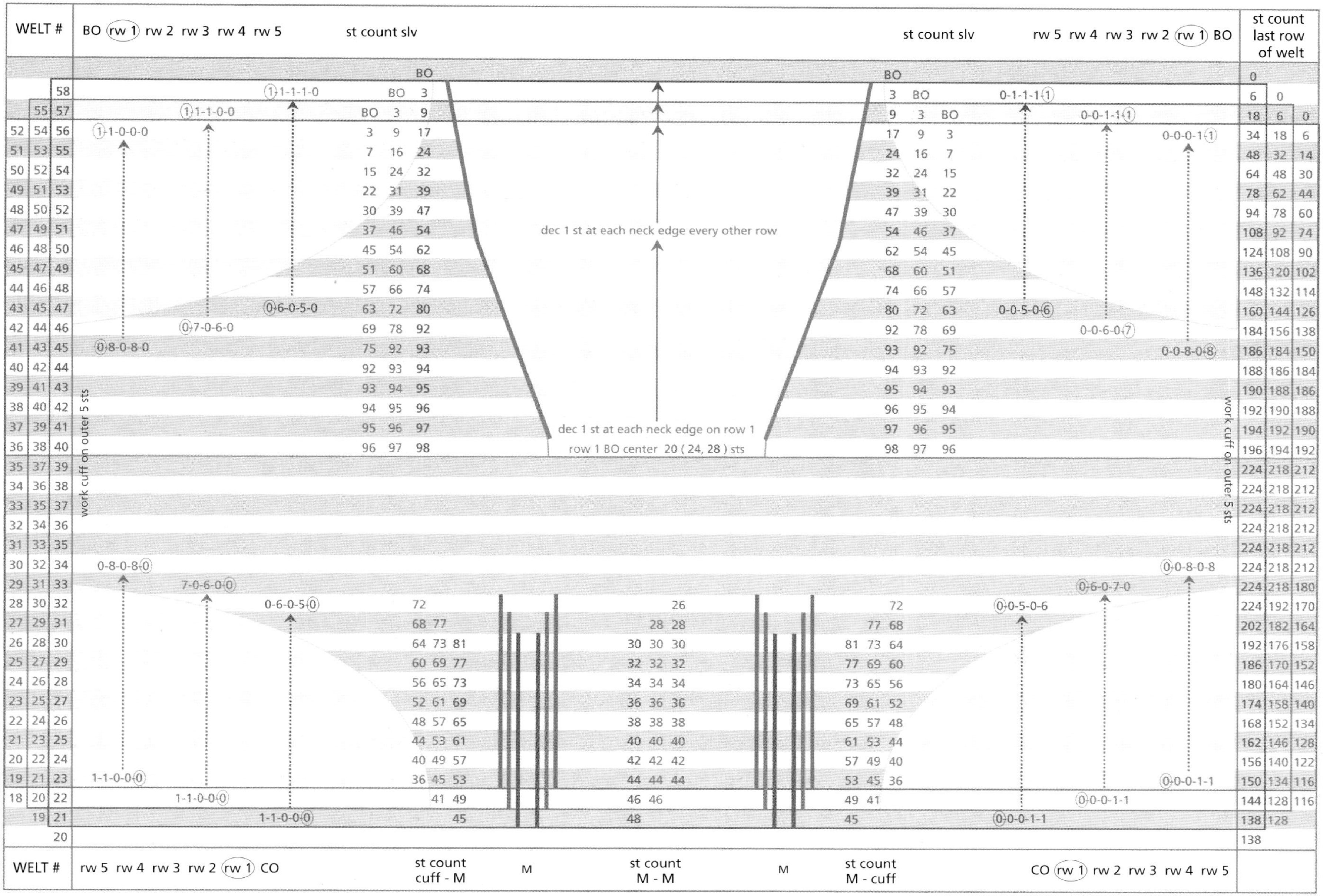

WELT #			BO (rw 1) rw 2 rw 3 rw 4 rw 5	st count slv						st count slv			rw 5 rw 4 rw 3 rw 2 (rw 1) BO	st count last row of welt		
						BO				BO				0		
		58	①-1-1-1-0		BO	3				3	BO		0-1-1-1-①	6	0	
	55	57	①-1-1-0-0	BO	3	9				9	3	BO	0-0-1-1-①	18	6	0
52	54	56	①-1-0-0-0	3	9	17				17	9	3	0-0-0-1-①	34	18	6
51	53	55		7	16	24				24	16	7		48	32	14
50	52	54		15	24	32				32	24	15		64	48	30
49	51	53		22	31	39				39	31	22		78	62	44
48	50	52		30	39	47				47	39	30		94	78	60
47	49	51		37	46	54	dec 1 st at each neck edge every other row			54	46	37		108	92	74
46	48	50		45	54	62				62	54	45		124	108	90
45	47	49		51	60	68				68	60	51		136	120	102
44	46	48		57	66	74				74	66	57		148	132	114
43	45	47	⓪-6-0-5-0	63	72	80				80	72	63	0-0-5-0-⑥	160	144	126
42	44	46	⓪-7-0-6-0	69	78	92				92	78	69	0-0-6-0-⑦	184	156	138
41	43	45	⓪-8-0-8-0	75	92	93				93	92	75	0-0-8-0-⑧	186	184	150
40	42	44		92	93	94				94	93	92		188	186	184
39	41	43		93	94	95				95	94	93		190	188	186
38	40	42		94	95	96				96	95	94		192	190	188
37	39	41		95	96	97	dec 1 st at each neck edge on row 1			97	96	95		194	192	190
36	38	40		96	97	98	row 1 BO center 20 (24, 28) sts			98	97	96		196	194	192
35	37	39												224	218	212
34	36	38	work cuff on outer 5 sts										work cuff on outer 5 sts	224	218	212
33	35	37												224	218	212
32	34	36												224	218	212
31	33	35												224	218	212
30	32	34	0-8-0-8-⓪										⓪-0-8-0-8	224	218	212
29	31	33	7-0-6-0-⓪										⓪-6-0-7-0	224	218	180
28	30	32	0-6-0-5-⓪	72					26			72	⓪-0-5-0-6	224	192	170
27	29	31		68	77			28	28		77	68		202	182	164
26	28	30		64	73	81	30	30	30	81	73	64		192	176	158
25	27	29		60	69	77	32	32	32	77	69	60		186	170	152
24	26	28		56	65	73	34	34	34	73	65	56		180	164	146
23	25	27		52	61	69	36	36	36	69	61	52		174	158	140
22	24	26		48	57	65	38	38	38	65	57	48		168	152	134
21	23	25		44	53	61	40	40	40	61	53	44		162	146	128
20	22	24		40	49	57	42	42	42	57	49	40		156	140	122
19	21	23	1-1-0-0-⓪	36	45	53	44	44	44	53	45	36	⓪-0-0-1-1	150	134	116
18	20	22	1-1-0-0-⓪		41	49	46	46		49	41		⓪-0-0-1-1	144	128	116
	19	21	1-1-0-0-⓪			45	48			45			⓪-0-0-1-1	138	128	
		20												138		
WELT #			rw 5 rw 4 rw 3 rw 2 (rw 1) CO	st count cuff - M		M	st count M - M		M	st count M - cuff			CO (rw 1) rw 2 rw 3 rw 4 rw 5			

= size one
= size two
= size three
= all sizes

= Reverse Stockinette stitch welt, 5 rows
= Stockinette stitch welt, 5 rows

M = marker

= decrease 1 stitch per welt 2 stitches out from marker on last row of welt

= decrease at neck edge as directed above

= work as directed to this point

= increase 1 st at sleeve edge each row (below center line); decrease 1 st at sleeve edge each row (above center line)

Note: All stitch counts refer to the number of stitches at completion of the last row of the welt

bountiful thanks...

to Cat Bordhi, mentor extraordinaire, who provides enthusiastic, comprehensive and insightful guidance to aspiring and accomplished designers alike through her annual Visionary Retreat; without her, this book would not be in your hands today; and to the Visionary designers who, to a person, embraced my project and helped in every way imaginable; particular thanks to Cookie A, Jared Flood, Janel Laidman, Sundara Murphy, Emily McKeon, J.C. Briar, Myrna Stahman, Carol Breitner, Jeny Staiman, Carson Demers, and Marta McCall;

to Jeane deCoster, editor of all things technical and otherwise, whose keen analytical mind, ever present sense of humor and willingness to consider any and all possibilities were essential ingredients in the creation of this book;

to Zoë Lonergan, photographer and book designer, who possesses a wide range of talents, not the least of which is the ability to look through a lens and compose not just a photograph, but the page of a book as well; to Ashley Lonergan, lead model, who perched in precarious positions, wore alpaca in 100° heat and posed amongst cobwebs without complaint; and to Courtney Lonergan who, like her sister, contributed her native modeling skills to making this book as beautiful as they are;

to Annelle Karlstad and the staff of the Mendocino Yarn Shop whose support has been unwavering since day one; and to Susan Mitchell who served as test knitter and proof reader, contributing her valuable observations and ever-sharp eye to the cause;

to Ricia Araiza who provided the spark for this book and lent her radiant smile to its pages; to her husband Michael Leventhal, together they created the paintings you see throughout; and to Sallie McConnell, Linda and Fedele Bauccio, Beth Richmond, Sonya Smith, Karen Tanner and Suzy Pingree who each made meaningful contributions;

to my mother, who invented "make it day" just for me, taught me to knit, and introduced me to the world of beautiful fabric; to my daughters, Erica and Lauren, who are my best friends, truest guides, and most ardent fans; and, lastly, to my husband Bill, my perfect partner, the love of my life, who patiently listened to my many "Swirl theories," read and edited every page of this book several times over and picked up the loose ends of our lives so that I could complete *knit, Swirl!*

resources

Your LYS

A knitter's greatest resource is a Local Yarn Shop where information, inspiration, encouragement and community are always available. This book would not exist were it not for the encouragement I received at my LYS, the *Mendocino Yarn Shop*.

Books

*Knitter's Handbook: A Comprehensive Guide to the Principles and Techniques of Handknitt*ing, by Montse Stanley
If I could have only one knitting reference book, this would be it. Included within its informative pages you will find 5 variations of the cast-on method recommended for Swirls.

Knitspeak: An A to Z Guide to the Language of Knitting Patterns by Andrea Berman Price
This handy little book is not only a dictionary of knitting terms but a great how-to resource that speaks to almost every aspect of Swirl knitting.

The Knitter's Book of Yarn: The Ultimate Guide to Choosing, Using and Enjoying Yarn, by Clara Parkes
An invaluable reference book I recommend as a guide when making fabric development and yarn substitution decisions.

Online

www.knitswirl.com
Check *www.knitswirl.com* for illustrated tutorials of the techniques used in this book.

www.knitty.com
A free online magazine that provides excellent technical instruction including information on Jeny's Surprisingly Stretchy Bind Off and the use of duplicate stitch to weave in ends.

www.verypink.com
A master knitter's website that offers clear, sharp, step-by-step video tutorials including long tail cast on (thumb method) and the use of duplicate stitch to weave in ends.

www.techknitting.blogspot.com
A blog devoted to the technical aspects of knitting presented in detailed written form with illustrations and a user-friendly index.

Yarns

These fine yarn companies generously provided yarn for *knit, Swirl!* Please visit their websites and treat yourself to the pure enjoyment of working with their extraordinary yarns.

Alchemy Yarns of Transformation *www.alchemyyarns.com*

Blue Sky Alpacas *www.blueskyalpacas.com*

Curious Creek Fibers *www.curiouscreek.com*

Great Northern Yarns *www.greatnorthernyarns.com*

Karabella Yarns *www.karabellayarns.com*

Mountain Colors Yarns *www.mountaincolors.com*

Sundara Yarn *www.sundarayarn.com*

abbreviations

BO:	Bind off
CO:	Cast on
dec:	Decrease
inc:	Increase
JSSBO:	Jeny's Surprisingly Stretchy Bind Off
k:	Knit
k2tog:	Knit 2 together
M:	Marker
p:	Purl
p2tog:	Purl 2 together
rem:	Remaining
RS:	Right side*
rw:	Row
slv:	Sleeve
st:	Stitch
WS:	Wrong side*
YO:	Yarn over - Yarn travels up and over the top of the needle with the leading leg at the front.
YO in reverse:	Yarn over in reverse - Yarn travels up and over the top of the needle in the opposite direction of a standard yarn over, with the leading leg at the back.

*See No "Right Side", page 14

YOKE MEASUREMENT

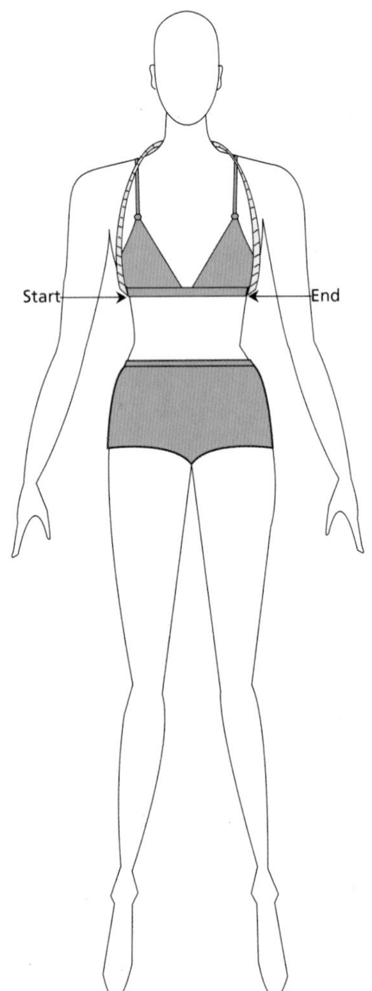